THE HISTORY OF THE SUDAN

A HISTORY OF THE
SUDAN

FROM THE COMING OF ISLAM
TO THE PRESENT DAY

Fourth edition

P. M. HOLT

*Professor Emeritus of the History of the Near and Middle East
in the University of London*

M. W. DALY

*Associate Professor of History, Arkansas
State University*

LONGMAN
London and New York

Longman Group UK Limited,
Longman House, Burnt Mill, Harlow,
Essex CM20 2JE, England
and Associated Companies throughout the world.

Published in the United States of America
by Longman Inc., New York

First Published 1961
Second Edition 1963
Third Edition 1979
Fourth Edition 1988

British Library Cataloguing in Publication Data

Holt, P. M.
   A history of the Sudan: from the
   coming of Islam to the present day. –
   4th ed.
   1. Sudan–History
   I. Title   II. Daly, M. W.
   962.4   DT155.6

ISBN 0-582-00406-3

Library of Congress Cataloging-in-Publication Data
Holt, P. M. (Peter Malcolm)
   A history of the Sudan, from the coming of Islam
to the present day.

   Bibliography: p.
   Includes index.
   1. Sudan–History–1820–   . I. Daly, M. W.
II. Title.
DT156.4.H64   1988   962.4′03   87–3857
ISBN 0-582-00406-3 (pbk.)

Set in 10/12 Times

Produced by Longman Group (FE) Limited
Printed in Hong Kong

CONTENTS

v

Contents

Part V: The Independent Sudan

MAPS

PREFACE TO THE FIRST EDITION

The first steps towards the making of the modern Sudan were taken, nearly a century and a half ago, when the soldiers of Muhammad 'Ali Pasha, the Ottoman sultan's viceroy in Egypt, brought under their master's rule the Muslim cultivators, merchants and tribesmen of Nubia, Sennar and Kordofan. A common administration, the shared glories and disasters of the Mahdist Revolution, and renewed experience of alien rule under the Anglo-Egyptian Condominium, welded the Sudanese peoples together, and stimulated the development of Sudanese nationalism. On New Year's Day, 1956, the Sudan emerged into independent statehood.

This is in brief the story which the following pages attempt to tell in more detail. Three factors predominate in modern Sudanese history. The first is the indigenous tradition, itself the product of the intermingling of Arab Muslims with Africans. The fusion began over a thousand years ago, and, as allusions to the problem of the southern Sudan will show, is still a continuing process. This lies at the base of Sudanese nationality, religion and culture. I have therefore dealt at some length with the earlier stages of the fusion in the Introduction, and have returned to the theme of the indigenous tradition in the Conclusion.

The two other factors are the influence of Egypt, which in its earlier phases was late Ottoman rather than purely Egyptian in quality, and the influence of Britain. The effect of these two influences upon the Sudan is seen in its history from the time of Muhammad 'Ali's conquests until the present day. Egyptian rule ended with the Mahdist Revolution, British administration with the coming of independence, but the modern Sudan is politically and materially very largely the heir of these earlier regimes. The cultural influence of both Egypt and Britain is unaffected by the transformation of their former dependency into a sovereign state. The play upon each other of these three factors is the theme of this book.

In the difficult problem of the transliteration of Arabic words, I have adopted a compromise. For the place-names of provinces and larger towns, I have used conventional forms, e.g. Khartoum, Kordofan, El Obeid. The conventional Kassala and Bahr El Ghazal have, however, been slightly modified to the more accurate forms Kasala and Bahr al-Ghazal. Personal names (except for Neguib and Nasser, which have a firmly established conventional spelling) and technical terms are rigorously transliterated, but diacritical marks have been omitted for the sake of simplicity. Ottoman titles which are not purely Arabic in origin, e.g. *defterdar, hükümdar*, are spelt according to modern Turkish conventions.

In conclusion, I wish to express my gratitude to all those who have helped me in the preparation of this book; in particular the General Editor of this series, Professor Bernard Lewis; my former colleague, Mr A. B. Theobald, and Sayyid Osman Sid Ahmed Ismail of the University of Khartoum. All these read the book in draft, and assisted me with their comments and criticisms. Dr G. N. Sanderson, also of the University of Khartoum, kindly provided information on the diplomatic background to the Reconquest. While acknowledging their very real help, I accept, of course, all responsibility for the statements and opinions expressed in my book. Material for the illustrations was generously provided by Dr J. F. E. Bloss and Mr F. C. A. McBain from their private collections of photographs, and by Mr R. L. Hill from the Sudanese archive of the University of Durham. Sayyid Mohamed Kamal El Bakri, First Secretary of the Sudan Embassy in London, was most helpful in making available, or obtaining, further photographic material. I am grateful to the following publishers for permission to reprint short passages from copyright works: Oxford University Press for *Egypt in the Sudan* by R. Hill, Messrs D. van Nostrand Inc., New York for *Diplomacy in the Near and Middle East* by J. C. Hurewitz, and Cambridge University Press for *Sudan Arabic Texts* translated by S. Hillelson. Lastly, I am forever indebted to the Sudanese people for the many happy and formative years which I spent in their land.

1961   P. M. Holt.

PREFACE TO THE SECOND EDITION

In the second edition, I have brought the story of events down to the beginning of 1963. The publication in 1961 of Dr Richard Gray's important study, *A history of the southern Sudan 1839-1889* (O.U.P.), has enabled me to revise and recast my account of developments in the south in Chapters 4 and 5. I have brought the Bibliography up to date. My thanks are due to reviewers who pointed out slips and misstatements in the first edition of this book.

June 1963   P.M.H.

PREFACE TO THE THIRD EDITION

When the second edition of this book was published, the independent Republic of the Sudan had not yet completed its first decade. The passage of time since then has made necessary our collaboration in this new edition, in which the story of events has been brought down to 1978, while the account of previous Sudanese history in the twentieth century has been rewritten in the light of the more copious source-materials and greater body of research now available. The opportunity has been taken also to describe more fully the history of the region, from the first contacts between the Muslim Arabs and the Christian Nubians to the invasion by the forces of Muhammad 'Ali Pasha. The revised and expanded bibliography indicates the greater abundance of works on the Sudan now at the reader's disposal.

February 1979   P.M.H.
                                                                                    M.W.D.

PREFACE TO THE FOURTH EDITION

Since the publication of the Third Edition of this book in 1979 important and dramatic political changes have occurred in the Sudan, notably the collapse of Jaafar Nimeiri's regime in 1985. The appearance of a new edition under a new imprint has made possible both a fresh look at that regime, and an outline of subsequent developments down to the restoration of parliamentary rule in April 1986. The Bibliography has also been brought up to date.

April 1987   P.M.H.
                                                                   M.W.D.

INTRODUCTION: THE LAND
AND THE PEOPLE

The medieval Muslim geographers gave the name of *Bilad al-Sudan*, 'the land of the Blacks', to the belt of African territory to the south of the Sahara Desert. In the more restricted sense of the territories lying southwards of Egypt, which formed the Anglo-Egyptian Condominium from 1899 until 1955, and which now constitute the Republic of the Sudan, the term is of nineteenth-century origin, a convenient administrative designation for the African empire acquired by Muhammad 'Ali Pasha, the viceroy of Egypt, and his successors.[1] The Sudan in this sense excluded the vast regions west of Darfur which in the late nineteenth and early twentieth centuries were to pass under French and British colonial rule; on the other hand it included territories which did not form part of the Sudan as traditionally understood – Nubia, the land of the Beja, and the Ottoman ports of the Red Sea coast.

Traditionally the name of Nubia was applied to the whole riverain region from the First Cataract to the Sabaluqa Gorge, not far north of the confluence of the Blue and White Niles. It fell into two portions, which had separate histories from the early sixteenth to the early nineteenth century. Lower Nubia, called by the Ottomans *Berberistan*, 'the land of the Barabra',[2] extended from the First to the Third Cataract, and thus included territory both north and south of the modern Egyptian-Sudanese frontier. It was, nominally at least, dependent upon the Ottoman viceroys of Egypt. Upper Nubia, above the Third Cataract, was under the suzerainty of the Funj rulers of Sennar.

East of Nubia, in the Red Sea Hills, were the Beja, recognized by medieval Muslim writers as a distinct ethnic group, not Nubians, nor Arabs, nor *Sudan* ('Blacks'). Suakin and its sister-port of Massawa (which was annexed by Italy in 1884) looked to the Red Sea and Arabia, rather than to the Nile valley, from which they were separated by the barrier of the Red Sea Hills and the intractable Beja.

1

The area of the present-day Republic of the Sudan is very nearly one million square miles – about one-quarter the size of Europe. Geographically, the greater part of the country is an immense plain. This may be divided into three zones: in the north is rocky desert and semi-desert; south of this is a belt of undulating sand, passing from semi-desert to savanna; south of this again a clay belt, which widens as it stretches eastwards from the south of Darfur to the rainlands and semi-desert lying east of the Blue and main Niles. The Red Sea Hills, a northerly prolongation of the Ethiopian highlands, separate the great plain from the narrow coastal strip.

The Sudanese plain is drained by the Nile and its tributaries. Both the White and Blue Niles rise outside the country. The White Nile enters the Sudan (where its upper reaches are known as Bahr al-Jabal, 'the Mountain River') at Nimule, and after a course of a hundred miles, passes into the clay plain. Here it is obstructed, and enlarges into an enormous swampy area, known as the Sudd (Arabic: *sadd*, 'barrier'). After a winding course of four hundred miles, it is joined by its western tributary, the Bahr al-Ghazal, which collects the waters of a multitude of smaller rivers, draining the south-western plain and originating in the ironstone plateau which forms the Nile-Congo divide. About eighty miles further on, it is joined by the Sobat from the east.

A broad, slow river, the White Nile emerges from the swamps into a region of acacia forests which at one time fringed its banks as far as Khartoum, but now the last part of its journey lies through open, almost treeless plains. From the confluence of the White Nile and Bahr al-Ghazal to Khartoum is a distance of about six hundred miles. The Blue Nile is a shorter, swifter and more beautiful river. Its course within the Sudan covers nearly five hundred miles. The peninsula which lies between the Blue and White rivers, as they converge at Khartoum, is known as the Gezira (Arabic: *jazira,* 'island' or 'peninsula'). Once the granary of Khartoum, the Gezira is now the site of the principal cotton-growing area of the Sudan.

The main Nile flows in a generally northward direction from Khartoum through increasingly arid country. Two hundred miles below Khartoum, it receives the seasonal waters of the Atbara, its last tributary. About a hundred and fifty miles further on, at Abu Hamad, it makes a great bend to the south-west before resuming its northerly course by Dongola to the Egyptian frontier.

THE TRIBES OF THE SUDAN

There exists a broad distinction, which is nevertheless slowly being modified by the processes of history, between the northern and southern parts of the modern Sudan. The north is, with certain important exceptions, Arabic in speech, and its peoples are largely arabized in culture and outlook. Its indigenous inhabitants are universally Muslim; a minority of Arabic-speaking Christians is composed of the descendants of immigrants from Egypt and Lebanon since the Turco-Egyptian conquest. The southern Sudan contains a bewildering variety of ethnic groups and languages. Unlike the northerners, its peoples are not generally Muslims, nor do they claim Arab descent; although there has been some degree of islamization and arabization. These tendencies were restrained during the Condominium period, when European and American missionaries effected a limited christianization of the region.

Three southern tribes will appear fairly frequently in the following pages. The Shilluk now occupy a comparatively small area on the western bank of the White Nile, but formerly their range was much more extensive. As late as the mid-nineteenth century their northern limit was the island of Aba, thirty years later to be the cradle of the Mahdia. Until the early years of the Turco-Egyptian regime, they raided the Arab settlements down the White Nile, and one such raid is said to have led to the foundation of the Funj kingdom by a band of Shilluk warriors.[3] Until the coming of firearms and steamers, they were able to meet their northern neighbours on equal terms.

The Dinka occupy a much more extensive territory than the present-day Shilluk, but lack their unity: they are a group of tribes, some of which dwell on the eastern bank of the White Nile, others, the majority, in the grassy flood-plains of the Bahr al-Ghazal, where they herd their cattle. Further south, on the higher land of the Nile-Congo divide, live the Azande, now divided by the international boundary between the Republic of the Sudan and Zaire.

The arabization of the northern Sudan resulted from the penetration of the region by tribes who had already migrated from Arabia to Upper Egypt. The process will be described in the following chapter. With certain comparatively minor exceptions, those northern Sudanese who claim Arab descent belong to one or other of two extensive, if somewhat artificial, divisions: the arabized Nubians, mainly sedentaries of the main Nile, composed of the Barabra and the Ja'ali Group; and the mainly nomadic or semi-nomadic Juhayna Group.

The Barabra, as we have seen, inhabit Lower Nubia. Their representatives in the modern Sudan are the Sukkut and Mahas, who still speak related Nubian dialects. South of them are a series of tribes, inhabiting the old Upper Nubia, who belong to the Ja'ali Group. These tribes claim as a common ancestor an Arab named Ibrahim Ja'al. Whether this eponym is historical or not, the traditional pedigree indicates an element common to all these tribes. Since the Arab irruption into this region, Arab descent has been a source of pride and distinction: hence it is not surprising that stress is laid on a common Arab ancestor. A further genealogical sophistication makes Ibrahim Ja'al a descendant of al-'Abbas, the Prophet's uncle. Thus the epithets Ja'ali and 'Abbasi have become virtually synonyms in the genealogies of the eastern *Bilad al-Sudan*. In spite, however, of the anxiety of the genealogists to provide the Ja'ali Group with a common Arab ancestor, it would be more realistic to regard the submerged Nubian substratum as the common ethnic element among these tribes. This hypothesis does not, of course, reject the undoubted historical fact of Arab ancestry as such: the result of intermarriage between Arab immigrants and the older Nubian population. From this intermingling the present Ja'ali Group derive their markedly Arab characteristics and their Muslim cultural inheritance.

The name of Ja'aliyyin (plural of Ja'ali) is specifically applied to one tribe of this Group, dwelling between the Atbara confluence and the Sabaluqa Gorge. The Ja'aliyyin in this restricted sense formed from the sixteenth century until the Turco-Egyptian conquest a tribal kingdom, dominated by a royal clan known as the Sa'dab. North of them, the region of Berber is the homeland of the Mirafab, another tribe of the Ja'ali Group, who also used to form a tribal kingdom. Further north still are other tribal members of the same Group, the Rubatab and Manasir, inhabiting the banks of the Nile down to and beyond the great bend at Abu Hamad.

The reach of the Nile between the Fourth Cataract and al-Dabba is the homeland of a tribal confederacy, the Shayqiyya, which does not claim Ja'ali origin. Many observers have noted what their history confirms, the difference between their character and that of their neighbours. In the eighteenth century the predatory, equestrian aristocracy of the Shayqiyya dominated Nubia. In 1821, they alone of the riverain tribes resisted the Turco-Egyptian invasion. Their subsequent service to the new regime as a force of irregular cavalry led to the establishment of Shayqiyya colonies around the junction of the Niles and elsewhere.

The most northerly tribes of the Ja'ali Group lie downstream of the Shayqiyya, between al-Dabba and the country of the Barabra. Their homeland is the historical region of Dongola (Arabic: *Dunqula*), whence these tribesmen are known collectively as *Danaqla* (singular: *Dunqulawi*), i.e. 'men of Dongola'. Among them there is far more consciousness of Nubian origin than among the tribes of the southern Ja'ali Group, and a Nubian dialect continues to be spoken.

The arabized Nubians are primarily sedentary cultivators, inhabiting the narrow strip of riverain land and the islands (some of which are very extensive) which can be watered by the Nile flood or irrigation. Their territories lie outside the normal rain-belt. Hence the pressure of population on the land has always been heavy, especially among the Danaqla and Barabra. This economic limitation, in association sometimes with political instability, has made temporary or permanent emigration a recurrent feature of the history of these peoples. The Barabra have provided Egypt with its 'Berberine' servants. In the sixteenth century, Mahas migrated to the confluence of the Niles and established themselves as religious teachers.

Various ruling groups, basically neither Nubian nor Arab, have claimed a Ja'ali (or synonymously, an 'Abbasi) ancestry. The royal family of Taqali, a small Muslim state in the pagan Nuba Mountains, derives its origin from the marriage of a Ja'ali holy man with an indigenous princess. A similar story is told of the origin of the Nabtab, the dominant clan of the Beja Banu 'Amir. The royal Kayra clan amongst the Fur claimed 'Abbasi ancestry, as did the neighbouring rulers of Wadai. The rise of the Shayqiyya in the eighteenth century produced an emigration of Danaqla to Darfur, which seems to have led to a development of trade between that state and Egypt. In the nineteenth century Ja'ali *jallaba* (petty traders) were ubiquitous in southern Kordofan and Darfur, on the southern fringe of Arab territory, while Danaqla and other members of the great Ja'ali Group played a prominent part in the opening-up of the White Nile and Bahr al-Ghazal. Al-Zubayr Rahma, the merchant-prince of the western Bahr al-Ghazal in the reign of Khedive Isma'il, prided himself on his 'Abbasi descent.

Mention should also be made of several tribes, outside the confines of ancient Nubia, which claim membership of the Ja'ali Group. These are probably synthetic tribes, formed by the accretion of heterogeneous fragments around Ja'ali leaders. It is significant that five of them have names derived from the Arabic root *jama'a*, 'to collect'.

In Sudanese genealogical usage, the term *Juhayna* is practically a comprehensive term for all tribes claiming Arab descent but not asserting a Ja'ali-'Abbasi origin. Arabs of the Juhayna of Arabia, who had migrated to Upper Egypt, played a leading part in the breakthrough into Nubia in the fourteenth century[4], and there has been a tendency for elements of varied (and even non-Arab) origins to link themselves with this successful tribe.

Even the confused and sometimes tendentious genealogical materials available today make it clear, however, that at least two important sub-groups can hardly be linked ancestrally with the Juhayna. The Rufa'a, found on the Blue Nile, preserve some memory of a distinct origin. Their ancestors lived in geographical proximity to the ancestral Juhayna, both in the Hijaz and in Upper Egypt; and this has probably led to their inclusion in the Juhayna Group. In the late fifteenth century an Arab population, probably of varied origins, became sedentarized at the junction of the Blue and White Niles under a chief from the Rufa'a named 'Abdallah Jamma'. He and his successors, the 'Abdallab, became prosperous from the tolls levied on the desert Arabs during their annual nomadic cycle, and were recognized by the Funj rulers of Sennar (1504–1821) as paramount chiefs of the Arabs[5]. The bulk of the Rufa'a were almost entirely nomadic until the nineteenth century, when the northern section became partly sedentarized. The town of Rufa'a on the Blue Nile was originally a tribal settlement. The southern section, on each side of the upper Blue Nile, is still largely nomadic.

A second sub-group which can hardly belong to the Juhayna by descent is the Fazara. This term, now obsolete in Sudanese usage, included until the last century most of the camel-nomads of northern Kordofan and Darfur. The historical Fazara tribe was of north-Arabian origin, whereas the Juhayna were south-Arabian.

Among the numerous tribes of the Juhayna Group, two have played a sufficiently important part in Sudanese history to be given specific mention. The leading tribe of the southern Butana (i.e. the quadrilateral bounded by the main Nile, the Atbara, the Blue Nile and the Ethiopian foothills) is the Shukriyya, camel-owning nomads. They rose to importance during the eighteenth century as Funj power declined, under the leadership of the Abu Sinn family.

Ahmad Abu Sinn (*circa* 1790–1870) lived on good terms with the Turco-Egyptian regime, was given the rank of bey, and for ten years was governor of Khartoum. Their territory included the grain-producing rainlands of the Qadarif, where a tribal market developed. This place, originally called Suq Abu Sinn ('Abu Sinn's Market') has now taken over the name of the region, anglicized as Gedaref.

Another important nomadic tribe is the Kababish. These inhabit a region suitable for sheep and camel rearing in the semi-desert north of Kordofan. They are a synthetic tribe, formed from diverse elements by a common way of life, which is reflected in their name (from Arabic: *ka sh*, 'a ram'). Their wide range, across the north-western trade-routes, made the tribe a factor of some importance in the commercial and political history of the Sudan, especially during the nineteenth century.

An important sub-group of tribes claiming origin from the Juhayna is the Baqqara of southern Kordofan and Darfur. As their name (from Arabic: *baqar*, 'a cow') implies, these are cattle-nomads: the frontier-tribes of Arabdom, inhabiting regions where camel nomadism is climatically impossible. The route by which they arrived in their present habitat is a subject of controversy, but broadly speaking they seem to be a southern offshoot of the great Arab irruption into the lands west of the Nile. The furthest wave of these immigrants was carried as far west as Lake Chad, whence a return-movement towards the east deposited the ancestors of the modern Baqqara tribes.

Between the Baqqara in the south and the camel-Arabs of the north were enclaves of non-Arab sedentaries. From one of these, the Fur, protected by the mountainous bastion of Jabal Marra, developed the important Muslim sultanate of Darfur ('the land of the Fur'). The non-Arab tribes to the south of the Baqqara country were frequently raided for slaves, and intermarriage has considerably modified the physical type of the Baqqara, although they have preserved their Arabic speech and tradition. Two tribes played a particularly important role in the history of the last century: the powerful Rizayqat of southern Darfur, athwart a principal route from the Bahr al-Ghazal region to the north; and the Ta'aisha, an unimportant tribe until the Mahdia, when they were used by their kinsman, the Khalifa 'Abdallahi, as an instrument of his domination in the Sudan.

The Beja are Hamitic-speaking tribes, now inhabiting the Red Sea

Hills and parts of the plains sloping down to the main Nile. Their ancestors confronted and, to some extent, intermarried with the Arab immigrants into Upper Egypt in the early Middle Ages. They are camel-nomads, although there has been some degree of sedentarization, especially in connection with the modern agricultural development of the Gash and Tokar deltas. Like the riverain Nubians, the Beja became Muslims, and have undergone varying degrees of arabization. In its lightest form, this amounts to little more than claiming an Arab pedigree; the early Muslim heroes, Khalid ibn al-Walid and al-Zubayr ibn al-'Awwam being preferred as adoptive ancestors.

The most northerly of the modern Beja, the 'Ababda, now divided between Upper Egypt and the Sudan, are, however, Arabic-speaking. As protectors of the route across the Nubian Desert, from Sudanese territory to the Nile at Kurusku, a clan of the 'Ababda played a part of some importance before the construction of the railway, and their chiefs were in close relations with the Turco-Egyptian administration. The more southerly and less arabized Beja underwent a period of expansion in the eighteenth century, moving south-westwards from their mountainous habitats towards the plains of the Atbara and the Gash. The most aggressive of these tribes, the Hadendowa, had established itself in the Taka, the region of the Gash, by the early nineteenth century.

Of the other non-Arab peoples of the northern Sudan, the Fur have already been mentioned. Although surrounded by a flood of immigrant Arab tribes, they succeeded in establishing a dynastic Muslim state which was not finally extinguished until 1916. Between Darfur and the White Nile, the hilly region of the Nuba Mountains provided a refuge for another indigenous people as Arab tribes gradually occupied the plain of Kordofan. The name of Nuba is applied in Arabic both to these people and to the historical Nubians of the main Nile. The nature of the relationship between these two homonymous groups has long been a matter of controversy. Here it is enough to note that the hill-Nuba never succeeded in asserting themselves against the Arabs, as did the Fur. Their hill-top communities were divided and isolated. They remained for the most part pagan, although the greater security of the present century has opened the way both to organized Christian missionary activity and the more amorphous but effective influence of contact with Muslims. In the north-eastern foothills lay the kingdom of Taqali, whose rulers encouraged the immigration of settlers and established their suzerainty over a considerable area. The kingdom continued to exist in semi-autonomy after the Turco-Egyptian conquest; and was integrated into the local government system of the Condominium.

THE ANCIENT TRADE-ROUTES

The territories which now form the northern Sudan were traversed by a number of trade-routes. These found their outlet through Upper Egypt and the Red Sea. The commerce of the eastern *Bilad al-Sudan*, extending to Darfur or a little further west, was thus quite distinct from that of the central *Bilad al-Sudan*, which found an outlet by way of the Fezzan to North Africa.

The routes of the eastern *Bilad al-Sudan* lay along two main axes. One, running roughly from south to north, linked Sennar with Egypt. The other, roughly from west to east, linked Darfur with Suakin. Commercial relations existed between Sennar and western Ethiopia, centring on Gondar. From Sennar a route ran along the western bank of the Blue Nile through the Gezira to the ancient market-town of Arbaji.[6] Further to the north, the river was crossed, and the way continued along the eastern bank of the Blue and main Niles by al-'Aylafun and Halfayat al-Muluk ('Halfaya of the Kings'), the later capital of the 'Abdallab chiefs.

Beyond Qarri, the old 'Abdallabi capital, there were alternative routes to the north. The western route was apparently the more used in the earlier Funj period. The Nile was crossed near Qarri or al-Diraya (i.e. either above or below the Sabaluqa Gorge), and travellers then struck across the Bayuda Desert in a north-westerly direction, cutting off the great bend of the Nile and avoiding the country of the predatory Shayqiyya. Before the rise of the Shayqiyya, in the late seventeenth century, caravans may well have followed the river all the way. The desert route met the Nile again at Kurti, and continued along its western bank, through the vassal-kingdom of Dongola, to the frontier-post of Mushu, some way south of the Third Cataract. Here the caravans turned into the desert.

At the Salima Oasis, the Nile route was joined by the great artery of trade between Darfur and Egypt, the *Darb al-arba'in* ('the Forty Days' Road'). This began at Kubayh, the principal commercial centre of Darfur, ran to the frontier-post of Suwayna, and thence went north-eastwards across the desert to Salima. From Salima the route went by way of the alum-producing watering-point of Shabb to the Kharja Oasis, which was an outpost of Ottoman Egypt. Thence it ran to the Nile at Asyut.

The eastern route seems to have developed during the eighteenth century, in consequence of increasing political instability in the riverain territories downstream of Berber. From Qarri it went along the eastern bank to Shendi and El Damer, and over the Atbara into the territory of Berber. It then left the river, and crossed the Nubian Desert until Ottoman territory was reached in the neighbourhood of Aswan. After Muhammad 'Ali's conquests, a shorter desert-crossing was usual, from Abu Hamad, at the great bend of the Nile, by the wells of al-Murrat to Kurusku in Lower Nubia. The line of the modern railway, between Abu Hamad and Wadi Halfa, is the latest variant in this historic route.

The routes of the west-east trade axis were also liable to vary in accordance with political conditions. Kordofan was a debatable land between the rulers of Sennar and Darfur, and the situation of the untamed Shilluk on the White Nile combined to render unsafe the direct route from Kubayh to Sennar via El Obeid. Caravans therefore took a more northerly route from El Obeid to Shendi. From Shendi caravans went to Egypt by the desert-crossing described above. Merchants travelling from Shendi to Suakin went up the river Atbara to Quz Rajab, a market-town ruled by an 'Abdallabi chief. A direct route from Sennar also ran to Quz Rajab, but this was rendered dangerous by the Shukriyya nomads. From Quz Rajab, one route went direct to Suakin, while another made a diversion into the Taka.

By the early nineteenth century, Shendi, the point of intersection of the two route-axes, had become the principal commercial centre of the eastern *Bilad al-Sudan*. In the years immediately preceding the Turco-Egyptian invasion it was under the strong autonomous rule of *Makk* Nimr,[7] the Sa'dabi chief. Its populace was composed of indigenous Ja'aliyyin and merchant settlers from Sennar, Kordofan, Darfur and Dongola, the last being the most numerous. In spite of the commercial activity over which they presided, neither the Sa'dab nor any other Sudanese dynasty coined their own money. Millet and *dammur,* the local cotton cloth, the staples of local commerce, formed the media of exchange, while foreign silver coins (in Burckhardt's time,[8] the Spanish dollars of Charles ɪᴠ) were used for larger transactions.

Shendi was a centre both for the internal trade of the various regions cf the eastern *Bilad al-Sudan*, and for external trade. Amung the principal commodities produced and consumed within the region were millet and *dammur*, while slaves were of pre-eminent importance, both in internal and external trade. The slaves were not, of course, taken from among the Muslim peoples, but were obtained chiefly by raiding the pagan fringe of Ethiopia and the tribes to the south-west of Darfur. A certain number of them came from servile families settled in the neighbourhood of Sennar. Although many slaves were retained permanently in the Sudanese territories, as domestic servants, field workers and armed bodyguards, there was a considerable export trade to Egypt and Arabia. A smaller, more specialized trade, was in horses from Dongola, which were exported to the Yemen.

Although there was little commercial intercourse between the eastern *Bilad al-Sudan* and the countries west of Darfur, a steady stream of Muslim pilgrims, known generally as Takarir, or Takarna (singular, Takruri), passed from the central and western *Bilad al-Sudan* into Darfur, where their numbers were still further augmented from the local peoples. From Darfur they went eastwards by a variety of routes. Some went north, to Asyut and Cairo, where they joined the Egyptian Pilgrimage Caravan. Others made their way to Sennar and Gondar, and thence to the seaport of Massawa. The most favoured route in the early nineteenth century was however the great commercial artery by way of Shendi to Suakin. This pilgrimage-route, linking the central and eastern portions of *Bilad al-Sudan*, can hardly have been older than the sixteenth century, when Muslim dynasties were established in Sennar, Darfur and Wadai.[9]

Many of the pilgrims were excessively poor, and depended on charity or earnings from manual labour to complete their journey, which in some cases lasted for years. Their successors in the present century, now generally called Fallata, have provided much of the labour force for the cotton-fields of the Gezira, and are a semi-permanent element in the population of the modern Sudan. At some time, probably in the early nineteenth century, a colony of Takarna established a vigorous frontier-state in a district of the Abyssinian marches known as the Qallabat. The name of their territory is perpetuated in the modern frontier-town of al-Qallabat, anglicized as Gallabat.

PART I

BEFORE THE TURCO–EGYPTIAN CONQUEST

*At Bujarâs [Faras], the capital of the province of Al-Marîs,
which is a well-populated city, there is the dwelling-place of
Jausâr, who wore the turban and the two horns and the
golden bracelet.*

Abu Salih, *History*
(early thirteenth century), translated B. T. A. Evetts.

*The Sultan of the Muslims, the Caliph of the Lord of the
Worlds; who undertakes the affairs of the world and the
Faith; who is raised up for the interests of the Muslims;
who supports the Holy Law of the Lord of the Prophets;
who spreads the banner of justice and grace over all the
worlds; he by whom God corrects His servants and gives
light to the land; the repressor of the race of unbelief and
deception and rebellion, and the race of oppression and
corruption; the mercy of God (praised and exalted be He!)
to the townsman and the nomad; he who trusts in the King,
the Guide: the sultan, son of the sultan, the victorious, the
divinely aided Sultan Badi, son of the deceased Dakin, son
of the Sultan Badi.*

*May God, the Compassionate, the Merciful, grant him
victory by the influence of the great Qur'an and the noble
Prophet.   Amen. Amen. O Lord of the Worlds.*

From a charter of
Sultan Badi vɪ (1791).

1

THE EASTERN *BILAD AL-SUDAN*
IN THE MIDDLE AGES

At the time of the coming of Islam in the early seventh century, there were three territories on the Nile, south of the Byzantine province of Egypt. The first of these, the land of the Nobadae or Nubians proper, extended upstream from the First Cataract. Beyond it lay the country of the Makoritae with its capital at Old Dongola. Still further south was the kingdom of the Alodaei, the capital of which, Soba, lay on the Blue Nile, not far from the modern Khartoum. Christian missionaries had made converts, including the ruling families; and at an uncertain date before 891 the two northern territories were combined into one kingdom, usually called by its Arabic name, al-Muqurra (i.e. the Makoritae). The term al-Nuba (the Nubians), although properly restricted to the people of the more northerly of the two territories, was generally applied to the combined kingdom, and even extended to the inhabitants of its southern neighbour, known in the Arabic sources as 'Alwa.

The conquest of Egypt by the Muslim Arabs between 639 and 641 brought to the border of Nubia a militant power, but one whose control over Upper Egypt was still precarious. Frontier raiding by both sides took place, and in 651–2, the governor of Egypt, 'Abdallah ibn Sa'd ibn Abi Sarh, led an expeditionary force to besiege Dongola. The campaign and its outcome are known to us only from later Arabic accounts, which represent the Nubians as suing for peace, but it is clear that 'Abdallah was unable either to inflict a decisive defeat or to extend Muslim territory south of the frontier-town of Aswan. As the history of the following centuries was to show, invaders from the north were checked both by the resistance of the Nubians and by the long and difficult lines of communications from advanced bases in Egypt. In the end Christian Nubia succumbed to gradual erosion and infiltration rather than to organized military invasion.

Medieval Arabic writers attach to 'Abdallah ibn Sa'd's expedition the conclusion of a formal treaty of peace, which, we are given to understand, henceforward regulated the relations between Muslim Egypt and al-Muqurra. The story presents some anomalies. In the first place, the alleged instrument is known as the *baqt* – a word which is unique in Arabic diplomatic terminology, and (in spite of the exertions of medieval etymologists) is derived from no Arabic root but from the Latin *pactum* by way of Graecized *pakton*, in Hellenistic usage 'a compact of mutual obligations and its connected payments'. In the second place, the stipulations of the *baqt* are curious. They are described with increasing elaboration as time goes on, so that al-Maqrizi, writing in the first half of the fifteenth century, eight hundred years after the event, gives what purports to be the authentic text, signed, sealed and delivered. Since it includes the provision that the Nubians shall maintain in good order the mosque which the Muslims have built in the centre of the city of Dongola, one need not hesitate to stigmatize this as a medieval forgery. The earlier accounts of the *baqt*, however, which go back to the ninth century, indicate that the essence of the compact was an annual exchange of slaves from Nubia for provisions from Egypt. The number of slaves is given (with some variation) as 360, and the kind and qualities of the provisions are specified in one source. The assertion by one writer that the supply of these provisions originated as an act of grace by the Muslim governor of Egypt may be disregarded as a face-saving presentation of a state-controlled barter-trade between the two territories. The survival of the Hellenistic term suggests that 'Abdallah ibn Sa'd's invasion did not originate this annual transaction but rather re-established, perhaps after interruption, a trade of long standing. As the Shari'a crystallized in the first three centuries of Islam, Muslim jurists had difficulty in accommodating within their categories this anomalous relationship with a Christian state. It has been suggested that al-Maqrizi's 'treaty' represents such an adaptation of historical fact to legal fiction.

To the east of Lower Nubia lay the barren and mountainous territory, the source of gold and emeralds, known to medieval geographers as *bilad al-ma'din*, 'the land of the mines'. This was a region outside the effective control of the Egyptian and Nubian rulers alike, inhabited by the sparse and fragmented tribal groups of the Beja, but by its nature attractive to adventurers. Clashes between the Beja and immigrant Arab miners were inevitable, and led in 854 to a full-scale military expedition from Qus, supported by a supply-fleet in the Red Sea. The Beja chief, 'Ali Baba, was defeated, and taken to the caliph in Baghdad as a tributary ruler. He was honourably received, and sent home with gifts. Such campaigns and the resultant undertakings to pay tribute were of transient effect; of more significance was the continued immigration of tribal Arabs to the land of the mines.

The career of one Arab adventurer in the third quarter of the ninth century illustrates the state of the frontier society there. 'Abdallah al-'Umari was (or claimed to be) a descendant of the third caliph, 'Umar ibn al-Khattab. A man of family and education, he bought a gang of slave-labourers and went off to make his fortune in the gold mines. He built up a following among the miners by exploiting (not always successfully) the tribal rivalries and resentments of the Arabs. His presence was disturbing to the Nubians, and repeated hostilities ensued. Finally Ahmad ibn Tulun, the autonomous governor of Egypt, alarmed at the unrest on his southern frontier, sent to Aswan an expeditionary force, which was defeated by al-'Umari. His prestige in the land of the mines was now, in 869, at its height, but his authority was precarious, resting as it did on the unstable Arab grouping in the region. In the end he fell a victim to tribal assassins. His head was carried to Ahmad ibn Tulun, who was, no doubt, as gratified as the Nubian king to learn of his death.

Al-'Umari's principality, if it may so be styled, died with him, but his career was an indication of increasing arabization of the region. One of the leading tribal groups in the land of the mines was Rabi'a, which in the time of al-'Umari had allied with the Beja against him, and suffered from his reprisals. By the middle of the tenth century, Rabi'a, who had intermarried with the Beja, were paramount throughout the region, and their chief was styled *Sahib al-Ma'din*, 'the Lord of the Mines'.

In 969 Egypt was conquered on behalf of a dynasty, the Fatimids, who had set up a caliphate in North Africa in opposition to the 'Abbasids of Baghdad. Shortly afterwards an envoy was sent to the court of Dongola. His name, Ibn Sulaym al-Aswani, suggests that he was a native of Aswan, and hence familiar with the Nubians. The object of his mission was twofold: to re-establish trading relations, which had been interrupted by the change of regime in Egypt; and to seek the conversion of the Nubian king to Islam. The latter aim may seem surprising, and indeed was not achieved, but it must be remembered that the Fatimid propagandist organization was highly developed and had contributed largely to the success of the dynasty.

Ibn Sulaym returned to Egypt to write an account of the Nubians. The extant portions of this, transmitted by later authors, are the most important single literary source concerning medieval Nubia.[1]

Ibn Sulaym describes the country through which he passed on the way to Dongola. Five miles upstream of Aswan, beyond the First Cataract and the island of Philae, was the frontier-post of al-Qasr, 'the fortress', held by a garrison and forming the gateway to Nubia. Beyond lay the great province of Maris, the old land of the Nobadae, extending along the Nile to a village above the Fourth Cataract, which marked the boundary between Maris and al-Muqurra. The most northerly part of Maris was open to the Muslims, who held land in the vicinity of the frontier, and traded upstream. Intermarriage and conversion to Islam are suggested by Ibn Sulaym's comment that a group of the Muslim inhabitants did not speak good Arabic. A narrow strip of land by the river was irrigated by water-wheels turned by oxen, and was cultivated in small patches of one to three acres. The land gave several crops in the year: wheat was uncommon, but barley, millet, sorghum, sesame and beans were grown. There were palm-trees, and upstream, where the cultivated area broadened out, vineyards.

In this northern district of Maris were two fortresses, one being Ibrim, and Bajrash (now known as Faras), the residence of the governor who was styled 'the Lord of the Mountain'. Stationed at the approach of the Second Cataract, he controlled the transit-trade and passage upstream. The Muslim merchants bartered goods (sometimes under the guise of 'presents') for the slaves which he provided. A port called Taqwi at the foot of the Second Cataract marked the limit for boats coming from al-Qasr, and no one could go further into Nubia without the Lord of the Mountain's leave. Beyond the Second Cataract lay the narrow and barren reach of the Nile, later to be known as Batn al-Hajar, 'the Belly of Stone', which is vividly described by Ibn Sulaym. This region was in effect the military frontier of Nubia. Six stages beyond the commercial frontier at Taqwi was the garrison of the Upper Maqs. Although the district formed part of Maris and was within the jurisdiction of the Lord of the Mountain, the commandant of the garrison held authority from the king himself to exercise the most rigorous control over all who passed. Indeed the death penalty awaited those who penetrated further into Nubia without the king's permission. Here no Muslim currency circulated, for there were no Muslim merchants, and local trade was carried on by the barter of slaves, cattle, camels, iron and grain. It was the existence of this closed military zone which enabled the Nubians to launch surprise raids on their neighbours.

The garrison of the Upper Maqs was separated by another cataract from the town of Say, an episcopal see. The next district, Saqluda, resembled that lying south of Aswan, and produced date-palms, vines, olives, and cotton which was woven locally. The governor apparently held office by direct royal appointment, and had authority over a number of sub-governors – Ibn Sulaym tells us that Saqluda means 'the Seven Governors'. Passing beyond this last part of Maris, Ibn Sulaym came to the district of Baqum, 'the Marvel', where the Nile spread out among a number of islands. A succession of villages with cultivation, cattle and dovecots lined the banks, for this was the granary of the capital, and the king's favourite holiday resort. Parrots and other tropical birds abounded in the trees, and crocodiles (allegedly harmless) swam in the streams. A further district, Safad Baqal, was equally fertile and well-populated – the churches and monasteries are particularly mentioned – and equally favoured by the king, whose capital, Dongola, lay at its southern extremity, fifty days' journey from Aswan.

As far as his mission was concerned, Ibn Sulaym had only limited success. A disputation with King George of Muqurra over the rival merits of Christianity and Islam was fruitless, as might have been expected. While Ibn Sulaym was in Dongola, the celebration of the Muslim Feast of Sacrifice fell due, and he organized public prayers for his co-religionists, who were about sixty in number, outside the city. In spite of the objections of some courtiers, the king allowed the prayers to be held. The incident is interesting evidence that the number of Muslim residents in Dongola was at that time very small, since some of the sixty must have been Ibn Sulaym's own suite; and that presumably no mosque existed in the city, despite the alleged provisions of the *baqt* treaty.

Ibn Sulaym must, however, have been more successful in restoring the slave-trade between Nubia and Egypt, since black troops formed an important part of the Fatimid army, and played a political role in the history of the dynasty. Earlier regimes in Egypt had similarly recruited black slave-soldiers. In the early Islamic period, the country had been garrisoned by Arab tribal warriors, the descendants of the conquerors. But the 'Abbasid Caliph al-Mu'tasim (833–42) ended this system: the Arabs lost their salaries and pensions. Henceforward the standing armies of rulers in Egypt were recruited from a variety of sources, chief among them being white slaves, mainly at this time of Turkish origin and known as Mamluks, and black slaves brought in from (or through) Nubia, called *Sudan* – a term which is sometimes rendered 'Sudanese', but which simply means 'Blacks' and lacks any national significance. Ahmad ibn Tulun, the first of the autonomous governors of Egypt, himself of Turkish Mamluk descent, reportedly had 24,000 Turkish Mamluks and 40,000 Blacks. The founder of the second gubernatorial dynasty, the Ikhshid (also of Turkish origin) likewise had black slave troops, and a black eunuch, Kafur, was the regent after his death. Under the Fatimids, Berber tribal warriors, Turks and *Sudan* formed the forces of the caliphate, and the last group attained particular importance in the reign of al-Mustansir (1035–94), whose mother was a black slave-girl. During the last century of Fatimid rule, when the caliphate was seriously weakened, the *Sudan* underwent various changes of fortune. At its very end, when in 1169 Saladin was military governor of Egypt, he had to put down a desperate revolt of the black troops, and expel their remnants from Cairo to Upper Egypt. For several years their risings there necessitated the sending of expeditions to suppress them. On one of these in 1173, Saladin's brother, Turan Shah, penetrated into Nubia, where he captured Ibrim, which, however, was evacuated by the Ayyubid garrison two years later. An ambassador was at this time sent to Dongola, ostensibly on a mission to the Nubian king, actually to spy out the country in case Saladin and his brothers needed to retreat there.

Since the tenth or early eleventh century, the chief power in the vicinity of Aswan and the northern part of Maris had been a clan originating from the Arab tribe of Rabi'a, linked with the group who dominated the Land of the Mines. Its chief performed in 1007 a notable service to the Fatimid caliph of Egypt, al-Hakim, by capturing a troublesome rebel known as Abu Rakwa. For this, he was awarded the honorific of *Kanz al-Dawla*, 'the Treasure of the State', which later chiefs inherited, and from which the clan as a whole was called Banu'l-Kanz. In 1174 an alliance between the rebel *Sudan* and the reigning Kanz al-Dawla was suppressed by another of Saladin's brothers. Banu'l-Kanz were driven out of the Aswan region southwards into Nubia.

The period of the Fatimid caliphate saw the rise of an important port on the Red Sea coast. This was 'Aydhab, near the northern frontier of the modern Sudan, and from it routes ran across the desert to the river ports of Qus and Aswan. 'Aydhab had a share in the international trade between Egypt and the Indian Ocean, which developed considerably under the Fatimids, and also in the pilgrimage traffic to the holy cities of Mecca and Medina. The older route had passed by way of Lower Egypt and Sinai, but this presented increasing difficulties in the later eleventh century, particularly after the establishment of the Latin Kingdom of Jerusalem by the Crusaders. 'Aydhab had obvious disadvantages – the lack of a fertile hinterland to supply provisions, the hazardous desert-journey through Beja territory to the Nile, the remoteness of the town from Cairo, so that its revenues and administration were shared with a Beja chief of the locality. Nevertheless the port enjoyed, with some vicissitudes, a busy commerce and much prosperity until the late fourteenth century.

Apart from the campaigns of Saladin's brothers, which, as we have seen, were undertaken primarily to suppress the fugitive *Sudan*, the period of Ayyubid rule of Egypt seems to have been one of peaceful relations with Nubia. The situation began to change, however, in the second half of the thirteenth century, when Mamluk rulers displaced the Ayyubids. Two of the early Mamluk sultans, Baybars (1260–77) and Qalawun (1279–90), began their careers as Turkish military slaves in the household of the penultimate Ayyubid ruler of Egypt. As warrior-kings and converts to Islam, they saw their principal duty as the protection of Muslim territory against the infidel – the Mongols in Iraq and Persia, the Crusaders on the coast of Syria-Palestine, the Nubian Christians in the far south. It is not therefore surprising that the Mamluk period saw the adoption of a sustained aggressive policy towards Nubia, designed to bring al-Muqurra under the control of the Mamluk sultanate. To this there were contributory causes. Upper Egypt had been for centuries the refuge of insubordinate Arab tribes, and there were recurrent revolts of greater or less significance throughout and beyond the Mamluk period. Banu'l-Kanz reappeared on the scene, seeking to regain their former seat at Aswan, but from 1380 a counterbalance to their power was provided by Hawwara, a fraction of the great tribe of that name, arabized Berbers who had moved into Egypt. Throughout the fifteenth century and well into the Ottoman period, Hawwara were dominant in Upper Egypt. Furthermore, as will appear, the decline of al-Muqurra was accelerated by quarrels and rivalry within the ruling family.

This dangerous symptom first appeared when, in 1268, King David, who had usurped the throne from his maternal uncle, sent a letter to Baybars informing him of this, and accompanied the letter with gifts. He was presumably seeking the sultan's support, but Baybars's reply was to demand the *baqt* – presumably this trade had lapsed with the change of regimes in Egypt, as it seems to have done at the Fatimid conquest. That Nubia might still be a dangerous neighbour was demonstrated in 1272, when David's forces carried out a damaging raid on 'Aydhab, still Egypt's principal Red Sea port. The governor of Qus carried out a counter-raid towards Dongola in the following year, but in 1275 he sent out a full-scale expedition including both Mamluks and Arab tribesmen, to install Shakanda, another Nubian prince, in place of David. A battle was fought in 1276 near Dongola, in which the Mamluk expeditionary force was victorious. It was the first Muslim army to penetrate so far into Nubia since 'Abdallah ibn Sa'd, over six centuries before. Shakanda was crowned in Dongola, and for the first time a Nubian king took an oath to a sultan in Egypt as his overlord.[2] From the point of view of the Egyptian chancery, Shakanda's status was assimilated to that of a provincial governor, and that of the Nubians to *dhimmis*, i.e. Christians living under Muslim rule and protection, and paying tribute. The two northern fortresses of Ibrim and al-Daw were placed under the sultan's jurisdiction, and their revenues went to his privy purse.

This pattern of events, the invasion of Nubia to install a pretender as vassal-king, was to recur on several occasions in the next forty years. At no time did the Mamluk sultans carry out, or even attempt, a permanent military conquest of al-Muqurra, although for a short time in the reign of Qalawun there was a Mamluk garrison in Dongola. Nevertheless the remote security of Nubia, which had impressed Ibn Sulaym three centuries before, was at an end. In 1292 one of these vassal-kings wrote bitterly to al-Ashraf Khalil, Qalawun's son, after an interruption of the *baqt*, that the land was wasted 'because of the invasions of the Muslim armies time after time after time', augmented by the destruction caused by the king of al-Abwab, the southern neighbour of al-Muqurra.

Another of Qalawun's sons, al-Nasir Muhammad, inaugurated the last stage in the history of al-Muqurra. Unlike his predecessors, al-Nasir Muhammad was not a warrior-king. The last of the Crusader territories had been conquered by Khalil: the Mongol rulers of Persia and Iraq had been converted to Islam, and no longer presented a threat to the Mamluk sultanate. The potential danger from Christian Nubia was also brought to an end. A Mamluk expedition to Dongola in 1316 installed as king a Nubian prince, 'Abdallah Barshambu, who had been converted to Islam while a hostage in Cairo. The sole significant act of his short reign was the turning of the church in Old Dongola into a mosque, an event commemorated in an inscription dated 16 Rabi' I 717 (i.e. 29 May 1317), which still exists. 'Abdallah Barshambu was soon overthrown and killed by a rival, none other than the current Kanz al-Dawla, whose clan had intermarried with the Nubian royal family. After further troubles, and another Mamluk expedition in 1323–4, the Kanz al-Dawla succeeded in establishing himself on the throne.

Thereafter little is heard of al-Muqurra in the Egyptian chronicles, and only one further Mamluk expedition (in 1366) seems to have been sent. The Nubian kingdom had ceased to offer a threat to the southern frontier of the Mamluk sultanate. The islamization of the rulers was under way, there was increasing Arab immigration into the cultivable riverain areas and the rainlands further south. It is significant that the expedition of 1366 occurred when a usurper had obtained the throne of Dongola with Arab tribal assistance, and had subsequently fallen out with his allies. Al-Muqurra was rapidly passing into a dark age. Its epitaph was written by the great contemporary historian, Ibn Khaldun, towards the end of the fourteenth century:—

Then the clans of the Juhayna Arabs spread over their country, and settled in it, ruling it and filling it with ruin and decay. The kings of the Nubians set about holding them back, but lacked strength. Then they proceeded to win them over by marriage-alliances, so that their kingdom broke up, and it passed to some of the offspring of Juhayna through their mothers, according to the custom of the barbarians by which possession goes to the sister and the sister's son. So their kingdom was torn to pieces, and the Juhayna nomads took possession of their land. They have no means of imposing royal control over the damage which could be stopped by the submission of one to another, and they are faction-ridden up to the present. No trace of sovereignty remains in their land, but now they are wandering bedouin who follow the rainfall like the bedouin nomads. No trace of sovereignty remains in their land, because the tincture of Arab nomadism has changed them through mixture and union.[3]

The history of the southern kingdom of 'Alwa is even more obscure than that of al-Muqurra, since it was more remote from Egypt, with which it had little direct contact. An account of it in the later tenth century is given by Ibn Sulaym, who cites as his informant a certain Samyun, the crown-prince of 'Alwa. The position of Soba, the capital, is correctly given, and the description continues:

In it are fine buildings and spacious residences, churches abounding in gold and gardens, and there is a suburb in which is a community of Muslims. The ruler of 'Alwa is wealthier than the ruler of al-Muqurra; he has a bigger army and more horses than the Muqurri. His land is more fertile and more extensive. They have few date-palms and vines; and their principal cereal is white millet resembling rice, from which they make their bread and beer. Meat abounds with them because of the abundance of their cattle, and the great wide plains, so that it takes days to reach the hill-country. They have excellent horses and brown Arabian camels. Their religion is Jacobite Christianity, their bishops being appointed by the patriarch of Alexandria, like the Nubians'. Their books are in Greek which they interpret in their own language. They have less understanding than the Nubians. Their king may reduce to slavery any of his subjects he wishes for any offence or no offence, and they do not hold that against him. Nay, rather they prostrate themselves before him, not resisting his order however repugnant, and call out, 'Long live the king! His will be done!' He wears a crown of gold, and gold is abundant in his land.[4]

The northern frontier province of 'Alwa, marching with al-Muqurra, is called by the Arabic writers al-Abwab, 'the Gates', a term which is still applied to the region of al-Kabushiyya in Ja'ali territory, south of the confluence of the River Atbara with the Nile. Here was a governor, who was sometimes referred to as the king of al-Abwab. During the thirteenth and fourteenth centuries, the rulers of al-Abwab frequently co-operated with the Mamluks against al-Muqurra. After his defeat in 1276, King David fled to Adur, king of al-Abwab, but was sent as a prisoner to Cairo. Ten years later, his captor, Adur, sent an embassy to Qalawun professing submission to the sultan and complaining about the king of al-Muqurra. His ambassadors came by way of 'Aydhab, and were accompanied by a Mamluk envoy, who had strayed from the route by Dongola, had been arrested, and threatened with the death penalty. At about the same time, another embassy arrived with gifts from Dongola, presumably to conciliate the sultan and to avert an alliance between him and the king of al-Abwab. The outcome of this was that at the beginning of 1287 an embassy was sent to King Adur and eight other potentates of the south, while another was sent to Dongola.

The subsequent decline of 'Alwa goes unrecorded in history, but after the collapse of the kingdom of al-Muqurra there was nothing to prevent the steady immigration of Arab tribesmen into the great plains to which Ibn Sulaym refers. Islamization, albeit at first of a very superficial kind, must have accompanied this population movement and the intermarriage of the Arabs with the native peoples. Christianity lingered on into the sixteenth century, however. A Portuguese source, connected with the embassy to Ethiopia in 1520–6, speaks of the recent existence of a hundred and fifty churches in 'Alwa, and witnessed the arrival of a delegation to ask for priests to be sent to their land.[5] Probably by this time Soba had ceased to exist.

Meanwhile, the Red Sea coastal areas remained more in touch with the outside world, although here too there was a decline in importance and prosperity during the Mamluk sultanate. King David's raid in 1272 does not seem to have inflicted lasting damage on 'Aydhab, but other causes contributed to its downfall. With the reduction of the Latin kingdom of Jerusalem to the coastal fringe of Palestine in the time of Saladin, the Muslim pilgrims returned to their old route by Sinai. The vital line of communication for trading caravans between Upper Egypt and 'Aydhab was frequently endangered by the lawlessness of tribesmen, both Arabs and Beja. Sultan al-Nasir Muhammad endeavoured to secure this sector of his southern frontier also by commissioning a punitive expedition against the desert tribes. In 1317 his force advanced from Qus to 'Aydhab, then along the coast to Suakin and inland in a great sweep to the River Atbara. They pushed upstream to Jabal Kasala, then made their way down the river to its junction with the Nile, returning to Egypt through al-Muqurra. It was a remarkable achievement, but it failed to repress the nomads. The hazards which they caused to caravans passing between 'Aydhab and Qus on the Nile appear to have ended trade through this port in the second half of the fourteenth century.[5]

2

THE EASTERN *BILAD AL-SUDAN* FROM THE EARLY SIXTEENTH TO THE EARLY NINETEENTH CENTURY

The period of Sudanese history from the early sixteenth to the early nineteenth century is for the most part obscure and lacking in firm historical data. The primary sources are few. The oldest literary source extant is a biographical dictionary (a genre characteristic of Islamic historical writing) containing nearly 300 notices of Muslim holy men. Muhammad wad Dayfallah, the compiler of this work, the *Tabaqat*, came from a family of religious scholars living at Halfayat al-Muluk. He is said to have been born in 1726–7, and he died in 1809–10.[1] The *Tabaqat* contains biographies going down to 1802–3. It is clear from internal evidence that these are not all the work of one hand, since they vary considerably in style, nature and language, some of them amounting to only a few lines, others to several pages, subdivided into chapters. It is therefore reasonable to assume that the *Tabaqat* includes older materials.

The second literary source available to us is conventionally called the Funj Chronicle, and it exists in a number of recensions.[2] The original chronicler was a certain Shaykh Ahmad ibn al-Hajj Abu 'Ali, better known as Katib al-Shuna, 'the clerk of the government grainstore'–an office he held after the Turco-Egyptian conquest. His home was in the eastern Gezira, near the Blue Nile, but all we know of him comes from a few references in his chronicle, the last of which dates from 1838. Internal evidence indicates that the original draft was made before the fall of the Funj sultanate in 1821, but the oldest extant recension goes down to 1838. Later continuations brought the chronicle down to 1871–2, with a good deal of editing and supplementing of the earlier material. The Katib's original version falls very clearly into two parts. The first, and much shorter, portion of the chronicle, deals with the origin of the Funj, and gives some information about the earlier rulers from the early sixteenth century to 1724. From that date, the accession of Badi IV Abu Shulukh, the information becomes increasingly copious, as the author draws on his own recollections and those of the generation of his father

(d. 1802). The Funj chronicle is thus a valuable and detailed source for the events of the last century of the Funj kingdom, although the author's field of vision is practically limited to the Gezira, and he has little to say about the important tribal polities of the main Nile. On the early Funj rulers his information is comparatively sparse, while his materials on the origins of the dynasty admit of no certain interpretations.

A source of a different kind is provided by Sudanese genealogies. A number of these were collected by the late Sir Harold MacMichael, and published in translation in his *History of the Arabs in the Sudan*. All these genealogies were compiled in the nineteenth or early twentieth century, although (like the *Tabaqat* and the Funj Chronicle) they incorporate earlier materials. It has not always been clearly realized that the intention of the compilers of genealogies was primarily to make a statement and a claim about the political and social relationships of the families at the time of writing. They were not prepared for the benefit of historians, or in the interest of historical accuracy. In this connection one may note that while, as we have seen, the medieval historical sources speak of the immigration of Rabi'a and Juhayna into the eastern *Bilad al-Sudan*, the later genealogists lay stress upon the descent of the Funj from the Umayyads, that of the riverain tribe of the Ja'aliyyin from the 'Abbasids, and of more than one holy family from the Prophet. The genealogical texts themselves offer evidence of this process of sophistication. In conclusion, it may be said that at best the genealogies offer firm historical data for only a few generations before the time of writing. Before that, as with the Funj traditions, it is a matter of interpretation.

A further problem of historical writing on the Sudan is the deficiency of documentary sources. Here some advance has been made in recent years, with the discovery and (to a small extent) the publication of land-charters and related documents.[3] The extant charters, so far as they are known, are all of comparatively late date, none being earlier than the eighteenth century, while most date from or after the reign of the Funj ruler Badi iv (1724–62). These charters throw some light on the social history of the Sudan in the period, systems of land-tenure, the position of religious teachers (who were the principal beneficiaries), and the great officers of state. Like the *Tabaqat* and the Funj Chronicle, they indicate an islamization of indigenous usages and institutions.

27

The fourth main source of information on the Sudan in these three centuries is the accounts of travellers. These are fairly few in number, and were for the most part written by men passing through the region to get to Ethiopia or to Egypt. The earliest such account is that given by the Jewish traveller, David Reubeni, who claimed to have spent some time in the entourage of 'Amara Dunqas, the first Funj ruler.[4] But Reubeni was an adventurer of uncertain origin, and his narrative should be regarded with caution. The same may be said of the account given by the seventeenth-century Turkish writer, Evliya Chelebi, which purports to describe a visit to Sennar in 1671–2, but the veracity of which has been impugned.[5] Once again, reliable information begins in the eighteenth century, and becomes increasingly detailed and valuable as time goes on. Of outstanding importance is the account given by James Bruce of his return from Ethiopia to Egypt by way of Sennar and the main Nile in 1772.[6] A detailed picture of society and conditions in Nubia as far south as Shendi was given by the Swiss traveller, John Lewis Burckhardt, who made two journeys in 1813 and 1814.[7]

The origins of the Funj have been a tantalizing problem for modern students of Sudanese history, and various interpretations have been placed on the scanty data available, not always with due criticism of the sources or caution in the deductions made. The Funj have been regarded as immigrants to the Blue Nile from the Shilluk of the White Nile (as stated by Bruce), from Bornu, or from Ethiopia.[8] More recently the White Nile hypothesis has been revived, but the immigrants are now presented as the bearers of ancient Nubian culture to their new homeland.[9] A recent contribution by an anthropologist suggests that the enquiry itself has been wrongly formulated, and that the origin of the Funj should not be sought in tribal migrations but in the status and function of the group so designated.[10] Essentially, however, the problem remains unsolved. Without fresh data (possibly from archaeology), and without a more rigorous investigation of the linguistic and historical data which have been adduced in support of the various hypotheses, further progress appears unlikely.

The establishment of the Funj kingdom, arabicized and islamicized as *al-Saltana al-Zarqa'* (the Black Sultanate), is ascribed to a certain 'Amara Dunqas, and is dated with curious precision to the *Hijri* year 910, i.e. 1504–5. He is described as the founder of Sennar, which became the Funj capital. If any reliance is to be placed on Reubeni's account, however, 'Amara and his court were constantly on the move throughout his domains, and the 'king's city' was Lam'ul, eight days' journey beyond Sennar – an unidentified site. The legend of the founding of Sennar given in the Funj Chronicle suggests that 'Amara and his people were cattle-nomads, who, in the early sixteenth century, were moving northwards down the Blue Nile. The permanent settlement of the dynasty at Sennar was perhaps not for another century, since, according to the Funj Chronicle, Sultan Irbat or Rubat (1616–45) founded the mosque there. His son, Badi II Abu Diqin (1645–80), completed it and built a five-storied palace.

Down to the reign of Badi II, the Funj Chronicle's account of the successors of 'Amara Dunqas is little more than a king-list, similar to the one which was written for Bruce in Sennar, and which is now in the Bodleian. The dates in the two lists are, however, not in agreement, although they concur in the order of rulers, with the exception of the second and third. From the accession of Badi II onwards, the Chronicle provides much more information.

While the Funj were establishing their power on the upper Blue Nile, its lower course and the territories of the southern reaches of the main Nile, i.e. substantially the kingdom of 'Alwa, had been overrun by Arab immigrants. Traditionally, the town of Arbaji on the Blue Nile was founded thirty years before Sennar by an Arab named Hijazi ibn Ma'in, which at least suggests Arab penetration so far south by the late fifteenth century. But a greater figure was the folk-hero 'Abdallah Jamma', who is shown as the leader of the Arabs (the epithet *Jamma'* means 'Gatherer'), and is presented in tradition as a champion of Islam. The great achievement ascribed to him is the capture of Soba, which sank into unimportance: according to Reubeni, in the time of 'Amara Dunqas it was in ruins, 'there they have wooden dwellings'. 'Abdallah's status as a Muslim hero is confirmed by the tradition which represents him as marrying the daughter of a holy man from the Hijaz, and he is represented as the eponymous ancestor of the ruling clan called the 'Abdallab.

The situation which these traditions seem to depict is of two immigrant groups, both perhaps nomadic, moving into the former kingdom of 'Alwa, Muslim Arabs from the north, pagan Funj from the south. Although Katib al-Shuna makes a brief reference to the co-operation of 'Amara and 'Abdallah to fight the 'Anaj (i.e. the indigenous people of the region), a tradition transmitted by Bruce is probably of great significance. This speaks of the defeat of the Arab

29

leader near Arbaji in 1504 by a pagan, black nation, subsequently known as the Funj. The chief of the Arabs 'thus became as it were their lieutenant'. Here there is perhaps some telescoping of developments. The tradition brings out the significance of the year 1504 as being that in which a military victory gave the Funj hegemony over the Arabs. The allusion to Arbaji points to its significance as an Arab frontier-settlement. But the Funj dominance did not remain unshaken. 'Abdallah Jamma', whose capital was at Qarri on the main Nile, died in the reign of 'Amara II Abu Sikaykin (1557–69), and the Funj king thereupon appointed 'Abdallah's son, 'Ajib al-Kafuta, to succeed him. Early in the seventeenth century 'Ajib revolted and drove out King 'Abd al-Qadir II, who fled to Ethiopia. His brother, 'Adlan I, regained the throne, and defeated 'Ajib at the battle of Karkoj in 1611–12. 'Ajib himself died in the battle, and his sons fled to Dongola. The mediation of a Muslim holy man, Shaykh Idris wad (i.e. son of) al-Arbab, obtained an amnesty for them. They returned to Qarri, where one of them was duly appointed shaykh.

In other respects the early Funj period was a time of territorial expansion and consolidation. Bruce has recorded the conquest of Jabal Moya and Jabal Saqadi, isolated hills in the central Gezira, by 'Abd al-Qadir I, a son of 'Amara Dunqas, who ruled in the mid-sixteenth century. Ethiopia was sometimes a dangerous neighbour. 'Abd al-Qadir II had apparently accepted Ethiopian suzerainty before 'Ajib al-Kafuta drove him into exile. His successors rejected Ethiopian claims, and relations deteriorated into inconclusive frontier warfare in 1618–19. The reign of Badi II saw a significant extension of Funj power westwards. A defeat was inflicted on the Shilluk, who at this time dominated much of the lower White Nile, and a bridgehead was established at Alays, now called al-Kawwa. Badi then made a difficult crossing of the plain of Kordofan, and besieged the little Muslim hill-state of Taqali, imposing tribute on its ruler.

Far to the north, Funj territory marched with Egypt, which became an Ottoman province in 1517. For some decades, however, much of Upper Egypt was beyond the effective control of Cairo, while Lower Nubia was similarly loosely dependent on the Funj sultan, so that at first there was no occasion for a clash between the Ottomans and the Funj. The extension of Ottoman rule into Nubia occurred late in the reign of Sultan Süleyman the Magnificent (1520–66), through the initiative of Özdemir (Azdamur) Pasha.

Özdemir was a relative of the former Mamluk sultan of Egypt, Qansawh al-Ghawri (1501–16), and served the new regime as governor-general of the Yemen. About the year 1550, he was authorized to recruit troops in Egypt for an expedition against Ethiopia. On his way from Upper Egypt to Suakin, he intervened in a tribal struggle in Lower Nubia, and captured Ibrim. Garrisons of Bosniak troops were installed there and also at Aswan and Say, while the administration of the region (primarily the collection of revenue) was committed to an official entitled the *kashif*. These remote representatives of Ottoman military power and governmental authority developed, during the next three centuries, into an hereditary caste which intermarried with the local people.[11] From Nubia, Özdemir proceeded to the Red Sea coast to establish an Ottoman base against the Portuguese on the one hand and the Ethiopians on the other. Suakin passed into his hands; Massawa was taken in 1557, and became his administrative centre; Zayla was conquered from the Portuguese. Özdemir died in 1559–60, during the course of an inland campaign, having thus established the Ottoman province of Habesh, i.e. Abyssinia.

Like Lower Nubia, Habesh in the seventeenth and eighteenth centuries became a weak and remote outpost. The Portuguese threat passed away, and the Red Sea became, in the seventeenth century, a quiet backwater of Muslim commerce. When Bruce visited Massawa in 1769, it no longer had an Ottoman governor but was ruled by a tribal chief, with the title of *na'ib* (Arabic: 'deputy'). As in Nubia, the Ottoman garrison had intermarried with the local people and their descendants formed an hereditary military caste. Although the *na'ibs* were nominally subordinate to the Ottoman governor of Jedda, they were in practice much more dependent on the rulers of Ethiopia, with whom they shared the customs revenue, while they had ceased to pay tribute to the sultans.

Burckhardt, in 1814, found a similar condition of affairs in Suakin. Suakin was governed by an *amir* chosen from the local patrician families of the Hadariba, a tribe of mixed Arab-Beja origin. The descendants of the Ottoman garrison-troops, who here claimed mostly a Kurdish ancestry, formed another element in the population. Ottoman authority in the port was limited to the granting of recognition to the *amir* by the governor of Jedda, and the appointment of a customs-officer, who had the title of *agha*.

The Funj king was thus the overlord of extensive Sudanese

territories, from the Third Cataract to the foothills of Ethiopia, and from the eastern desert to Kordofan. It was not a centralized or highly administered state, but rather a species of high-kingship, in which much power was held by subordinate rulers. Chief of these was the 'Abdallabi shaykh of Qarri, who bore the title *manjil* or *manjilak*, and was the viceroy over the north. Within this region were the tribal territories along the main Nile, notably that of the Ja'aliyyin, and the Shayqiyya confederacy, which defeated the forces of Badi II, and broke away from Funj suzerainty. Old Dongola was still a town of importance, and a colony of Funj in the vicinity strengthened the king's control in the north. In the southern territories, the heartland of the Funj kingdom, the provincial governors were appointed by the king, but there was a tendency for the office to become hereditary. Four of the chief governorates were the march-provinces of the Taka (the modern Kasala); Atbara, on the upper waters of that river; Khashm al-Bahr, controlling the riverain areas upstream of Sennar; and Alays, guarding the crossing of the White Nile into Kordofan.

The conversion of the Funj rulers to Islam seems to have taken place very early. Reubeni's account, for what it is worth, depicts 'Amara Dunqas as at least a nominal Muslim, showing great respect to self-styled descendants of the Prophet. His son and successor bore the Muslim name of 'Abd al-Qadir. As already mentioned, Rubat and his son Badi II built the mosque in Sennar. The islamization of the dynasty may have been due partly to political pressure from the 'Abdallab rulers in the north. 'Abdallabi tradition describes the revolt of 'Ajib al-Kafuta against 'Abd al-Qadir II as a holy war, which was followed by the building of mosques far up the Blue Nile and in the Ethiopian marches. 'Ajib is also represented as making the Pilgrimage to Mecca. Bruce, in a significant remark about the Funj invaders, says that 'They were soon after converted to Mahometism, for the sake of trading with Cairo.'[12] No doubt, here as elsewhere, merchants were bearers of Islam. Yet traces of its pagan, African origin can be discerned in the Funj monarchy until the end. The Funj Chronicle describes accession ceremonies which have nothing to do with Islam. The ruler's charters might describe him as 'our lord the sultan, the son of the sultan' on the Ottoman model, but the old, non-Arabic title of *makk* continued to be used. Bruce even asserted the existence of a custom of king-killing, the licensed regicide being a household officer from the royal clan entitled *sid al-qom* ('the lord of the kindred'), but the evidence in the Arabic sources for this practice is not clear.

The islamization of the peoples of the Funj sultanate was largely the work of individual holy men who settled in the countryside, taught the Qur'an, and endeavoured to bring social usages into conformity with the Sharia. Some of these teachers were already active before the coming of the Funj. One such was Ghulamallah ibn 'Ayid, whose father came from the Yemen, and who lived in the Dongola region, probably in the early fifteenth century. Another was Hamad Abu Dunana, who brought in the Sufi order (*tariqa*) of the Shadhiliyya to the Berber district in 1445. The marriages (whether real or alleged) of his daughters are interesting. One was the mother of the holy man Idris wad al-Arbab, while another is said to have been the wife of 'Abdallah Jamma' and the mother of 'Ajib al-Kafuta. There are some indications that 'Abdallah himself was primarily a holy man, although of a more militant character than was usual in the Nilotic Sudan.

The *Tabaqat* of Wad Dayfallah ignores the Muslim pioneers before the Funj sultanate, and its geographical range centres upon the main Nile. It offers, however, a glimpse of the islamization of the borderland between Funj and 'Abdallab in the northern Gezira, when, after speaking of the foundation of Sennar and Arbaji, Wad Dayfallah continues:

> And in that territory, no school of religious learning or of the Qur'an was known. It is said that a man would divorce his wife, and another marry her on the same day without '*idda*, until Shaykh Mahmud al-Araki came from Egypt, taught people about the '*idda*, and dwelt on the White Nile. He built a castle called the castle of Mahmud.[13]

There are two points of interest here. First, the Muslim missionary is shown as being primarily a teacher of Islamic law, the Shari'a, and introducing Muslim usages in regard to divorce and remarriage. In this connection, it is significant that the Sudanese word for a religious teacher or holy man is *faki*, from the Classical Arabic *faqih*, 'a jurist'. Secondly, living on the White Nile, Mahmud had a fortified dwelling, since he was on the very frontier of Islam. The notice of Mahmud al-'Araki tells us further that his castle was 'between the Hassaniyya and Alays',[14] i.e. between the Arab tribal land in the northern Gezira and the future Funj bridgehead. How precarious Islamic institutions were in this region is illustrated by the remark that between Khartoum and Alays were seventeen schools, all of which were destroyed by the Shilluk and *Umm Lahm*, the year of famine and smallpox in 1684.

Wad Dayfallah represents the second half of the sixteenth century, the time of the joint rule of 'Amara II and 'Ajib, as being a period of active islamization. Holy men coming from Egypt, Baghdad and the Maghrib taught the Shari'a and the religious sciences, and initiated their followers into the Sufi orders. Particularly important was the Qadiriyya order which was introduced into the Gezira by a visitor from Baghdad, Taj al-Din al-Bahari, in the second half of the sixteenth century. Natives of the Nilotic Sudan early played a part in these activities. Mahmud al-'Araki studied in Egypt before returning to his homeland on the White Nile. The territory of the Shayqiyya was an important centre of Islamic teaching in the reign of 'Ajib. Four brothers, the Sons of Jabir, three of whom had studied in Cairo, maintained a mosque-school in which they taught the Shari'a, but which in the end broke up when the last of the brothers married a queen of the Shayqiyya. The succession of teachers continued in the descendants of their sister.[15] This development, the establishment of a holy family consisting of the kinsfolk of a religious teacher or Sufi guide, was characteristic of Sudanese Islam in this period.[16]

The *fakis* had a distinctive and important role in Sudanese society and politics. Some of them, especially the local heads of Sufi orders, possessed considerable political influence. Badi II Abu Diqin granted the *faki* Bishara al-Gharbawi, a holy man in the Shayqiyya territory, exemption from all taxes and dues throughout the Funj dominions; these privileges were confirmed in the following century by Badi IV Abu Shulukh to his successors. Other *fakis* were endowed with grants of land and, perhaps in connection with these, were invested with Funj symbols of authority, the stool and turban, and even in one case with the *taqiyya umm qarnayn*, the horned cap which was the distinctive sign of secular authority. The holder of this exceptional privilege, Shaykh Hasan ibn Hassuna, who died in 1664–5, was the grandson of a Tunisian immigrant. He was possessed of great herds and traded in horses. He dominated the country around the village which still bears his name, north-west of Khartoum, like a feudal lord, having a private army of slaves, 'each one of whom bore a sword with scabbard-tip and plate and pin of silver'.[17]

In the eighteenth century, when Funj-'Abdallab control over the main Nile was weakening, the Majadhib, a family of hereditary *fakis*, established a tribal theocracy among the Ja'aliyyin, south of the

Atbara confluence. The founder of the state was Hamad ibn Muhammad al-Majdhub (1693–1776), who, after studying under Sudanese teachers, made the Pilgrimage and was initiated into the Shadhiliyya order. He acquired enormous prestige among the Ja'aliyyin as a teacher and ascetic, and became the effective ruler of a district centring upon his residence at El Damer.

Burckhardt, who visited El Damer in 1814, has left a description of the Majdhubi theocracy in its last phase. Its ruler, *al-faki al-kabir* 'the great teacher', was Muhammad al-Majdhub (1796–1831), a grandson of the founder. Burckhardt comments on the neatness, regularity and good condition of El Damer. It contained several schools, drawing pupils from a wide area in the Sudan; the teachers had many books on theology and law, brought from Cairo. Many of the *fakis* had themselves studied at Cairo, in al-Azhar, or at Mecca. The great religious prestige of the Majadhib was widely acknowledged and served as a passport to travellers on the route to Suakin.

Relations between the *fakis* and the rulers were not always harmonious. The holy men frequently acted as mediators or protested against oppression. An outstanding example of opposition is provided by Hamad al-Nahlan, called Wad al-Turabi, an ascetic who, while on Pilgrimage at Mecca, declared himself to be the *mahdi*. On his return, he protected the nomad Arabs and the villagers of the eastern Gezira during a great tax-gathering expedition commanded by the *wazir* of Sultan Badi III al-Ahmar about the end of the seventeenth century. The episode, demonstrating the miraculous power of Wad al-Turabi, is described at length in the *Tabaqat*.[18] In comparison with these venerated and influential men, the cult officials of the Funj period are insignificant.

The reign of Badi III (1692–1716) was troubled in other respects. He was at one time confronted by a revolt of his minister, Irdab, who appears to have commanded the Funj warriors, and who was supported by the 'Abdallabi chief. The rebels appointed a new sultan and marched against Badi. Although their forces were much larger than his, he succeeded in defeating them, and killing Irdab. Another revolt of the Funj took place under his son and successor, Unsa III, who was deposed in 1720, and sent away with his son and family. His successor, Nol, was connected on the female side with the Unsab, the previous succession of sultans. His reign, until 1724, was short and peaceful, but under the son who succeeded him, Badi IV Abu

35

Shulukh, power was finally to pass from the hands of the Funj sultans.

In the meantime, a new state had arisen in the west. The Keira sultanate in Darfur began as a tribal kingdom in the mountainous region of Jabal Marra, and emerges into history about the middle of the seventeenth century. We have no indigenous literary sources to chronicle its development as the Funj Chronicle does for the sultanate of Sennar, but this lack is partly compensated by the traditions and observations recorded by travellers. Since the sultanate survived until 1874, and was restored from 1898 to 1916 by 'Ali Dinar, we are much better informed on Keira institutions than we are on those of the Funj. The first European traveller to reach Darfur was W. G. Browne, who was there between 1793 and 1796, much of which time he unfortunately spent in confinement.[19] A much more informative account is that of Muhammad ibn 'Umar al-Tunusi, who went to Darfur in search of his father, and dwelt there from 1803 to 1811.[20] Shortly before the overthrow of the sultanate, it was visited by the German traveller, Gustav Nachtigal, who has left a valuable record of its historical traditions and its condition in 1874.[21] After its annexation to the Egyptian Sudan, Darfur was administered from 1881 to 1883 by the Austrian, Rudolf von Slatin, who also summarized its history in his book, *Fire and sword in the Sudan*.[22] Another corpus of traditions was recorded by Na'um Shuqayr, the Lebanese historian of the Sudan, his principal informant being the *imam* of the last sultan before the Egyptian annexation.[23] In the last few years, the range of primary source-materials on the Keira sultanate has been significantly extended by the publication of land-charters, a work which is still continuing. These, like their counterparts from the Funj sultanate, do not antedate the eighteenth century.

In the Keira sultanate we can see more clearly than in the Funj the expansion of a tribal kingdom into a Sudanic empire, accompanied by the evolution of the rulers from African divine kings to Muslim sultans, and by the progressive islamization of their institutions and subjects. The ascendancy of the Keira was preceded by two semi-legendary tribal power-structures in the region, traditionally and conventionally represented as the dynastic kingdoms of the Daju and Tunjur. The Keira clan and the rulers of Wadai are represented as the successors of the Tunjur rulers. The original centre of the Keira was in the northern part of Jabal Marra, whence successive waves of expansion made them dominant over the rest of the hill-country and the surrounding plains. The first of their rulers who seems an historical figure was Sulayman, called Solongdungo, perhaps meaning 'the Arab'. He lived probably in the second half of the seventeenth century, and his reign coincided with (or, in traditional terms, caused) a tribal split, part of the Keira (represented as a defeated faction) moving out of Jabal Marra, eastwards into the plains. This group, the Musabba'at, was to play an important part in the history of both the Funj and Keira sultanates in the eighteenth century. The reign of Sulayman is also traditionally seen as the beginning of the islamization of Darfur.

The principal phase of expansion was concluded in the reign of Sulayman's grandson, Ahmad Bukr, who probably died about 1730. This brought the Keira sultanate up against neighbours who could make effective resistance against conquest and absorption: Wadai to the west, the Zaghawa nomads to the north, the Musabba'at to the east. South of Darfur was the territory of the negro peoples. These provided the slaves, who were an important element in the society of the sultanate, and were also the principal article in commerce with the north. On his deathbed, Ahmad Bukr obtained an oath from his magnates securing the passage of the sultanate to each of his sons in turn. This attempt to regulate the succession was, in the event, productive of a series of struggles during the ensuing decades.

Kordofan was, in the eighteenth century, a buffer territory between the Funj and Keira sultanates. The eastern part was to some extent within the Funj sphere of influence. As we have seen, Badi II had reduced the kingdom of Taqali to tributary status in the later seventeenth century, while the Ghudiyat tribe in southern Kordofan (north of the Nuba Mountains) was closely identified with Funj suzerainty. Their chief bore, like the 'Abdallabi ruler, the title of *manjil,* and paid tribute to Sennar. Western Kordofan received the Musabba'at immigrants, who established there a sultanate of their own.[24] Engaged alternatively in warfare against their kinsmen in Darfur and in attempts to conquer central Kordofan, the Musabba'at were a disturbing element to both the greater sultanates. Shortly before the middle of the eighteenth century, 'Isawi, the sultan of the Musabba'at, defeated the representatives of the Funj in central Kordofan. Meanwhile, a faction of the Musabba'at under the leadership of Khamis ibn Janqal, a son of the previous sultan, had made their way to Sennar, where they formed an element in the forces of Badi IV. Thanks largely to them, an invasion by the Ethiopian ruler, Iyasu II, was halted at the River Dinder in 1744.

The reign of Badi IV ended, as has been mentioned, in disaster. The reasons for his downfall are implied in the charges made against him by Katib al-Shuna. Basically, it seems that he tried unsuccessfully to erect a new monarchy on new foundations. He proscribed the Unsab, the former royal clan which his father had supplanted, and granted the lands of the old families to his supporters – the Nuba and the followers of Khamis. It is probable that the earlier risings of the Funj against Badi III and Unsa III had been revolts of free-born tribal warriors against sultans who were seeking a new military power base in slave-troops. When Badi II returned from his victorious campaign against Taqali, he settled his captives, many of whom were Nuba, 'some of them in the east, and some of them in the west; and they built villages surrounding Sennar, like a wall about it'.[25] So writes Katib al-Shuna, and Bruce saw these villages when he passed. Their garrisons and the sultans' slave-troops were no doubt further recruited from the tribute which Badi II imposed on Taqali. A similar shift to reliance upon aliens and slaves characterized the rule of Badi IV's contemporary, Sultan Abu'l-Qasim of Darfur (*c*. 1749–77).

As Badi's reign went on, his arbitrary rule (as the chronicler describes it) became more intolerable. Once more a rising of the Funj took place, but its outcome did not follow the pattern of the previous military revolts. The victory of the Musabba'at in central Kordofan had been reversed by a new leader of the Funj forces, Muhammad Abu Likaylik, whom Badi had appointed as shaykh (perhaps meaning governor of Kordofan) in 1747. The commanders of the Funj forces occupying Kordofan were dismayed at the news reaching them of their ruler's behaviour, and agreed with Abu Likaylik to depose him. The army, under his leadership, crossed the White Nile at Alays, where they were joined by the sultan's son, Nasir. They advanced on Sennar and surrounded the town. Badi was allowed to leave under an amnesty, and Abu Likaylik installed Nasir as sultan (1762). This was the end of the effective Funj sultanate: as Katib al-Shuna remarks:

> From that time, the Hamaj held the power to loose and bind. They gained the mastery over the Funj. Shaykh Muhammad slew their magnates, and appointed and removed from office among them. The date was reckoned by the period of the shaykhs of the Hamaj, without reference to the kings.[26]

This was the irony of the revolution of 1762, that it redounded to the success neither of the Funj warriors who had plotted it, nor of the

'Abdallab, who for over two and a half centuries had represented the Arab element in the Funj sultanate. Whoever the Hamaj, the kinsfolk of Muhammad Abu Likaylik, were, they were neither Funj nor Arab. His and their victory may be seen as the resurgence of an autochthonous group, now islamized and Arabic-speaking. The Hamaj regency was thus inaugurated.

The withdrawal of the Funj garrison from Kordofan under Abu Likaylik in 1762 presaged the loss of the province. The power of the Musabba'at revived under their chief, Hashim ibn 'Isawi, who defeated the Ghudiyat in 1772, and regained control of central Kordofan. The real danger to Hashim came, not from the Nile valley, but from the Keira ruler of Darfur, Muhammad Tayrab, who, at the end of his reign in 1786–7 invaded Kordofan, and perhaps even reached the Nile at Omdurman. Henceforward until the Turco-Egyptian conquest, Kordofan was a dependance of the Keira sultanate. The memory of the Funj still lingered on: Browne, writing near the end of the eighteenth century, recorded that: 'A king, of the name of Abli-calik, is the idol of the people of Kordofan, where he reigned about fourteen years ago, and is renowned for probity and justice.'[27]

Muhammad Abu Likaylik was a strong and capable ruler, although illiterate. Eight years after his seizure of power, he deposed Nasir, and banished him from the capital. The ex-king plotted with the Funj against the regent, but Abu Likaylik learnt of the conspiracy, and had him put to death. His successor was his brother, Isma'il, whom Bruce visited, and described unflatteringly: 'He had a very plebeian countenance, on which was stamped no decided character; I should rather have guessed him to be a soft, timid, irresolute man.'[28]

When Abu Likaylik died in 1776–7 he was succeeded in the regency by his brother, Badi wad Rajab. A political crisis ensued in another conspiracy of the Funj with their king against the regent, and once again the conspirators were unsuccessful. Isma'il was deposed and sent to Suakin, and his son, 'Adlan II, was installed as king. A still more ominous development took place in 1780, when the sons of Abu Likaylik, resenting their treatment by their cousin, conspired with two other malcontents, the 'Abdallabi shaykh and the governor of Khasm al-Bahr, both of whom had been deprived of office, and had joined forces with 'Adlan. In the fighting that followed, Badi wad Rajab was defeated and killed, and one of the sons of Abu Likaylik,

Rajab, assumed the regency. 'Adlan was now intent on regaining the full royal power, and in 1784–5, while Rajab was on campaign in Kordofan, he carried out a coup against the regent's brother and deputy in Sennar. Rajab, returning from Kordofan, was killed in battle with the king (November 1785), and the Hamaj dispersed in disarray. Their eclipse was brief. Another son of Abu Likaylik, Nasir, became regent, and moved against Sennar. In 1788–9 the royalist forces were defeated in a battle, and 'Adlan died (it was said of grief, poison or witchcraft) a few days later.

The ascendancy of the Hamaj, thus restored, was never again lost until the Turco-Egyptian conquest, but it was an ascendancy over a declining and diminished kingdom. For the weakness of the Hamaj regency in this period, there were several reasons. The internal rivalries in the ruling clan, which had already appeared in the revolt against the Regent Badi, recurred frequently and disastrously. The Regent Nasir was opposed by his brothers, Idris and 'Adlan, and after several months of fighting, he was put to death in 1798 by the son of the Regent Badi, to avenge his father. 'Adlan himself became regent in October 1803, but two of his nephews, sons of former regents, conspired against him, and he was killed in an affray at the end of the same year. One of the conspirators, Muhammad wad Rajab, succeeded him, but his regency ended in anarchy in 1808, when he was killed by his cousin, Muhammad, the son of the Regent 'Adlan, in pursuit of a vendetta against his father's killers. Muhammad wad 'Adlan then became regent himself, his long rule lasting until 1821, when he too fell victim to a rising headed by his cousin, the son and brother of earlier regents. Shortly before the murder of the Regent Muhammad wad 'Adlan, in the words of Katib al-Shuna,

The approach of the son of the ruler of Egypt, Isma'il Pasha, had been confirmed to him. He had assembled the notable *fakis* and others to make enquiries, and had summoned the king of the Ja'aliyyin, the Kunjara and other tribes to war, with their rendezvous at Khartoum.[29]

His death plunged the Funj kingdom into anarchy at the very moment of the Turco-Egyptian invasion.

During these unhappy decades, when the Funj kings were ciphers, and the Hamaj regents were destroying themselves with internecine quarrels, their nominal vassals grew in power, and intervened in the politics of Sennar. Chief among these vassals were the 'Abdallabi shaykhs, the kings of the Ja'aliyyin, and the governors of Khashm al-Bahr. Each of these positions of power was disputed by rivals within the ruling families, and the kaleidoscopic and transient alliances of their factions with those among the Funj and the Hamaj characterize this last period of the history of the kingdom. One of the most successful was *Makk* Nimr wad Muhammad of the Ja'aliyyin, who established himself as the tribal king in Shendi in 1801–2, and whose long and prosperous reign lasted until the Turco-Egyptian conquest. His later, tragic history will appear. Meanwhile, the Majadhib theocracy in El Damer controlled the region around the junction of the River Atbara and the Nile, while Berber was the capital of the tribal kingdom of the Mirafab. Further north, the territories controlled by the Shayqiyya had long since been lost to the Funj.

The sultanate of Darfur, by contrast, was at this period at the height of its power. The warrior-sultan, Muhammad Tayrab, died at Bara on his return from his victorious campaign in Kordofan. A succession struggle ensued, in which the successful faction installed their candidate, a pious posthumous son of Ahmad Bukr named 'Abd al-Rahman al-Rashid. 'Abd al-Rahman was sultan at the time of Browne's visit to Darfur, and the traveller describes him as 'a man rather under the middle size, of a complexion adust or dry, with eyes full of fire, and features abounding in expression. His beard is short but full, and his countenance, though perfectly black, materially differing from the negro; though fifty or fifty-five years of age, he possesses much alertness and activity.'[30]

The reign of 'Abd al-Rahman al-Rashid marked the apogee of the Keira sultanate. Territorially, it was now at its widest extent. The royal court, which under previous rulers had migrated to a succession of sites from the original homeland of the Fur, was now permanently settled east of Jabal Marra and gave its name, El Fasher (al-Fashir), to the capital of the sultanate. Islam was striking deeper roots: 'Abd al-Rahman had been a *faki* before he became sultan, and the divine kingship of his ancestors was becoming overlaid with the formalities of an Islamic monarchy. Holy men, among them immigrants from the Nilotic regions, received estates, and supplied the sultanate with religious teachers and clerks in the administration. The country was still almost completely secluded from the lands to the north, although slaves (captured in raids on the pagans of the south) were sent to Upper Egypt along the great desert-route called *Darb al-arba'in*. Apart from these regular commercial contacts, the first attempts to establish political communications begin about this time. Browne tells us that 'Abd al-Rahman, on his accession, sent a present to the Ottoman sultan:

It consisted of three of the choicest eunuchs, and three of the most beautiful female slaves that could be procured. The Othman emperor, when they were presented, had, it is said, never heard of the Sultan of Dar-Fûr, but he returned an highly-ornamented sabre, a rich pelisse, and a ring set with a single diamond of no inconsiderable value.[31]

Bonaparte, when in Egypt in 1799, received a letter from 'Abd al-Rahman, and replied asking the sultan to send with the first caravan two thousand black slaves, over sixteen years old.[32] But this attempt to form an army of negro Mamluks came to nothing. Under 'Abd al-Rahman's successor, Muhammad Fadl, the Keira sultanate was at last to be brought into violent confrontation with a superior military power.

The early nineteenth century, before the Egyptian conquest, saw the appearance of new influences in the religious life of the Sudan. These were the repercussions of that great wave of revival and reform, which arose in the heart of Islam during the late eighteenth century, and which produced, among other less-known phenomena, the fanatical Wahhabi movement in Arabia. One aspect of the revival was the appearance of a new activist spirit in the Sufi orders. The Khalwatiyya order, founded in the fourteenth century, took on fresh life in the eighteenth, when missionaries were sent to propagate its teachings in Africa. One of these, al-Sammani (1718–75), established a new sub-order, which was brought to the Sudan about 1800, by a Sudanese, Ahmad al-Tayyib al-Bashir, who had been initiated in Medina. He won many adherents in the Gezira, particularly along the White Nile, for the Sammaniyya *tariqa*.

Another religious teacher whose followers were to have great influence in the Sudan was Ahmad ibn Idris al-Fasi, who originated from Fez in Morocco but spent much of his career in Arabia, where he died in 1837. Like the Wahhabis, he was a reformer who sought to restore the primitive model of Islam, purged of superstitious innovations. He influenced Muhammad al-Majdhub, when the latter was an exile in Mecca after the Turco-Egyptian conquest. Another of his disciples was Muhammad 'Uthman al-Mirghani (1793–1853), who was sent by Ahmad ibn Idris as a missionary to the Sudan. He won an enormous following among the Nubian tribes between

Aswan and Dongola, and in 1816–17 reached Sennar. Here he seems to have gained little success, and he left the Sudan, never to return. While on his missionary journey, however, he had married a woman of Dongola, by whom he had a son, al-Hasan.

After Ahmad ibn Idris's death, al-Mirghani organized his own adherents, in Arabia and the Sudan, as a new order, the Mirghaniyya or Khatmiyya. Further proselytization was carried out in the Sudan by his son, al-Hasan, and the order was favourably viewed by the Turco-Egyptian rulers. But the coming of the Egyptians had brought an important change into the structure of Sudanese Islam, as will appear.

PART II

THE TURCO – EGYPTIAN PERIOD
1820–81

You are aware that the end of all our effort and this expense is to procure negroes. Please show zeal in carrying out our wishes in this capital matter.

Muhammad 'Ali to the *Defterdar*
(23 September 1825).

I have granted you . . . the government of the provinces of Nubia, Darfour, Kordofan, and Sennaar, with all their dependencies – that is to say, with all their adjoining regions outside of the limits of Egypt. Guided by the experience and wisdom that distinguish you, you will apply yourself to administer and organize these provinces according to my equitable views, and to provide for the welfare of the inhabitants.

Ferman of Sultan 'Abd al-Majid
to Muhammad 'Ali Pasha
(13 February 1841).

3

THE INAUGURATION OF THE
TURCO – EGYPTIAN REGIME
1820–25

Muhammad 'Ali's conquest of the Sudanese provinces has some similarity to Özdemir Pasha's conquest of Lower Nubia and the Red Sea littoral, nearly three centuries previously. Both expeditions were primarily private ventures of ambitious servants of the Ottoman sultan. Their armies fought in the sultan's name, the territories acquired were formally annexed to his dominions, but lay in practice outside the bounds of his effective control. But there were certain differences between Özdemir's status and that of Muhammad 'Ali which were to affect the future history of their conquests. In 1820 Muhammad 'Ali Pasha was the autonomous viceroy of Egypt, and could draw on considerable military and economic resources in order to secure his rule over the Sudanese provinces. Unlike Özdemir, he was the founder of a dynasty, which, until the double calamity of the Mahdist revolution and the British occupation of Egypt, held tenaciously to the territories he had acquired. He was, in the third place, influenced by current European ideas, and sought not merely to acquire territory in the traditional Ottoman fashion, but to exploit its resources of men and its natural products.

Muhammad 'Ali's primary motive in undertaking the invasion of the Sudan was probably political. In the early days of his rule over Egypt, his most dangerous opponents had been the Mamluks, the survivors of the military and governing élite whose chiefs had been, in the previous century, the real masters of Egypt. By massacre and proscription, he had succeeded in 1811 in breaking their power in Egypt, but a remnant of the Mamluks had escaped beyond his control and established themselves in the petty state of Dongola, at that time a dependency of the Shayqiyya confederation. Their headquarters, which they called *Ordu* (Turkish: 'the Camp', a name corrupted by the Sudanese to *al-'Urdi*), and which is more generally known as New Dongola, stood on the west bank of the Nile, not far south of the old frontier between *Berberistan* and the Funj dominions. Here they built a walled town, recruited black slaves to

47

replenish their own dwindling numbers, and clashed with the Shayqiyya for the control of the region.

The history of the previous century had many times demonstrated the extraordinary vitality and tenacity of the Mamluks; it was commonplace for a defeated faction to withdraw upstream until a convenient opportunity occurred for a descent on Cairo and a political revolution. Although the Mamluks of Dongola were perhaps too insignificant in numbers and too remote to follow the traditional pattern, their inviolability was certain to cause anxiety to the viceroy of Egypt.

In 1812, therefore, Muhammad 'Ali Pasha sent an embassy to urge the Funj sultan to expel the Mamluks from the dominions he nominally ruled. Neither the sultan nor the Hamaj regent any longer possessed effective authority in Dongola, as Muhammad 'Ali was doubtless well aware. The embassy served a more practical purpose in spying out the military weakness and political fragmentation of the Nilotic Sudan. The situation was also made known to the viceroy by *Makk* Nasr al-Din, a member of the ruling family of the Mirafab of Berber, who sought the support of Muhammad 'Ali against his dynastic rivals. The political disorder on the middle Nile had almost stopped trade with Egypt, and the desire to revive commerce was one of Muhammad 'Ali's motives in making the conquest.

The viceroy had, however, greater ambitions than simply to restore the old trading relations. A conquest of the Nilotic Sudan would bring under his control a principal channel of the slave-trade. At this time Muhammad 'Ali's military situation was precarious, and the idea of a slave-army, docile, trained in the European manner and personally loyal to him, was most attractive. The Albanian troops, who had raised him to power in Egypt, were dangerously insubordinate, and could well be put to the arduous task of conquering and pacifying the remote Sudan. A further attraction of the region was its fabled gold mines, which, could they be located and exploited, would provide the viceroy with the means to assure his position in Egypt and his independence of the sultan.

It is difficult to find a convenient designation for the conquest of 1820–21. It was prepared in Egypt by the ruler of Egypt. Yet to speak of 'the Egyptian conquest' is liable to call up anachronistic associations. The Arabic-speaking Egyptian nation-state with its national army did not then exist: the government of the Ottoman province of Egypt was in the hands of Turkish-speaking Ottoman subjects, a ruling élite linked by a complicated web of ties to the Arabic-speaking population.

On the other hand, to speak of 'the Ottoman conquest' is equally unsatisfactory. It was, as has been said above, a private venture by Muhammad 'Ali. Although after the conquest the new provinces were governed by the same Turkish-speaking élite that ruled Egypt, and although Ottoman suzerainty was recognized, the sultan's power was even more tenuous in the Sudan than in Egypt itself. Perhaps the clumsy adjective 'Turco – Egyptian' best describes both the conquest and the administration which followed.

To the Sudanese, at any rate, the invaders and the new rulers were *al-Turk*, 'the Turks', and their regime was *al-Turkiyya*. These terms, which at first were linguistically justifiable, subsequently came to include all members of the ruling and military élites who were not of Sudanese origin. It lost its linguistic connotation and never acquired a purely ethnic significance: the Condominium administration set up in 1899 was 'the second *Turkiyya*' and, to the unsophisticated Sudanese at any rate, the British officials were 'Turks'.

The force, which left Cairo early in July 1820, was composed of about four thousand actual combatants. Different sources give varying accounts of the strength of the contingents, but all bring out their extraordinarily varied composition. Albanians and 'Turks' of unspecified origin were prominent. Another element was the Maghribis – Arabs of north-west Africa, who had long provided soldiers of fortune for the Ottoman Empire. The most genuinely Egyptian element in an ethnic sense was the Bedouin tribal forces, but the Egyptian *fallahin*, as yet unconscripted, had no part in this military venture. Of particular importance, because of their knowledge of the Nubian marches, were the 'Ababda tribesmen, who provided the camel-transport. The commander of the expeditionary force was the viceroy's third son, Isma'il Kamil Pasha, who was then about twenty-five years of age. He was accompanied by the usual household staff of a governing pasha, including a secretary, Muhammad Sa'id Efendi, who was to play a part of some importance. Three *'ulama'* travelled with the expedition, to summon the Sudanese Muslims to obey the agent of the Ottoman sultan. The officers included George Bethune English, a renegade American, who served as an officer of artillery and wrote an account of the expedition. A much more detailed and scientific description was written by a French observer, Frédéric Cailliaud, a distinguished traveller and archaeologist. Two English amateurs of antiquities, George Waddington and the Rev. Barnard Hanbury, also attached themselves to the advancing army and penetrated as far as Marawi, whence they were peremptorily ordered to return by Isma'il Pasha.

On 20 July 1820 Isma'il and his staff joined the army at Aswan. The timing of the start of the campaign was governed by the flood of the Nile, during which season alone it would be possible to haul the boats over the Cataracts. The *kashiflik* of Lower Nubia had long been autonomous of Cairo, and Husayn *Kashif*, one of the brothers who ruled the region, would have disputed the advance of the expedition but, finding himself unsupported, he fled to Kordofan. His brother, Hasan *Kashif*, submitted to Isma'il, and was confirmed in office.

The Second Cataract was passed, and the ruler of Say made his submission, only to revolt later and to be killed in the fighting. English was not a little surprised to find the people of Say, the descendants of the Bosniak soldiery, 'as white as the Arabs of Lower Egypt, whereas the inhabitants of Nubia are quite black, though their features are not those of the Negro.'[1] The Mamluks of New Dongola made no resistance. A few came in to surrender, but the majority of them fled further south and sought refuge with the Ja'ali ruler, *Makk* Nimr of Shendi. The petty rulers of the Danaqla submitted to Isma'il, and were confirmed in their positions.

The destruction of the military power of the Shayqiyya had been a principal object of the expedition. A summons was sent to their chiefs to surrender their horses and arms, but this was rejected. The Shayqiyya confederacy was at this time headed by two chiefs, *Makk* Subayr, the principal ruler of the Hannakab, in the western part of the territory, and *Makk* Jawish, whose capital was Marawi. On 4 November a battle took place near Kurti, in which the Shayqiyya were defeated. The remnant of their forces, which escaped from the battlefield, crossed the Nile and took refuge in a stone fortress at the foot of Jabal Dayqa (now called Jabal Ibn 'Awf), where they were bombarded by Isma'il, and routed once again.

This was the end of serious military resistance. *Makk* Subayr submitted to the pasha, while Jawish fled southwards, to seek asylum among the Ja'aliyyin. Isma'il's victory over the Shayqiyya was largely a consequence of his superior armament. The Shayqiyya were armed principally with long swords and lances. They carried shields of hippopotamus or crocodile hide, while some of their leaders wore coats of mail.

A very few had pistols; but the possession of guns was confined to the Chiefs, and it is a singular proof of their attachment to the weapons of their fathers, that having it always in their power to be tolerably supplied with firearms . . . they would never consent to adopt them.[2]

One is reminded of the similar conservatism of the Mamluks of Egypt, whose cavalry were routed by the fire-power of the Ottomans in 1516. Faced with this resistance, Isma'il showed for the first time a degree of ruthlessness, but an amnesty was offered to all who would surrender themselves, and in the vicinity of his camp order and security prevailed.

Having concentrated his forces, Isma'il prepared for a further advance. A river column of boats, with a protective escort moving along the bank, was sent upstream, while the pasha marched with the bulk of his troops across the peninsula of the Bayuda Desert on the left bank of the Nile. He set out on 21 February 1821, and reached the river seven days later at al-Buqayr. On 5 March the desert column reached al-Ghubush, opposite the residence of *Makk* Nasr al-Din, the ruler of Berber,[3] who made his submission and was confirmed in office.

Isma'il was in the meantime negotiating with *Makk* Jawish and the fugitive Mamluks at Shendi. All made their submission, with the exception of a small remnant of the Mamluks, who continued their flight and vanished from history. The amnestied Mamluks returned honourably to Egypt. On 19 May *Makk* Jawish made a capitulation no less final than honourable. 'I have fought against you,' he said to Isma'il, 'to the utmost of my means and power, and am now ready, if you will, to fight under the orders of my conqueror.'[4] He was given an army rank and accompanied Isma'il on the rest of the expedition, while Shayqiyya cavalry were enlisted under the command of their chiefs as irregulars.

The two rulers of the Ja'aliyyin, *Makk* Nimr of Shendi and *Makk* al-Musa'id of Metemma, also submitted and were confirmed in their positions. A similar submission was made by the sick and aged chief of the 'Abdallab, Shaykh Nasir wad al-Amin. His son and *Makk* Nimr accompanied Isma'il as hostages. Hitherto the advance had been up the western bank of the Nile, but it was now necessary to cross into the Gezira. The passage of the White Nile took from the early morning of 20 May to the afternoon of 1 June, and was a difficult operation since only nine small boats had been able to pass the Third Cataract. The horses and camels were swum across, or floated with inflated water-skins. Had the kingdom of Sennar possessed an effective army, Isma'il's troops could have been caught at a serious disadvantage, but there was no enemy in the vicinity, the passage was unopposed, and the remainder of the advance was a military parade.

The Regent Muhammad wad 'Adlan, who had sent a defiant message to Isma'il, had been killed by conspirators supporting his cousin, Hasan wad Rajab, about the beginning of April. The following weeks were wasted by an internecine struggle between the two factions. From this, Hasan emerged victorious only to flee to the Ethiopian frontier on hearing of the approach of Isma'il. Such authority as remained in Sennar was held by the old minister, the *Arbab* Dafa'allah, and the brother of the murdered regent. As the expeditionary force approached Sennar, they began to negotiate a capitulation. English describes the arrival of Dafa'allah and his colleague as ambassadors:

I saw these personages when they arrived. They were two, one a tall thin elderly man of a mulatto complexion, dressed in green and yellow silks of costly fabric, with a cap of a singular form,[5] something resembling a crown, made of the same materials, upon his head. The other was the same young man who had come a few days past to the Pasha. He was dressed today in silks like the other, except that his head was bare of ornament. They were accompanied by a fine lad about sixteen, who was, it is said, the son of the predecessor of the present Sultan. All three were mounted on tall and beautiful horses, and accompanied by about two hundred soldiers of the Sultan, mounted on dromedaries, and armed with broadswords, lances and shields.[6]

On the next day, the last Funj sultan, Badi VI, came in person to Isma'il's camp to make his submission. He was well received and honourably entertained. He apparently obtained recognition of his position from the pasha, like the other Sudanese rulers, but politically this meant nothing. A pension, granted to him and the royal family, continued to be paid until the Mahdist revolution. On the following day, probably 13 June, the expeditionary force entered Sennar. The town was far gone in ruin and decay. Even the mosque had been profaned by the scrawled drawings of pagan raiders. The old royal palace was derelict, and Badi's own residence was a large courtyard containing low brick buildings. The condition of Sennar was visible evidence of the debility of the Funj state at the time of the conquest.

After the reduction of Dongola and the Shayqiyya country,

Muhammad 'Ali Pasha sent out a new expeditionary force of three or four thousand troops and a battery of artillery to conquer the sultanate of Darfur. The commander of this second army, Muhammad Bey Khusraw, the *Defterdar*, left Cairo to join his troops on 20 April 1821.[7] The force assembled at al-Dabba, on the left bank of the Nile, below Kurti, and, with the assistance of Shaykh Salim, the chief of the Kababish, struck south-westwards across the Bayuda Desert towards Kordofan. The Furawi governor, the *Maqdum* Musallim, was invited to surrender and replied with a letter protesting against this unprecedented invasion of a Muslim country which was not subject to the Ottoman sultan. The two armies clashed at Bara, where the horsemen of Darfur and tribal warriors of Kordofan were routed by the firearms and artillery of the invaders. The *maqdum* was killed in the fighting, and the *Defterdar* entered El Obeid, the provincial capital.

On hearing of the loss of Kordofan, Sultan Muhammad Fadl sent an army to recover the province. This too was defeated. The inhabitants of the plain of Kordofan were soon reduced to submission and the harsh brutality of the *Defterdar* and his troops was long remembered,[8] but the Nuba hillmen of Jabal al-Dayir, as well as those of the remoter mountains to the south, remained unsubdued. The ultimate objective of the expedition, the subjection of Darfur itself, was also beyond the powers of the invaders. Muhammad 'Ali Pasha later tried to gain his end by supporting the claims of a brother of Muhammad Fadl, named Abu Madyan, but this attempt to install a puppet sultan in El Fasher[9] also ended in failure.

The first impressions which the people of Sennar had of their new ruler were by no means wholly unfavourable. The conquest had been achieved practically without bloodshed, and Isma'il Pasha deliberately presented himself as a mild and accessible administrator. His coming was to mark a new era: he would listen to no petitions concerning events before his arrival. To this rule, however, one important exception was made: Hasan wad Rajab and the killers of the Regent Muhammad wad 'Adlan were pursued and captured. Hasan himself was imprisoned and treated with leniency, but some of his underlings were put to death by impalement – a punishment that was a disagreeable innovation to the Sudanese.

The conquerors had already attained their military objectives: the destruction of the independent power of the refugee Mamluks and the Shayqiyya. Muhammad 'Ali Pasha could now seek to realize his further aims: the exploitation of the wealth of the Sudan, especially its gold and slaves. Towards the end of 1821, Isma'il was joined at Sennar by his elder brother, the famous Ibrahim Pasha, as commander-in-chief of the troops of Sennar and Kordofan. They were repeatedly urged by Muhammad 'Ali to send slaves to Egypt. The two brothers decided to make expeditions into the pagan territories to the south of Sennar, but Ibrahim soon fell ill and returned to Cairo. Isma'il went on and established his authority over the auriferous region of Fazughli, where a levy of gold was laid on the traders.

Meanwhile preparations were going forward for the taxation of the riverain districts. A census of the slaves and flocks held by the Sudanese had already been made, but apart from a levy of fodder no taxes had yet been demanded. During Isma'il's absence, however, the arrangements were completed. The fiscal system was organized by a committee of three, the pasha's secretary, Muhammad Sa'id Efendi, the *Mu'allim*[10] Hanna al-Tawil (a Coptic financial official) and the *Arbab* Dafa'allah. Taxes were to be paid by owners of slaves and animals at the rate of fifteen dollars per slave, ten dollars per cow, and five dollars per sheep or donkey.[11] The burden would fall on the settled people of the riverain villages, not on the nomads (there was no mention of a camel-tax), who were still virtually outside the control of the regime.

It has rightly been said that this taxation appears 'almost unbelievably onerous, and to amount to something approaching confiscation'.[12] Confiscation rather than revenue was indeed probably the real intent. Specie was rare in the Sudan, and the taxes could be paid in strong male slaves instead of cash. Thus Muhammad 'Ali's incessant demand for slaves to train as soldiers could be met by draining the reservoir of slave-labour available in the newly conquered provinces, until such time as sufficient recruits could be obtained by raiding the pagan tribes of the upper Blue and White Niles and the Nuba Mountains.

This device, if carried out, would however have grave social and political consequences. It would destroy the slave-retinues of the petty rulers who had accepted Muhammad 'Ali's suzerainty, and it would jeopardize the livelihood of all but the very poorest families, since slaves were universally employed in the households and the fields. The results were curiously similar to those which ensued from Khedive Isma'il's attempts to abolish slavery, nearly sixty years later. The Sudanese rose in rebellion.

The first symptoms of revolt appeared at once. A rumour spread that Isma'il Pasha was dead in the southern mountains, and there were sporadic attacks on Egyptian troops. The situation was saved for the time being by the return of Isma'il to Sennar. He acted with wisdom and discretion. The rebellious Sudanese were treated with clemency, and he tried to modify the assessment. He was too late; the books had already been sent to Cairo. Among his troops disease was widespread, and he removed his headquarters downstream from Sennar to Wad Medani, supposedly a healthier site. But the mortality continued, among those who died being the *Qadi* Muhammad al-Asyuti, who had been sent as judge with the invading army. While Isma'il was at Wad Medani, Hasan wad Rajab escaped from confinement to play a part in the crisis which was developing.

In October or November 1822 the incident occurred which sparked off the rising. Isma'il left for the north and arrived by river at Shendi. Here he demanded a heavy contribution of money and slaves from the Ja'aliyyin, and insulted their chief, his former hostage, *Makk* Nimr. The following night his quarters were set on fire and he perished among his retinue.

At once revolt flared out among the riverain Sudanese from Shendi southwards to Wad Medani. The small local garrisons on the main and Blue Niles, at Karari, Halfaya, Khartoum, al-'Aylafun and al-Kamlin, evacuated their posts and made their way, not without difficulty, to general headquarters at Wad Medani. Here the secretary, Muhammad Sa'id Efendi, who had been appointed deputy governor (*kâhya*) by Isma'il Pasha before his departure, assumed command. He fortified his position and sent a reconnaissance party to the confluence of the Niles.

Alarming though the situation was, two factors favoured the Turco-Egyptian regime. Its troops, although inferior in numbers, were superior in their possession of firearms and their military experience to their opponents – a mixture of settled peasantry, tribal warriors and the private slave-armies of the Sudanese magnates. Secondly, the revolt was never either a general or a unified movement. Mahu Bey held the province of Berber against the rebels upstream. Dongola and the far north were totally unaffected. The Shayqiyya remained loyal to their new masters, and their irregulars served in the operations against the rebels. Even within the area of the revolt, the garrison of Khartoum was assisted by the people of the nearby village of al-Jirayf, whose chief guided the troops to Wad Medani.

The rebels never had unity of leadership. There were three principal centres of revolt, each dominated by local magnates. The Ja'aliyyin had as leaders their chiefs *Makk* Nimr and *Makk* al-Musa'id. The 'Abdallab revolted under their chief, Nasir wad al-Amin. In the Gezira the resistance was headed by those two survivors of the Funj-Hamaj regime, Hasan wad Rajab and the *Arbab* Dafa'allah. The latter, on the outbreak of the revolt, had fled from Wad Medani to 'Ibud, whither the rebels began to muster.

In these circumstances, it was possible for Mahu to hold out in Berber, and for Muhammad Sa'id to undertake local operations in the vicinity of Wad Medani. A cavalry squadron was sent from Wad Medani to 'Ibud, and the rebels there dispersed without a fight. The *Arbab* fled up the Blue Nile, and joined forces with his old enemy, Hasan wad Rajab. The deputy governor sent out another force, which included Shayqiyya levies, which defeated them at Abu Shawka, south of Sennar. Hasan wad Rajab was killed. The *Arbab* Dafa'allah escaped and made his way to the Ethiopian marches.

Neither Mahu nor Muhammad Sa'id was, however, strong enough to undertake the general suppression of the rebellion. This was the work of the *Defterdar* who, on hearing of the death of Isma'il hastened from Kordofan with a body of his troops and a contingent of Fur warriors. Entering the Ja'ali country, he found that Nimr and al-Musa'id were blockading Mahu in Berber, but their sons and a large number of followers were at Metemma. They negotiated an amnesty, but an unsuccessful attempt by a tribesman to assassinate the *Defterdar* provoked him to fury and a massacre ensued. He then marched north to relieve Berber. The Ja'ali chiefs advanced to meet him, crossed the Nile, and were defeated in a battle on the west bank. Freed from the blockade, Mahu left Berber and met the *Defterdar* at El Damer.

After their conference, the *Defterdar* advanced along the east bank into the 'Abdallabi country. He found Halfaya deserted, and burnt it. Another massacre took place on Tuti island, at the confluence of the Niles, while al-'Aylafun, which offered resistance, was burnt and looted. Shaykh Nasir had fled before him, but as the *Defterdar* continued to pursue him up the Blue Nile, he doubled back to Qubbat

Khujali, near the modern Khartoum North, and crossed to Omdurman, where he was joined by the survivors of the battle of Abu Shawka. Having reached Wad Medani, the *Defterdar* sent out an expeditionary force which completed the task of reducing the Gezira to submission. Meanwhile the *Defterdar* returned to Kordofan.

During his absence another force had dispersed the concentration of 'Abdallab and Hamaj at Omdurman, but the rebels fled to Shendi, to which *Makk* Nimr had returned. It was clear that further measures would be needed to suppress the revolt among the Ja'aliyyin, and the *Defterdar* again set out for the river. On hearing of his approach the rebels dispersed, but the main body of them under Nimr and al-Musa'id fled to al-Nasub in the Butana, near Abu Dilayq. Here they were defeated. Nimr and al-Musa'id fled, and a vast number of prisoners, including many members of Nimr's family, were taken.

Returning to the river, the *Defterdar* made his camp at Umm 'Uruq, a site now uncertain.[13] A last rebel force under al-Musa'id and Shaykh Nasir was still at large east of the Blue Nile. In September 1823 the *Defterdar* advanced against it. The rebels were defeated at Makdur, between the rivers Rahad and Dinder. The *Defterdar* now struck north-eastwards as far as Sabderat, just across the present Eritrean border, whence he returned to the Nile.

His term of command was drawing to a close. In January 1824 Muhammad 'Ali Pasha informed him of his impending recall. In his last few months the *Defterdar* ordered all the prisoners of war, whether slaves or freemen, to be sent to Cairo. A new deputy-governor was appointed to Wad Medani, while Muhammad Sa'id Efendi returned to Cairo with the remainder of the household and possessions of Isma'il Pasha. At Umm 'Uruq the *Defterdar* awaited the arrival of his successor; then, at the beginning of the new Muslim year (August–September 1824), himself departed for Egypt.

He was succeeded as commander-in-chief (in effect, as military governor) by 'Uthman Bey the Circassian, who was accompanied by five battalions of infantry. These were soldiers of a new type, the *Jihadiyya*, regular troops recruited from the slaves obtained in the Sudan, and drilled on European lines in the training camp established at Aswan in 1821. Muhammad 'Ali's great project of a new model army in place of the motley troops of Egypt was only partially achieved: the slave recruits perished by hundreds in the Egyptian climate, and by 1824 conscription of the Egyptian peasantry had begun. Nevertheless, the Negro *Jihadiyya* could fulfil a useful function as garrison troops in the Sudanese provinces. Henceforward the military strength of the Turco-Egyptian regime was mainly derived from two sources, the regular *Jihadiyya*, of slave origin, originating from what would now be called the southern Sudan; and the Shayqiyya irregulars, serving mainly as cavalrymen under their own chiefs.

'Uthman Bey realized at once the strategic importance of Khartoum, the trunk of land[14] at the confluence of the Blue and White Niles. He decided to build a fort and garrison a regiment there. This was the beginning, from which in a few years Khartoum was to develop as the military and administrative capital of the Egyptian Sudan. As yet, however, army headquarters remained at Wad Medani, whither 'Uthman proceeded. The new commander-in-chief, an elderly Mamluk, regarded his task with the eyes of a soldier rather than of an administrator. To repress revolt and get in the taxes were his sole aims, and he emulated the *Defterdar* in harshness and brutality. The consequence was a flight of cultivators from the Nile valley to the remote district of the Qadarif in Shukriyya territory. Here they were pursued by government troops and shot down.

'Uthman's few months in office were made more difficult by natural calamities. An epidemic of smallpox coincided with drought, famine, and the migration of refugees to produce severe depopulation. The commander-in-chief was ailing and left the responsibility of government to a deputy. But this man was a mere subaltern and the high-ranking officers refused to obey his orders. The army was drifting into anarchy, with consequent suffering for the people of the Sudan, when 'Uthman Bey died on 11 May 1825. The deputy-governor prudently concealed the fact of his death until he had summoned the experienced governor of Berber, Mahu Bey, to take over the command.

SETTLEMENT AND STAGNATION
1825–62

Mahu Bey, who had been governor of Berber since 1822, was a cavalry officer of Kurdish origin. His fortitude during the great revolt had prevented his province from falling to the rebel Ja'aliyyin. He took over the command of troops in the province of Sennar: the command in Kordofan, which had been held by the *Defterdar* and 'Uthman Bey jointly with Sennar, was now detached.

Mahu's brief period of authority marks a turning-point in the history of the Turco-Egyptian regime. He adopted a policy of conciliation towards the frightened and resentful Sudanese. Taxes were reduced, and the licence of the *Jihadiyya* was repressed. The novelty of his approach appeared when he summoned an assembly of the remaining Sudanese-notables in the Gezira, and consulted with them on the means of restoring order and bringing back the emigrants. He particularly approved of the advice of a minor shaykh, 'Abd al-Qadir wad al-Zayn, whom he raised in rank and employed as his adviser on native affairs. Shaykh 'Abd al-Qadir accompanied Mahu on a tour to the Qadarif, the asylum of many of the refugees. Mahu sent grain from the Qadarif to the stricken Gezira, thereby winning the gratitude of its people.

The rule of Mahu Bey marks another stage in the advance of Khartoum to the status of a capital. It was his habitual residence, and he stationed his troops at Qubbat Khujali, across the Blue Nile. His period of office ended in June 1826, when 'Ali Khurshid Agha arrived at Omdurman after serving under Ibrahim Pasha against the Greeks.

Khurshid's exceptional ability as an administrator is indicated by his long term of office in the Sudan, as well as by the successive extensions of power and elevations of rank conferred on him by the grateful Muhammad 'Ali. His appointment seems to have been designed to inaugurate a new period of civil administration, rather than military rule: he bore at first the title of 'governor of Sennar', whereas his predecessor had been commander-in-chief. His authority did not at this time extend to the northern provinces of Dongola and Berber, nor to Kordofan, but his own province of Sennar, including the Gezira and surrounding territories, the heart of the old Funj-'Abdallab dominions, presented administrative and political problems of far greater gravity than those which confronted his colleagues.

His policy was essentially the continuation and fulfilment of that practised by Mahu, a continuity symbolized by the circumstances of the meeting of the two men in Omdurman:

> The Amir Mahu Bey met him in Omdurman, and they conferred together in private there for a while. Then Mahu Bey ordered Shaykh 'Abd al-Qadir to be brought forward, and he presented him with his own hand to Khurshid Agha, saying, 'If you desire the prosperity of the country, then act according to the opinion of this man.'[1]

The restoration of prosperity was indeed the first object of the new governor. To achieve it, the lands abandoned during the revolt and subsequent repression had to be brought back into cultivation, and the thousands of emigrants, many of whom had made their way to the hill-country of the Ethiopian marches, persuaded to return to their villages. In the Ja'ali districts, much riverain land was given to the loyal Shayqiyya, who paid no taxes but received a forage ration in consideration of their service as cavalry.

Khurshid's new deal was devised with the assistance of Shaykh 'Abd al-Qadir, who was instructed to convoke an assembly of notables, and draw up a list of the villages, showing whether they were inhabited or lying waste. Letters of amnesty were sent out inviting the fugitives to return, and promising them freedom from disturbance. One of the most inveterate opponents of the Turco-Egyptian regime was Shaykh Idris wad 'Adlan, the brother of the murdered Regent Muhammad wad 'Adlan, who had fled at the conquest to the mountains upstream of Sennar, and had unflinchingly refused to recognize the new masters of his country. To him as an envoy came Shaykh 'Abd al-Qadir in the summer of 1826, with the offer of an amnesty from the governor. Idris accepted the invitation, and accompanied 'Abd al-Qadir to Berber, where he was welcomed by Khurshid and formally recognized as shaykh of the Funj mountains.

In the following twelve months another assembly of Sudanese notables was held in Khartoum. Its purpose was to advise the governor on taxation, but before proceeding to this the members were instructed to elect one of their own number as paramount shaykh, to be their official intermediary with the governor. Not surprisingly, their choice fell on 'Abd al-Qadir, who was invested with the paramountcy from Hajar al-'Asal to the further limits of the Funj mountains. The election really did no more than regularize 'Abd al-Qadir's position as native adviser to the governor. Khurshid had also a corps of experienced officers, the *mu'awins* (assistants), who formed a kind of intelligence branch. He regularly consulted them and also his Coptic financial intendant.

In 1828 Khurshid began a serious attempt to bring back the refugees from the Ethiopian marches. Some of them came in to him while he was on tour in that region. He was advised by Shaykh 'Abd al-Qadir to exempt the chief notables and *fakis* from taxation, in order to gain their support for his policy. He did so, and the stratagem proved highly successful. Under the influence of the Sudanese notables, many of the emigrants returned, to the great benefit of cultivation and the profit of the revenue.

A refugee leader of particular importance was Shaykh Ahmad al-Rayyah al-'Araki, a member of a family which had great religious prestige. During the troubles, he had led thousands of his tribesmen, the 'Arakiyyin, from their homes on the Blue Nile, into exile in the Ethiopian marches. He now came in to submit to Khurshid. After an honourable reception, he was sent back to proclaim an amnesty to the emigrants, and took letters from Shaykh 'Abd al-Qadir promising freedom from disturbance. But the governer also threatened that he would shortly make an expedition to the region, and kill those who had not submitted. He quickly fulfilled his promise and, freely or under compulsion, thousands of emigrants returned to the Blue Nile. Another consequence of this expedition was the extension of Egyptian rule over the Qallabat and its colony of Takarir settlers from the western *Bilad al-Sudan*.

Another crisis threatened in 1835. Khurshid returned from a visit to Cairo during which he had been instructed by Muhammad 'Ali Pasha to conscript Sudanese freemen for military service. This project, no doubt devised because of the pressure laid on Muhammad 'Ali's man-power by his occupation of Syria, appeared administratively simple, since it merely extended to the Sudanese provinces a system which had been applied in Egypt proper since 1824. The appearance was deceptive, and the rumour of Khurshid's intention filled with dismay an assembly of administrative officials and Sudanese notables which he summoned to meet in Khartoum. After two days of private consultation with Shaykh 'Abd al-Qadir, who insisted that conscription would start a fresh wave of emigration and damage the new prosperity of the country, Khurshid abandoned the project. Instead an alternative proposal was accepted, that the people of every locality should contribute a quota of their slaves as recruits for the *Jihadiyya*.

Khurshid devoted much energy to the development of Khartoum. Settlers in the town were rewarded with grants of privileges, and the population rose so rapidly that the mosque which he had built in 1829–30 was demolished seven years later to give place to a larger one. A barracks and military storehouse were constructed for the *Jihadiyya* garrison, and a dockyard was set up on the Nile. The townspeople were encouraged to build permanent houses in place of their tents of matting and hides, and were provided with building materials. Commerce was encouraged: trade routes were protected and Khurshid resisted Muhammad 'Ali Pasha himself to prevent the revenue and products of the Sudan being exploited for the benefit of Cairo. His period of office witnessed a local boom in trade, some petty merchants making great fortunes. But the prosperity of the Sudan was always precarious, being linked closely with the state of the harvest in the areas of rain cultivation. The inception of Khurshid's new deal had been favoured by the good rains of the summer of 1826; the difficulties of his last years were increased by drought and famine, beginning in 1836 and accompanied by a cholera epidemic.

Khurshid was less distinguished as a soldier than as an administrator. In the late summer of 1827, he led an expedition from al-Rusayris, on the upper Blue Nile, into the Dinka country. As a slave-raid this was no great success, only five hundred captives being brought in, while the Dinka put up a very stiff resistance, using arrows and spears, and routed Khurshid's cavalry. Nevertheless, Khurshid pushed on by force of arms as far as the Sobat, whence he returned to al-Rusayris. Three years later, in the autumn of 1830, he organized a river expedition against the Shilluk, whose raids in canoes were still troubling the Arabs of the White Nile as they had done in the sixteenth century. As Khurshid's ships moved upstream, the Shilluk deserted their islands and fled to the interior, and the expedition penetrated as far as the mouth of the Sobat. On the return journey, the Shilluk attacked the expedition with arrows. Artillery fire dispersed them and the troops were able to take booty and slaves, but the Shilluk returned to the attack, recovered their booty and compelled the expedition to withdraw with a mere two hundred captives.

Khurshid's third great expedition, in 1831–2, was against the Hadendowa of the Taka. Sabderat was his objective, but he seems never to have got so far. After crossing the Atbara at Quz Rajab, the expedition became entangled in the bush, and was heavily defeated by the Hadendowa under their chief, Muhammad Din. Unable to advance, Khurshid established a fortified camp and beat off another attack, but he was glad to be able to extricate himself and return to Khartoum.

The last years of his rule were marked by a series of frontier wars with Kanfu,[2] the Ethiopian ruler of the district of Kwara. The Ethiopian marches were always a critical area, remote from the centres of Turco-Egyptian power and a convenient refuge for malcontents. One of these was Shaykh Rajab wad Bashir al-Ghul, a chief of the Hammada Arabs, whose brother, Abu Rish, had been preferred by the authorities as head of the tribe. Rajab conspired with Kanfu to invade the Egyptian Sudan, and warning of the plot was sent to Khurshid by Ahmad *Kashif* Ghashim, the district officer of the Qadarif. Khurshid at the time was slave-raiding in Fazughli, and could not personally lead an expedition to the threatened area, but he sent off reinforcements. In the battle which took place, the Ethiopians were completely defeated and Rajab fled. He was, however, betrayed by Kanfu to Khurshid, who had him put to death in Khartoum in the spring of 1836.

Ahmad *Kashif* now took the initiative and raided Ethiopian territory. His first expedition was successful in capturing a number of prisoners, but on his second raid he was unexpectedly confronted by a large army under Kanfu. Ahmad's own troops had been augmented by reinforcements sent by Khurshid, but their commander resented his subordinate position and would not co-operate with Ahmad. The Turco-Egyptian troops were heavily defeated, but Ahmad escaped with his life, and the Ethiopians withdrew. This engagement, the battle of Wad Kaltabu, took place in April 1837.

Khurshid was now thoroughly alarmed. He believed that Kanfu was seeking to annex the frontier districts around the Qallabat, which would then once more become an asylum for emigrants. He asked

Muhammad 'Ali to send him reinforcements, so that he could mount a counter-attack on Kanfu. The viceroy agreed to do so. In the meantime, Khurshid gathered his own forces, and marched from Wad Medani to the Qallabat. Here he paused, and his campaign came to an inglorious conclusion. The British government intervened to warn Muhammad 'Ali against attempting conquests in Ethiopia. The reinforcements had, however, been despatched under the command of Ahmad Pasha Abu Widan,[3] who met Khurshid on his return from the Qallabat.

Khurshid's rule was now near its end, although he continued to enjoy the favour of Muhammad 'Ali Pasha. In February 1834 he had been raised to the rank of bey and appointed governor (*mudir*) of the four Sudanese provinces, Sennar, Berber, Kordofan and Dongola. In the following year he paid a visit to Cairo and was created a pasha. The unique nature of his appointment was indicated by the grant of a special title (*hükümdar*,[4] usually translated governor-general), which differentiated the head of the administration in the Sudan from the governors (*mudirs*) of the provinces of Egypt proper. In May or June 1838 he was recalled to Cairo and Ahmad Pasha Abu Widan took over as acting governor-general. Khurshid was expected to return after medical treatment. He never did so,[5] and some six months later Abu Widan was confirmed in office as *hükümdar*.[6]

Under Abu Widan, the administration continued on the lines laid down by Mahu and Khurshid. Shaykh 'Abd al-Qadir was again commended by the outgoing ruler to his successor, and continued as the governor-general's chief native adviser. Abu Widan soon distinguished himself by a rigorous investigation of the fiscal system, which had been relaxed under Khurshid to the great profit of the financial officials. Several of these suffered distraint and punishment. An edict, issued soon after Abu Widan's accession to power, ordered all tenants of riverain land to bring their holdings fully under cultivation. Derelict land was to become the property of the first claimant who cleared and irrigated it, while land thus brought into cultivation was given a three years' exemption from tax.

Abu Widan's stringency in fiscal matters produced two serious incidents. The first was with the Shayqiyya settlers, who had been allowed to colonize the derelict lands of the Ja'aliyyin rebels and emigrants. Abu Widan cancelled the forage allowance which these cavalrymen had received, and demanded the payment of land-tax with arrears from the time they had taken possession. The chiefs of the Shayqiyya produced their charter, but Abu Widan refused to relent. They then proposed to abandon their lands, but undertook to pay the arrears of tax if they might still receive their fodder rations. This compromise was also rejected by the governor-general, who insisted that they should continue to occupy their holdings. Very reluctantly, the Shayqiyya accepted the order, with the exception of one chief, *Makk* Hamad, who with his family and two hundred followers set off from Shendi for the Ethiopian marches.

On the way, the emigrants fell in with Shaykh Ahmad Abu Sinn, the chief of the Shukriyya, who informed the governor-general. Abu Widan set out in pursuit, attacked Hamad, and captured his baggage together with most of the women and children. Hamad himself escaped, with a few followers, and raided the camp of Abu Widan. The governor-general was himself accompanied by a contingent of Shayqiyya, whose chief, *Makk* Kanbal,[7] he suspected of having a secret understanding with Hamad. Kanbal was shot, probably at Abu Widan's instigation, and the Shayqiyya troops were sent home. Failing to catch up with the refugees, Abu Widan consulted his Sudanese advisers, Shaykh 'Abd al-Qadir, Shaykh Ahmad Abu Sinn and Shaykh Abu Rish of the Hammada. On their advice, he offered an amnesty to the refugee chief, who finally submitted on condition that the Shayqiyya should be allowed to vacate their lands, while those who wished to remain should pay a fixed annual tax, but without arrears. The fodder allowance remained cancelled.

The second crisis over taxes concerned Shaykh Abu Rish himself. When, probably early in 1842, Abu Widan demanded a double payment from the Hammada, the chief fled to the Ethiopian marches, and joined forces with a band of freebooters. He and his allies re-entered Sudanese territory, and inflicted a defeat on the local district officer. Although it was now the rainy season and movement in the region was extremely difficult, Abu Widan set out from Wad Medani to punish the raiders. At this juncture Abu Rish was abandoned by his allies and decided to submit to the governor-general. He came to Abu Widan's camp, and was pardoned after the intervention of Shaykh 'Abd al-Qadir and other notables.

The last important territorial expansion of the Egyptian Sudan in the reign of Muhammad 'Ali Pasha was achieved by Abu Widan's occupation of the Taka. Although the area had been invaded by the *Defterdar* and also by Khurshid, neither of them had succeeded in establishing their authority permanently, and Khurshid's campaign against the Hadendowa had been, as we have seen, an ignominious military failure. In 1840 Abu Widan determined to make a fresh expedition and to obtain the payment of tribute by the Beja. The two tribes which formed his principal objective were the Hadendowa under Shaykh Muhammad Din, in the wooded country of the northern Gash, and the Halanqa further south around Jabal Kasala.

Troops were assembled at El Damer, and on 20 March 1840 Abu Widan began his advance up the Atbara. On the way he was joined by Muhammad, the son of the *Arbab* Dafa'allah. In spite of his father's turbulent career, Muhammad wad Dafa'allah had been received into favour and was an important notable of the Gezira.[8] He brought with him his private retinue of troops. The expeditionary force halted at Quz Rajab, and then continued its advance in the direction of Jabal Kasala.

Although Muhammad Din had sent his son as an envoy, the first tribal chief to come in was Shaykh Muhammad Ila of the Halanqa. He was a parvenu to power, a *faki*, not related to the old chief, who had fled on the news of Abu Widan's approach. On 12 April the Turco-Egyptian force encamped on the Gash, near the village of Aroma, and two days later Muhammad Din arrived to make his submission in person. But to extract tribute from the unwilling and elusive Hadendowa was no easy matter, although Abu Widan seized Muhammad Din and other chiefs as hostages.

Finally the expeditionary force moved on to Jabal Kasala and encamped near the holy village of al-Khatmiyya, the headquarters of the Mirghani family. On the camp-site the town of Kasala subsequently developed, and became the chief administrative centre of the eastern Egyptian Sudan. Abu Widan now tried to defeat the Hadendowa by stratagem. Muhammad Ila suggested the damming of the river Gash, in order to prevent its floods from reaching the Hadendowa. Deprived of water for their lands and their crops, they would, the governor-general hoped, be compelled to submit and pay tribute. The device however failed, the floodwaters breaking the crudely constructed dam. An advance made against the Hadendowa was rendered ineffective by the scrub of the lower Gash. Abu Widan patched up an agreement with his opponents, and returned to Khartoum.

Although Abu Widan had failed to reduce the Hadendowa to submission, his campaign had been much more successful than that of Khurshid. Muhammad Din, the leader of the Hadendowa, was taken as a prisoner to Khartoum, where he died of smallpox in the following year. More important still, the Turco-Egyptian administration had obtained at Kasala a permanent foothold. The extension of the Egyptian Sudan towards the Red Sea inevitably gave a new importance to the old Ottoman ports of Suakin and Massawa, at that time nominal dependencies of the vilayet of the Hijaz. Abu Widan himself raised the question of their status, demanding that the governor of Suakin should pay taxes to the Sudanese treasury. In the face of opposition, both from the governor of the Hijaz and the Ottoman government, Muhammad 'Ali Pasha withdrew this claim. This was in 1843, but in 1846 the Ottoman Sultan 'Abd al-Majid granted the ports to Muhammad 'Ali on an annual lease. Three years later the lease was terminated and not until 1865, in the reign of Khedive Isma'il, were the two ports permanently annexed to the Egyptian Sudan.

While Abu Widan was *hükümdar*, an event occurred which was to have consequences of lasting importance for the history of the Sudan: the opening of the White Nile route to the south. This was the achievement of Salim, a Turkish sailor, usually called Salim *Kaptan* (in Arabic, *Qabudan*) from his naval rank as captain of a frigate. The situation on the river, southwards from Alays, of the fierce Shilluk warriors, and the hazards of navigation, prevented the penetration of Negro Africa from the north until the Turco-Egyptian conquest. Khurshid Pasha and Muhammad 'Ali had discussed an expedition up the White Nile in 1836, but the scheme was cancelled, and it was not until November 1839 that Salim and his boats passed into the unknown waters guarded by the Shilluk. After struggling through the sudd and up the Bahr al-Jabal, they returned to Khartoum. Salim led a second expedition in 1840, which, in January of the following year, reached the country of the Bari tribe, with whom they made contact near Gondokoro, near where Juba stands today. Salim's third expedition, in 1842, reached only a few miles further south.

Ahmad Pasha Abu Widan was a strong and effective governor: the Sudanese chronicler declares that his period of office was better than that of Khurshid, good though this was. He was perhaps too successful: it was rumoured that he was seeking to make himself independent, or alternatively that he was plotting with Sultan 'Abd al-Majid to separate the Sudanese provinces from Muhammad 'Ali's dominions. When he died suddenly in Khartoum, on 6 October 1843, the story quickly spread that he had been poisoned by his wife, the daughter of Muhammad 'Ali.

Whether or not Muhammad 'Ali instigated the death of Abu Widan, he took advantage of the situation to prevent his successor from attaining so powerful a position. A special commissioner, Ahmad Pasha Manikli, was sent to decentralize the administration. The appointment of *hükümdar* was abolished. Each province would be autonomous, under a governor of the rank of pasha, who would correspond directly with Cairo. A few months later, Muhammad 'Ali changed his mind. Manikli, who had remained in the Sudan to report on the gold of Fazughli, was ordered to reintegrate the administration. He himself was appointed *hükümdar*, a post which he held until 1845. His period of office was chiefly notable for a punitive expedition against the Hadendowa, carried out with a brutal vigour that won him the nickname of *Jazzar*, 'butcher'.

Muhammad 'Ali's uncharacteristic vacillation over these administrative changes marks the beginning of nearly two decades of feeble administration in the Egyptian Sudan. These are the years of the great viceroy's senility, of the retrogressive reign of 'Abbas I (1849–54), and of the capricious rule of Muhammad Sa'id (1854–63). Eleven representatives of the viceroy sat at Khartoum during the twenty years following the death of Abu Widan. Their abilities varied, but few of them held office long enough to rule effectively. The Sudanese chronicler has little to say of them. One of the greatest pioneers of Western culture in Egypt, Rifa'a Bey Rafi'al-Tahtawi, spent a few unhappy years in Khartoum, nominally organizing a school, in fact a victim of 'Abbas Pasha's jealous obscurantism. Bayard Taylor, the first American tourist in the Sudan, met him there in 1852 and heard the long tales of his woes. In the course of 1856 an epidemic of cholera broke out, which claimed, among many less distinguished victims, the great counsellor, Shaykh 'Abd al-Qadir wad al-Zayn.

At this juncture the Viceroy Muhammad Sa'id Pasha himself visited the Sudan. He went no further than Khartoum, but what he saw horrified him and he resolved at first to abandon the Sudanese provinces. By the time he had reached the capital, however, he had modified his views. The administration was again decentralized. Four provinces were established, one combining Khartoum and the

Gezira, another uniting Dongola and Berber, the others being Kordofan and the Taka. These were to be linked more closely with Egypt by a camel-post, while a railway from Wadi Halfa to Khartoum was projected. This second decentralization lasted until 1862, when Musa Pasha Hamdi was appointed *hükümdar*.

It was probably unfortunate that this period of hesitation and relaxation of control followed so closely on the opening-up of the White Nile route to the south. Muhammad 'Ali was unable to take any initiative in the development of the newly discovered regions, although the *hükümdars* sent small annual trading expeditions from Khartoum, to obtain ivory. Their monopoly of the White Nile trade coincided with the collapse of the general system of monopoly of Sudanese exports, which Muhammad 'Ali had maintained since 1824. The small but growing European trading community in Khartoum resented its exclusion from this last and potentially most profitable field of Sudanese commerce. Its spokesman was a Savoyard, Antoine Brun-Rollet, who was supported by the Roman Catholic mission to Central Africa. The foundation of this mission was a direct consequence of the opening-up of the White Nile, and it established its headquarters in Khartoum in 1848. Its leading figure was a young Slovene Jesuit, Ignaz Knoblecher (or Knoblehar), who, after a short visit to the Bari, returned to Europe, where he gained influential supporters in the Austrian Empire. The recall of the *hükümdar*, 'Abd al-Latif Pasha 'Abdallah, by 'Abbas I in 1851, removed the last obstacle to the free entry of both traders and missionaries to the south.

The Catholic mission at Gondokoro had a short and unsuccessful life. Permanently established in 1853, it was abandoned after about a year, the one surviving missionary founding a new station, called Holy Cross, among the Dinka, a hundred and fifty miles downstream. Knoblecher revived the station in 1855, but the missionaries failed almost completely to establish fruitful relations with the surrounding tribes. This frustration, combined with very heavy mortality, led to the closure of the mission at Gondokoro in 1860. Holy Cross had been abandoned in the previous year. An attempt by Franciscan missionaries to resume activity on the Upper Nile in 1862 met with no success.

The resentment and hostility which the missionaries encountered was partly due to the rapid deterioration of relations between the tribes and the European traders, who had come south in search of ivory. Their first field of activity was the Bari territory, but a stable trading system proved impossible to establish, and armed clashes soon began. The slave-trade as such played no part in this early friction, but during the later 1850s it developed as a by-product. The traders began to acquire ivory by force, since they could no longer satisfy their demands by peaceful exchange. Accompanied by bands of armed retainers, recruited largely from the Danaqla and Shayqiyya of the north, they set up fortified stations, known, from the thorn fences which surrounded them, as *zaribas*. These served them as headquarters, entrepôts for their goods, and garrison-posts in times of need. Slaves were needed to supply the domestic needs of the trading-communities, as concubines and porters, and were also used by the traders as a form of recompense to their retainers, thereby ɩeducing overheads. Thus, under the auspices of the ivory traders, a secondary slave-trade developed, which helped to supply the markets of the north. To obtain slaves, as well as cattle, which were indispensable for bartering for ivory, the traders allied themselves with hostile tribal groups, and promoted raiding.

For about a decade, the European traders dominated the White Nile, but their prosperity was transient. The real profits of the ivory-trade went to those who advanced the capital, and to the middlemen of the north. These were mainly Ottoman subjects – Egyptians, both Copts and Muslims, Syrians and Sudanese – who were better placed to grasp the secret levers of influence in Khartoum and Cairo. Western European firms were unable to break into the closed circle of the ivory export trade. The fortunate European traders on the White Nile made their quick profits, and withdrew; the unfortunate were killed by the climate. By the end of Muhammad Sa'id's viceroyalty, the White Nile trade had been almost wholly abandoned by the Europeans.

A similar sequence of developments was occurring at about the same time in the vast area, west of the Upper Nile, watered by the tributaries of the Bahr al-Ghazal. Here two lines of penetration, and two types of trader, converged and effected a symbiosis. The northern districts of this region, roughly speaking, along the line of the Bahr al-'Arab, had for centuries been the border between the Baqqara Arabs, and the Dinka and other non-Arab tribes. This territory was an old-established slave-producing area, and the typical merchants were the *jallaba*, small-scale Muslim traders coming from the north.

In the middle and later fifties, the passage up the Bahr al-Ghazal from the White Nile was discovered, and Syrian and Egyptian traders penetrated the interior in search of ivory. There was no phase of European-dominated commerce, as on the Upper Nile. The traders constructed their *zaribas* on the upper courses of the rivers, clear of the marshy clay plains inhabited by the Dinka. They easily subjugated the docile tribes living between the Dinka and the Azande of the Nile-Congo divide, to which the rivers gave access. Like the Dinka, the Azande did not easily succumb to the newcomers, but they were profoundly affected by them.

Ivory was the original attraction to the traders and their northern retainers, who were known as *bahhara*, because they had come from *al-Bahr* – the River Nile. As on the White Nile, however, the *zariba*-system necessitated slave establishments of some size. A special feature of the trader communities of the Bahr al-Ghazal were bodies of slave-troops, known as 'bazingers', which ultimately amounted to half the armed forces of the traders. Many Azande voluntarily joined their ranks. The *jallaba,* who had previously carried on a precarious trade, and had paid tribute to the tribal chiefs, now found protection and favourable opportunities for trade in the *zaribas*. While some of them remained small, independent merchants, others acted as agents for wealthy operators in Kordofan and Darfur. The *zariba*-owners also began to trade in slaves, like their counterparts on the White Nile. An extensive slave-trade developed, channelled through the overland route, northwards from the Bahr al-Ghazal. At its height, this was perhaps six times as great as the river-borne trade.

By the end of Muhammad Sa'id's reign, the Upper Nile and the Bahr al-Ghazal had thus been opened to a predatory commerce and over large areas the traditional tribal structure was in dissolution. European opinion was aroused by the great increase in the slave-trade, and the viceroy, a man more deeply influenced by European culture than his predecessors, tried to stop it. On his accession in 1854, he had instructed his provincial governors to prevent the introduction of slaves into Egypt from the south, and the public slave-market in Khartoum was closed. The village of Kaka, in Shilluk territory, now became the principal slave-market for the White Nile. In 1855, Sa'id endeavoured to extend his rule over the river. An expeditionary force was sent to establish a post at the mouth of the Sobat, and to search for slaves in boats passing down the river. The project had little success, and in 1857 the troops were withdrawn. The protests of the missionaries over the anarchic situation on the Upper

Nile stimulated Austrian and British pressure on the viceroy for renewed action. The *hükümdar*, Musa Pasha Hamdi, notified the traders, in October 1862, that boats would be allowed to leave Khartoum for the south for trade in ivory only. A capitation tax, equivalent to one month's pay, was made payable for each employee, while an officer with a small body of troops was appointed to inspect the traffic on the river.[9] Muhammad Sa'id's southern policy was not very successful, but it was to be taken up with greater effect (and disastrous consequences for Egyptian rule in the Sudan) by Khedive Isma'il.

Muhammad Sa'id Pasha also appointed the first Christian governor in the Sudan, Arakil Bey the Armenian, a relative of Nubar Pasha who played so prominent a part in the history of Egypt under Khedive Isma'il and his successors. Arakil was the first governor of Khartoum and the Gezira under the system of decentralization. The appointment of a Christian almost provoked a revolt of the powerful Shukriyya tribe, a threat which Arakil overcame by his personal courage. His rule was short, since he died in Khartoum in 1858.

The picture of political stagnation in these years is repeated in the field of economic history. Muhammad 'Ali began with an optimistic view of the resources awaiting development and exploitation in the Sudan. A period of disillusionment followed. The limited success of his attempts to recruit a slave army has already been described. Even more disappointing than the slave-soldiers was the gold of the Sudan. This was sought principally in two regions, around Fazughli and at Jabal Shaybun in the Nuba Mountains. European experts, pushed on by Muhammad 'Ali himself, prospected these areas, but to little purpose. The search was to be resumed in the Condominium period, but the profits were small. The iron deposits of Kordofan were slightly more productive, and provided nails for the government shipyard. An attempt to improve their exploitation, with the aid of English iron founders, was, however, a failure. The copper deposits of Hufrat al-Nahas, on the border between Darfur and the non-Arab peoples, were outside the range of Egyptian control until long after Muhammad 'Ali's time.

Attempts to improve Sudanese agriculture were rather more successful. In the early years after the conquest, Egyptian peasants were sent into the new territories to teach their methods to the Sudanese cultivators. Something was done to increase the irrigable areas by the main Nile. New fruit-trees were introduced, while plantations of sugar-cane and indigo were developed. The spread of cotton-production lay in the future, but Mahu Bey is said to have obtained from the Ethiopian frontier the seed which bears his name, and which was the parent of Egyptian cotton. One of the most valuable exports of the Sudan was, as it is today, the gum-arabic of Sennar and Kordofan, while the role of the ivory trade has already been described. Cattle and camels, brought from the Sudan, augmented Egyptian livestock, depleted by epizootics and warfare.

5

THE ERA OF KHEDIVE ISMA'IL
1863–81

The reign of Khedive Isma'il (1863–79) marked the culmination of Turco-Egyptian power in the Sudan. Under him the administration regained the vigour which it had lost since the later years of Muhammad 'Ali. In his time the territories of Egypt's African empire were enormously increased. But with all his ability, Isma'il lacked the caution of his grandfather. Moreover he ruled at a time when international interest in Egypt, and in Africa generally, was far more marked, and the issues at stake far greater, than they had been while Muhammad 'Ali lived. Hence the last years of Isma'il's reign are a period of increasing difficulty ending in disaster. Three years after his deposition, the fortunes of the khedivate reached their nadir, when his successor Muhammad Tawfiq was a pawn in the hands, first of 'Urabi Pasha[1] and his militant nationalists, and then in those of the victorious British invaders.

Three characteristic themes emerge from the story of the Egyptian Sudan during the two decades which may broadly be called the era of Isma'il. The first is a great expansion of the territories ruled by the khedive. The second, closely connected with this, is a prolonged struggle against the slave-trade. The third, which again is linked with the two preceding themes, is the increasing employment in high military and civil offices of men who were neither Muslims nor Ottoman subjects, but for the most part Europeans and, at least nominally, Christians.

Although Muhammad 'Ali, as we have seen, valued his Sudanese possessions largely because they tapped a reservoir of slaves whom he could use in his army, the lucrative and flourishing slave-trade became increasingly an embarrassment to his successors. Muhammad Sa'id and Isma'il were westernized rulers, with some genuine sympathy for that nineteenth-century humanitarianism to which Muhammad 'Ali had paid no more than occasional lip-service. The combination of anti-slavery idealism with schemes for colonial expansion, a frequent phenomenon of European imperialism in the last decades of the century, was, at a rather earlier period, characteristic of Khedive Isma'il. It is easy to dismiss his measures against the slave-trade as hypocrisy, a mere pretext for the acquisition of territories that he could not effectively govern, but this is an over-simplification. The campaign against the trade was begun years before the khedivial government had made any attempt to extend its power over the great slave-acquiring areas of the Upper Nile and the Bahr al-Ghazal, while the first suggestions of such an extension seem to have come from the British consul in Cairo.

The measures taken in Muhammad Sa'id's reign had been a pitiful failure. The slave-trade proceeded as vigorously as ever, since the source of the trade lay beyond the control of the administration. Further steps were taken late in 1863. The White Nile province was reconstituted with its headquarters at Fashoda, in Shilluk territory. This to some extent strengthened the hand of the authorities. Of the two merchant-princes who dominated the area, one fled while the other made terms with the administration. At the same time Musa Hamdi tripled the capitation tax on personnel. This action, coming just when the traders' boats were about to leave Khartoum, provoked a great outcry from the European trading community, who suspected that the governor-general was trying to drive them off the river. Within the next few years, in fact, the few remaining Europeans withdrew from their establishments in the south.

A further measure against the slave-trade, inaugurated in June 1864, was the establishment of a force of river police. This was equipped with four steamers and half a dozen armed sailing-ships, which intercepted the traders' boats on their return downstream. After the first shock, the river police seem rapidly to have lost their efficaciousness. An official inquiry in 1866 revealed that in spite of the seizure of 3,538 slaves, the traders had quickly learnt to elude or bribe the patrols, and that their operations were continuing on a large scale. The good intentions of the khedive were, in fact, being defeated by three factors: the existence of powerful and wealthy vested interests in the mercantile community; the lack of honest and well-paid officials; and the absence of any provision for the future of the confiscated slaves. Although in theory these should have been repatriated at the expense of the traders, they were in fact brought to Khartoum where many of them were enrolled in the army. Thus the administration itself was led to connive at a veiled form of slave-recruitment.

The withdrawal of the European traders from the White Nile and the Bahr al-Ghazal was followed by the emergence of a new generation of merchant-princes in the extensive regions still outside khedivial control. On the White Nile, the most successful of these was Muhammad Ahmad al-'Aqqad, who, probably with the financial backing of Isma'il himself, bought up most of his competitors' establishments. His partner in the firm of Agad and Company was his brother, Musa Bey, who had been a friend of Muhammad Sa'id. Muhammad Ahmad was succeeded, on his death in 1870, by his son-in-law, Muhammad Bey Abu'l-Su'ud, who was to have a disconcerting confrontation with the Mahdi on Aba Island. The enormous expenses of the trade in ivory led al-'Aqqad, as it had led his predecessors, to have recourse to slave-trading to recoup his losses. He sheltered under a khedivial decree which authorized the personnel of expeditions to bring their Negro concubines and children to Khartoum: a loophole which made possible the transport and sale of thousands of slaves annually.

The only answer to this recurrent problem seemed to be a further extension of khedivial rule, and the appointment as officials of men who stood outside the circle of vested and corrupt interests. The khedive sought to attain both these objectives when, in April 1869, he took into his service the distinguished British explorer, Sir Samuel Baker. Baker drew up his own contract of employment, which was however modified in some details by Isma'il. His tour of duty was to last for two years, during which he was to lead an expedition with the objects of annexing to Egypt all the territories in the Nile basin, suppressing the slave-trade and establishing a chain of military posts in the newly-acquired regions. Baker was given a princely salary and equipment, and provided with a flotilla of six steamers and several sailing ships.

If strength of body and force of character had sufficed for the task, Baker would have been an admirable choice. But he was deficient in administrative qualities and, a more serious defect in the circumstances, totally blind to his delicate and invidious situation. He was an Englishman and a Christian in the employ of a Muslim ruler. His mission was odious to the powerful and entrenched slave-trading interest with its numerous ramifications in the administration, the army and Sudanese society generally. As it was, he quarrelled with the governor-general, Ja'far Mazhar Pasha, with the slave-traders and with the tribes whose interests he was supposed to protect. Nevertheless, he carried the flag to the borders of Uganda, and left garrisons to mark the authority of the khedive along the Upper Nile.

While Baker was thrusting his way irascibly up the Nile, another expedition was marching to establish the khedive's authority in a different region. The Bahr al-Ghazal was dominated by the merchant-princes, whose *zaribas*, strung out along the routes to the north, were stages for the slave-caravans going to Kordofan and Darfur. Dar Fartit, to the south of Darfur, was an ancient slave-raiding area. About the middle of the century a Muslim named Muhammad al-Hilali, who claimed to come from Morocco, had acquired power in this region and established an autonomous kingdom under the overlordship of Darfur. Trouble had subsequently developed between the vassal and his suzerain, and Hilali sought asylum with Ja'far Mazhar, who proposed to the khedive to support his rights in Dar Fartit. Isma'il agreed, seeing in Hilali an instrument by which he might extend his power over the whole Bahr al-Ghazal. Hilali was formally appointed chief of the district of the Bahr al-Ghazal and, in spite of the protests of the sultan of Darfur, was sent off to bring the territory into submission.

The principal opposition which he had to fear was not from the enfeebled sultanate of Darfur, but from the powerful and independent merchant-princes of the Bahr al-Ghazal itself. Amongst these, the most important was a Ja'ali, al-Zubayr Rahma Mansur, who had made himself the principal trader in the western part of the Bahr al-Ghazal and sent his caravans into Darfur. Zubayr's relations with Hilali were at first friendly, but they soon deteriorated. The difficulties which the slave-trade was experiencing on the Nile worked to the profit of the traders in the remote Bahr al-Ghazal, who were unwilling to accept Hilali's credentials as the agent of the administration. In 1871 Hilali asked Khartoum for reinforcements, and when they arrived he began to attack and reduce the *zaribas* of the traders. Zubayr marched to the aid of his friends and kinsmen. The unfortunate Hilali was killed in battle. The khedive saved appearances, realizing that Zubayr was beyond his power, by constituting the Bahr al-Ghazal a province and appointing Zubayr as its governor (December 1873).

The Upper Nile and the Bahr al-Ghazal had thus been added, at least in name, to Isma'il's African empire. The administrative organization of the newly acquired territories on the Nile was the work of another Englishman, Charles George Gordon, who had already made a name for himself as an unorthodox but successful soldier in China. Appointed to succeed Baker, with the title of governor of the Equatorial province, in 1874, he established a provincial capital at Lado, organized the series of riverain garrisons which tenuously held the region, and strove to reconcile the tribes, rendered angry and resentful by the depredations of the slave-traders and the heavy-handed methods of Baker. When he resigned in 1876, Egyptian authority was still feeble. Once again, a basic problem was that of personnel. Although there were advantages in employing foreign administrators, their salaries were high, and they succumbed to the climate. The Danaqla, who filled many of the civil and military posts, had long been inured to the region; they were hardy and intelligent, but they felt little loyalty towards the administration, or sympathy for the campaign against the slave-trade.

Meanwhile Zubayr ruled in the Bahr al-Ghazal. As the principal operator in this region, he made an agreement with the Rizayqat tribe of Baqqara in southern Darfur to ensure a safe passage for his caravans. In 1873 the Rizayqat broke their agreement. Zubayr complained to their overlord, Sultan Ibrahim Muhammad of Darfur, and at the same time invaded the territory of the Rizayqat and defeated them. The strained relations that followed, between the sultan and Zubayr, led to further hostilities. Zubayr covered his aggression by informing the governor-general, Isma'il Ayyub Pasha, and through him the khedive, of a project to invade and conquer Darfur in the name of the Egyptian government.

While Isma'il Ayyub concentrated his forces in Kordofan, Zubayr struck into Darfur from the south. A Fur army was defeated in January 1874, and in October Sultan Ibrahim was killed at the battle of Manawashi. On 2 November, Zubayr entered El Fasher, where he was joined a few days later by Isma'il Ayyub. Thus Darfur became a province of the Egyptian Sudan, over half a century after Muhammad 'Ali had originally planned its conquest. Zubayr was granted the title of pasha, but his great triumph was rapidly to be followed by eclipse. A clash with Isma'il Ayyub was inevitable. When it occurred, Zubayr went to Cairo, to plead his cause in person, and there he was detained. He did not return to the Sudan until after the Anglo-Egyptian reconquest. With his removal, the Bahr al-Ghazal lost its master, at a time when the khedive's authority in the province was little more than nominal.

The reign of Khedive Isma'il witnessed also an expansion of the Egyptian empire in the east, when in 1865 the ports of Suakin and

Massawa were finally ceded by the Ottoman government to the viceroyalty of Egypt.[2] The acquisition of the Red Sea ports opened a new phase in the relations of Egypt and Ethiopia. In 1871 Isma'il appointed as governor of Massawa a Swiss, Munzinger, whose authority was subsequently extended over the whole Sudanese coast. Munzinger began to prepare for war against King John IV of Ethiopia. He died in an ambush, but Isma'il's aggressive policy continued. The outcome was unfortunate for Egypt. Two Egyptian expeditionary forces in succession were overwhelmed and defeated in the Eritrean highlands in 1875 and 1876 respectively.

Isma'il's failure in Ethiopia was the first of a series of calamities. The following year, 1877, saw a crisis in the three characteristic developments of his reign. In February Gordon was appointed governor-general of the Sudan, the first Christian and European to hold this post. At the outset he was faced with the legacy of Isma'il's expansionist policy – an unsettled frontier with Ethiopia, revolt in Darfur, and anarchy in the Bahr al-Ghazal. Finally, in August 1877, the khedive concluded the Anglo-Egyptian Slave Trade Convention, which provided, amongst other things, for the termination of the sale and purchase of slaves in the Sudan by 1880. Meanwhile the khedive's growing financial involvement was leading to increasing difficulties with his European creditors and the great powers that stood behind them. It was in the years following 1877 that the revolutionary situation was created which ultimately resolved itself in the Mahdia.

The appointment of Gordon as governor-general placed at the head of the Sudanese administration a man devoted to his duties and possessed of daemonic energies. In the course of a few months he attempted to reach a settlement with Ethiopia, pacified Darfur, and appointed as governor of the Bahr al-Ghazal the one man who might possibly have served as an instrument of Egyptian rule – Sulayman, the son of Zubayr. But Gordon's successes were superficial, and his later years of office were to show the complexity of the problems which he struggled to solve. His difficulties were partly personal, partly the result of circumstances. He was inexperienced in the routine of administration and contemptuous of bureaucracy. He was impulsive and relied on intuition, while his deeply personal religion tended to invest his decisions and his vacillations with a divine sanction in his own eyes. He was a fanatical Christian. He was illiterate in Arabic, and his command of the spoken language seems to have been meagre in the extreme. Yet far less honest and far less able men have succeeded in building and administering empires. Gordon was unfortunate in that he assumed power at a time when Isma'il, the one man whom he could trust, was declining in authority. He had neither sound finances nor effective forces to back him. He mistrusted his Egyptian subordinates, often with reason, but the caprice of his appointments and dismissals indicates a lack of judgement, while his reliance on inexperienced Sudanese and Europeans, often ill-equipped for their tasks, weakened an administration already defective in tradition and *esprit de corps*.

From July 1878 the tide turned against him. He was now solely responsible for the suppression of the slave-trade, a policy difficult in any circumstances and impossible in the conditions of those years. Sulayman, who had been superseded by a rival, revolted in the Bahr al-Ghazal, and risings broke out in Darfur and Kordofan. Gordon, acting in concert with two Italian subordinates, Gessi in the Bahr al-Ghazal and Messedaglia in Darfur, succeeded in restoring order, but the south-west was sullen and unreconciled to the rule of the khedive's officials. To cut off supplies from Sulayman, Gordon had authorized the Baqqara chiefs to harry the *jallaba* who traded in their districts. El Obeid and the other towns of Kordofan and Darfur were filled with the survivors and kinsmen of these traders, thus abruptly deprived of their stake in Egyptian rule.

In June 1879, as a result of European pressure, Isma'il was deposed by Sultan 'Abd al-Hamid II. Realizing that his one support was gone, Gordon sought to resign. Effectively his administration ended with Isma'il's reign, although his formal resignation did not come until 1880, after a further unsuccessful attempt to reach a settlement with Ethiopia. His successor as governor-general was Muhammad Ra'uf Pasha, a man of mixed Nubian and Ethiopian parentage, who had served under both Baker and Gordon. During his administration, in June 1881, the storm broke.

In economic matters, the reign of Isma'il was a period of unfulfilled promise. The story of the Sudan railway project is typical. His predecessor, Muhammad Sa'id, as mentioned earlier, planned the construction of a railway to link Upper Egypt with the Sudanese provinces, but the scheme was abandoned.[3] Isma'il took it up with new enthusiasm as a means of assisting administrative centralization. A British engineer, Sir John Fowler, made plans for opening the First

Cataract to shipping, and for constructing a railway from Wadi Halfa to Metemma. Work was begun on both schemes in 1873, but progress was delayed by the khedive's financial difficulties. However, in February 1875 work was resumed at Wadi Halfa. Labour difficulties and the deepening financial crisis again intervened. The line reached only thirty-three miles south of Wadi Halfa when the work was suspended. The project was finally abandoned after the British occupation of Egypt. Thereafter, apart from the abortive attempt to construct a line from Suakin to Berber in connection with the campaign against 'Uthman Diqna in 1885, there was no further railway-building in the Sudan until Kitchener's campaign in Dongola during 1896.

Two other grandiose schemes of Isma'il's time were equally unfortunate. At the beginning of his reign, he encouraged the formation of a private organization, the *Compagnie du Soudan*, to develop rail and river transport and assist the export trade. After an initial buying spree, the company got into difficulties, and in 1868 went into liquidation. His other great scheme has still left memories in the Sudan. The American Civil War caused a boom in Egyptian cotton, much to the khedive's profit. His governor in Suakin, Ahmad Mumtaz Pasha, rightly perceived that the Sudan also had areas eminently suitable for cotton-growing, and started an experimental plantation in the Tokar district. This was a success. Isma'il's interest was aroused and Mumtaz put 2,500 acres of the Gash delta under cotton. He had selected his areas well; under the Condominium, as we shall see, they became centres of cotton production; but by this time the Civil War was over and the boom was ending. Neither Mumtaz nor his master had good heads for business, so although in 1871 the pasha was put over the combined provinces of Khartoum, Sennar and the White Nile, in which he found wider scope for his cotton projects, his financial situation crumbled and he was dismissed from office after less than a year. Among the Sudanese country-people until quite recent times, the name of Mumtaz was used as a synonym for cotton.

Against these failures must be set some developments in the communications of the Sudan. The first steamers had appeared on the Sudanese Nile before Isma'il's time, but the creation of a fleet of government steamers took place in his reign. Most of them were sent upstream from Egypt, and had difficulty in passing the cataracts that lay between Aswan and Khartoum. They were serviced at a dockyard west of Khartoum, near the junction of the Niles. The surviving steamers and the dockyard were subsequently part of the physical legacy of the Egyptian administration to the Mahdist state.

The steamers played an important part in strengthening the hold of the administration over the country, particularly over the outlying provinces of the south. It was aided also by the development of the electric telegraph system. In 1866 Wadi Halfa was linked with Upper Egypt, and by 1874 the line had been extended to Khartoum. Another section, completed in 1875, linked this line with the Red Sea coast by way of Berber, Kasala and Suakin. A third section connected Khartoum with the west, running by El Obeid to the borders of Darfur. This system was a casualty of the Mahdist revolutionary war, since the long stretches of unprotected line were easily cut by the rebels. Under the Mahdist government, a fragmentary system, linking the treasury in Omdurman with the dockyard at Khartoum, survived and was operated by telegraph-clerks of the old administration.

PART III

THE MAHDIST STATE
1881–98

A Mahdi who since he arose never betrayed or deceived, who guided the blind and codified religious knowledge; who penetrated into the inmost secrets of the divine presence; who every day is revealed in the colour of a new light; who strives not after created things but after the Creator.

> From a verse panegyric by Ahmad Sa'd, translated by S. Hillelson.

The woe which befell us has now befallen the Ansar; English gunfire, and slaughter, and wretchedness. The Sirdar takes up his quarters in the Khalifa's courtyard. Shaykh al-Din is a prisoner, and Ya'qub carries firewood.

> From anonymous verses circulating after the defeat of the Khalifa, translated by S. Hillelson.

6
THE MAHDIST REVOLUTION
1881-85

It is frequently asserted that the Mahdia was due to the oppression and misgovernment of the Egyptians in the Sudan. This hypothesis has been too easily and uncritically accepted, since it fails to explain why the revolution began precisely when and where it did. Examples of oppression and corruption could be found in the Turco-Egyptian administration, although it may be queried whether these were as universal and offensive as is sometimes suggested. The savage pacification by the *Defterdar* was a regrettable but abnormal incident of the conquest; thereafter there was, as we have seen, a good deal of association of the Sudanese notables and men of religion with the administration. Corruption shocked the nineteenth-century European visitors, but it had long been endemic in Ottoman and Egyptian administration. To judge Turco-Egyptian administration by the standards of twentieth-century colonial rule, instead of seeing it as part of the pattern of late Ottoman provincial government, is unwarranted and unhistorical.

The accepted explanation would be more tenable if, on the declaration of the Mahdia, the revolt had flared out throughout the length and breadth of the Egyptian Sudan. But this was not the case. For two years it was practically confined to the southern fringe of the Arab provinces, centring in Kordofan, the conquest of which was the first major achievement of the Mahdi's followers. It spread only gradually to the other parts of the Sudan, last of all to those northern riverain provinces which had had the longest experience of Turco-Egyptian rule. This is a fairly clear indication that at the outset the reasons for the success of the Mahdia lay in local conditions.

The ascription of the Mahdia to the faults of Turco-Egyptian rule also fails to explain why it should have broken out in 1881. Why not sooner? The Sudanese had borne alien rule for sixty years; why did it suddenly become intolerable? There is no reason to assume that the burden had suddenly become heavier under the feeble rule of Muhammad Ra'uf. It had, however, become easier to throw off.

To explain the timing of the outbreak, one must look beyond the Sudan to events in Egypt, which followed to some extent a similar pattern. The khedivial autocracy had virtually ended with the deposition of Isma'il in 1879. His son and successor, Muhammad Tawfiq, was a puppet of the great powers. The change of rulers swept away the prestige which had surrounded the viceregal dynasty from the time of Muhammad 'Ali. In Egypt, the forces of opposition gathered around the army leader, 'Urabi Pasha, and effected by gradual stages a change in the centre of power; a genuine revolution which was abruptly nullified in September 1882 by the British occupation. The collapse of the khedivate in 1879 was as obvious to the Sudanese as to the Egyptians, and, by a turn of the screw, the revolutionary changes within Egypt made metropolitan control over Sudanese provinces weak and hesitant. There appears to have been no direct communication between the supporters of 'Urabi in Egypt and those of the Mahdi in the Sudan,[1] but both movements found their opportunity in the power-vacuum caused by the disappearance of Isma'il's autocracy.

The timing of the Sudanese outbreak may further be linked with the resignation of Gordon. Like Isma'il, Gordon was far from being an ideal ruler, but with all his faults of ignorance, caprice and misjudgement he was, like the khedive, a dynamic and masterful personality. His withdrawal from the Sudan after the deposition of Isma'il produced the classical situation for the outbreak of a revolution. Muhammad Ra'uf was the mild and gentle ruler who reaped the whirlwind sown by his energetic predecessor.

The Mahdia takes its name from its leader, Muhammad Ahmad ibn 'Abdallah, a man of Dunqulawi origin, who in June 1881 despatched letters from the island of Aba in the White Nile, informing the notables of the Sudan that he was the Expected Mahdi, the divine leader chosen by God at the end of time to fill the earth with justice and equity, even as it had been filled with oppression and wrong. He was then a man about forty years of age. From childhood he had been deeply religious and, although he had never been outside the Sudan, he had studied at the feet of more than one Sudanese teacher, and was initiated into the Sammaniyya order. His rigorous asceticism had led him to quarrel with one of his teachers, but for some years past he had lived at Aba, gaining among the surrounding tribes an increasing reputation for holiness and supernatural powers. He was attended by a small company of devout men like himself, and had been joined within the previous two or three years by a disciple who was to eclipse them all.

This was a certain 'Abdallahi ibn Muhammad, the son of the soothsayer of the Ta'aisha, a tribe of Baqqara living in the south of Darfur. 'Abdallahi shared the expectation of the coming of the *mahdi*, which was current in the Sudan in this period, and he had on one occasion hailed Zubayr with this title. But Zubayr refused to accept the role, and passed out of Sudanese history. 'Abdallahi's coming to Muhammad Ahmad may well have been the decisive event in turning the Dunqulawi teacher's thoughts towards assuming the Mahdiship. In these years also Muhammad Ahmad made two visits to Kordofan, and stayed a while in El Obeid, where political intrigue and resentment against the local administration were rife.

What were the motives that drove Muhammad Ahmad to lead a revolt against the Egyptian administration in the Sudan? To many modern Sudanese, he is *Abu'l-Istiqlal*, 'The Father of Independence', a nationalist leader who united the tribes of the Sudan by an Islamic ideology, drove out the alien rulers, and laid the foundations of a nation-state. This is an interpretation of the consequences of his revolt, rather than an appreciation of his motives. Another modern Sudanese view of Muhammad Ahmad sees in him a *mujaddid*, a renewer of the Muslim Faith, come to purge Islam of faults and accretions. Much in Muhammad Ahmad's own statements about his mission supports this opinion. A theme which occurs frequently in his pronouncements is that he was sent to establish the Faith and the Custom of the Prophet – the normative ideals of Islam. Seen from this point of view, Muhammad Ahmad is comparable to the Muslim reformers of the eighteenth and nineteenth centuries, such as Muhammad ibn 'Abd al-Wahhab, the founder of the Wahhabi movement in Arabia.

But Muhammad Ahmad went further than this. His mission as reformer developed eschatological overtones. He claimed for himself unique status, reflected in the three titles which he associated with his name – the Imam, the Successor of the Apostle of God, the Expected Mahdi. As Imam, he asserted his headship of the community of true Muslims. As Successor of the Apostle of God, he envisaged himself recapitulating the role of the Prophet, by restoring the community which Muhammad had established. As the Expected Mahdi, he was an eschatological figure whose advent foreshadowed the end of the age.

87

At times of crisis in the Islamic world, the appearance of a *mahdi*, claiming divine sanction to overthrow the old order and set up a new theocracy, is a not uncommon development. Two medieval *mahdis* had established durable political regimes, 'Ubaydallah, the founder of the Fatimid dynasty in North Africa and Egypt in the tenth century, and Muhammad ibn Tumart, whose followers, the Almohads, had conquered and ruled north-west Africa and Moorish Spain in the twelfth century. There had been others more recently, including one who assailed, and was defeated by, Bonaparte's French troops in Egypt at the end of the eighteenth century.

To an established government, the appearance of a *mahdi* is therefore a dangerous symptom. Muhammad Ra'uf apprehended the danger, but did not act with sufficient force to suppress it. An expedition sent to Aba in August 1881, to seize Muhammad Ahmad, miscarried, and the troops commanded by Muhammad Bey Abu'l-Su'ud, head of the White Nile firm of Agad and Company, were beaten off with some casualties by the Mahdi's followers. This victory of spears and clubs over firearms was hailed as a miracle and, as soon as the government steamers had withdrawn, the Mahdi and his little group of followers crossed the White Nile and made their way to Qadir, a remote hill in the south of Kordofan, on the fringe between Arab and Negro territory. Here the malcontents began to assemble. In this period three main groups may be distinguished among the *Ansar*,[2] as the Mahdi called his supporters.

There were, first, the genuinely pious men who were his disciples in a religious sense and, in some cases, had been with him for years. These men accepted him as the Expected Mahdi. They deplored the state of the Sudan because they were pietists and wished the conduct of its people to be governed by the Holy Law of Islam in its full rigour. The administration was odious, not so much because of oppression and corruption in the usual sense, but because any government not patterned on the primitive Islamic theocracy was inherently depraved. When the Mahdi and these men spoke of misgovernment and purification, they were thinking in theological rather than political terms.

A second group of the Ansar had more practical grievances. These were the Ja'aliyyin and Danaqla of the dispersion, who had settled on the southern fringe of the Arab Sudan, penetrated the White Nile and Bahr al-Ghazal, and worked as boatmen, traders and soldiers of fortune in the great opening-up of the south. Directly or indirectly, the livelihood of many of them was connected with the slave-trade, and Gordon's policy, culminating in the harrying of the *jallaba*, had struck at the roots of their prosperity. Now that Gordon and Isma'il were gone, the opportunity had come to resume their old ways of life. These men were neither theologians nor devotees, but they could cover their political and economic interests with a veil of religion, since the institution of slavery was not as such repugnant to Islam, and the wholesale employment of Christians by a Muslim government derogated from the prestige of their religion.

The third group consisted of the Baqqara nomads, who shared neither the religious ideals of the Mahdi's disciples nor the political grievances of the northerners of the dispersion. To them the Mahdia made its appeal in simple and elementary terms: 'Kill the Turks and cease to pay taxes.' To the nomad, control by any settled government is hateful, and the firmer its control, the more hateful it becomes. The nomads of the southern fringe had in the previous ten years become increasingly conscious of government. The Rizayqat had suffered from the superior armament and forces of Zubayr. Then came the conquest of Darfur, and the substitution of thoroughgoing Egyptian administration for the easy yoke of Sultan Ibrahim. It was the fickle, light-hearted Baqqara who formed the army of this pious revolution, and their importance is reflected in the unique status of their kinsman, 'Abdallahi, in the Mahdi's councils.

Qadir was still more difficult of access than Aba. An attempt to intercept the Ansar while crossing Kordofan failed, and an expedition organized by the governor of Fashoda against the orders of Ra'uf Pasha was annihilated in December 1881. Ra'uf was recalled in the following March, and the 'Urabist government in Egypt appointed as his successor an energetic soldier with long experience in the Sudan, 'Abd al-Qadir Hilmi Pasha. Meanwhile a much more serious attempt to crush the Mahdi had been organized by the acting governor-general, a German telegraph official named Giegler. In spite of its superior forces, this expedition also was overwhelmed in May 1882 by the Ansar. Each of these victories raised the prestige of the Mahdi, while the booty acquired augmented his meagre resources. The Baqqara began to turn increasingly to the new leader of revolt, among them the Rizayqat, who welcomed the prospect of a clash with the provincial authorities of Darfur.

Hitherto the Mahdi, in his refuge at Qadir, had been on the

defensive. He now turned to the offensive and led his followers in a holy war against Kordofan. He knew that in the provincial capital, El Obeid, he could count on a fifth column of sympathizers. The operations in Kordofan followed a pattern which was to be characteristic of the Mahdi's wars. Sporadic local tribal risings first occurred, and were dealt with, usually effectively, by the forces of the administration, but as fast as one was suppressed, another broke out. The immense distances and difficult circumstances of these petty engagements laid a heavy burden on the provincial troops. The second phase opened with the arrival of a Mahdist army in the province. This, combined with more general tribal risings, tried the Turco-Egyptian provincial forces to the utmost. In pitched battles they were still usually victorious, but they were unable to consolidate their successes and had to withdraw to their fortified bases, which, in the third phase, were gradually reduced by the Ansar. In Kordofan, by the autumn of 1882, only two garrisons still held out, at Bara and El Obeid.

The governor at El Obeid, Muhammad Sa'id Pasha, had taken early precautions by fortifying the administrative cantonment which, then as now, was separate from the commercial town. At the beginning of September 1882, the Mahdi with the main body of his supporters, augmented by large tribal levies, encamped near El Obeid. A general assault on the town, delivered in the Friday Battle of 8 September, was a failure: as so often in history, a tribal army found itself checked by a fortified garrison. But Muhammad Sa'id failed to press his advantage, and kept his troops in the cantonment. In the Mahdi's camp there were divided counsels. 'Abdallahi himself advised a retreat to Qadir, but was overruled. Instead the Mahdi moved his camp closer to El Obeid and the Ansar settled down to besiege the town. At the same time a new Mahdist force was organized, of what were in effect regular soldiers, neither fanatical devotees nor tribal warriors. These soldiers were mainly Sudanese originating from the south, who had served in the Turco-Egyptian forces, and had been captured in battle. Their status was interesting; they were commanded by Hamdan Abu 'Anja, who belonged to a servile tribe, clients of the Ta'aisha; they were known, not as Ansar, like the other troops, but by their former Turco-Egyptian designation of *Jihadiyya*; and they alone, it seems, were officially equipped with firearms.

As the year moved to its close, the situation of both Bara and El

Obeid deteriorated. A relieving force sent by 'Abd al-Qadir Hilmi from Khartoum was intercepted in October. After negotiations, the garrison of Bara surrendered on terms in January 1883, and swore allegiance to the Mahdi. A few days later, the determination of Muhammad Sa'id to resist was overborne by a council of his officers. On 19 January El Obeid capitulated and the Mahdi led the prayer of victory in the mosque. This was the first considerable town to fall into the hands of the Ansar, and its capture was followed by a ruthless search for treasure. The former governor and his chief officers had been granted their lives, but the Mahdi learnt that they were attempting to communicate with Khartoum. They were handed over to tribal chiefs, who made away with them.

While these events were taking place at Qadir and in Kordofan, there were sporadic risings in the Gezira and riverain districts south of Khartoum. These areas were however easily accessible by land or steamer, and the vigorous actions of Giegler and 'Abd al-Qadir Hilmi succeeded in holding in check the rebels on the Blue and White Nile. 'Abd al-Qadir indeed planned a vigorous counter-offensive against the Mahdists. He concentrated troops in Khartoum, organized three additional battalions of black *Jihadiyya*, and strengthened the chief administrative centres. He tried to counter the Mahdi's propaganda, and dealt harshly with officials whose loyalty he suspected. He appealed to Cairo for reinforcements, but the 'Urabist government was preoccupied with the threat of British intervention. 'Abd al-Qadir continued to hold office for a few months after the occupation of Egypt in September 1882, but, as a nominee of the 'Urabists, he was not in good standing with the new regime. He was recalled in February 1883, after a successful campaign against forces threatening Sennar.

Turco-Egyptian rule in the Sudan during its last two years, from the fall of El Obeid to that of Khartoum, was dominated by British policy towards Egypt. The British occupation of Egypt was at first regarded by Gladstone's government as a temporary measure, which would be ended as soon as Khedive Muhammad Tawfiq had been firmly re-established on his throne. The revolt in the Sudan was regarded as something outside the sphere of British responsibilities. The serious financial state of Egypt was an argument against large-scale measures to suppress the rebels and regain the lost territory. There was also the point of view expressed by Gladstone, that the Sudanese were a people rightly struggling to be free; against whom, therefore, military operations would be morally unjustifiable. Thus an illogical assemblage of political, financial and moral considerations led the British government, not only to evade involvement in the Sudanese problem, but also to check the attempts of the khedivial government to promote resolute action in the threatened provinces.

A success in the Sudan was, however, badly needed by Muhammad Tawfiq's ministers to restore the prestige of the khedivate and give it at least some semblance of autonomy *vis-à-vis* the occupying power. The Egyptian government was permitted by Britain to raise an expeditionary force entirely on its own responsibility. Many of the troops were demoralized survivors of 'Urabi's armies. A former British officer of the Indian Army, William Hicks, was appointed commander-in-chief, but on his advance into Kordofan he was accompanied by the governor-general, 'Ala' al-Din Siddiq Pasha.

The expedition, which marched out from Dueim on the White Nile on 27 September 1883, was doomed from the start. Hicks disagreed with his Egyptian colleagues, his men lacked hope, the route in its later stages ran through waterless scrub. As it advanced into Kordofan, the column was harassed by a reconnaissance force of Ansar, and proclamations from the Mahdi, scattered on the line of march, warned the troops that it was hopeless to fight against the soldiers of God. On 5 November, the expeditionary force was surrounded at Shaykan south of El Obeid, and cut to pieces by the Ansar and *Jihadiyya* of the Mahdi. Hicks and 'Ala' al-Din perished with all their chief officers. The last Egyptian attempt to hold the Sudan had failed.

The victory of Shaykan convinced the waverers all over the Sudan that Egyptian rule was doomed. The provinces neighbouring Kordofan were the first to fall. In Darfur an Austrian officer, Rudolf von Slatin, had been governor since 1881, and had struggled to repress the rebel Rizayqat in the south. After the fall of El Obeid his position became very precarious, although he publicly professed Islam in an attempt to secure the loyalty of his troops. One of his subordinates, a certain Muhammad Khalid, generally called Zuqal, was a kinsman of the Mahdi. After Shaykan the Mahdi invested him as governor of Darfur. On 23 December 1883 Slatin made his submission to Muhammad Khalid. For the next twelve years Slatin remained in the entourage of the Mahdi and his successor, sometimes an honoured councillor, sometimes a humiliated captive, always a secret enemy of the regime.

In the Bahr al-Ghazal the authority of the khedive was upheld, to the limit of his feeble resources, by a young Englishman, F. M. Lupton, formerly an officer in the British mercantile marine. Like his colleagues in Kordofan and Darfur, he succeeded at first in suppressing local revolts in which both the Dinka and the northerners of the dispersion took part. But the victory of the Mahdi at Shaykan doomed him, and he was cut off from Khartoum. A force sent by the Mahdi to invade the province reached the capital, Daym al-Zubayr, in April 1884, and Lupton had no choice but to surrender. He was sent to the Mahdi and died in Omdurman four years later.

The fall of El Obeid was followed by an extension of the revolt to a region hitherto untouched, one moreover of vital strategic importance, the hinterland of Suakin. The Beja tribes, isolated by their language and way of living from the Arab Sudanese, were unaffected at first by the Mahdia. Not until the summer of 1883 did an emissary reach them, to summon them to the holy war. The Mahdi's messenger and delegate was 'Uthman Diqna,[3] a Suakinese of partially Beja descent. He belonged to a mercantile family and had suffered arrest and imprisonment for slave-trading across the Red Sea. The Hadendowa, the leading Beja tribe of the region, had a grievance against the administration, since they had been bilked of part of the dues promised them for transport work in connection with the Hicks expedition, but neither this nor the personality of 'Uthman Diqna seems to have been the real factor which incited them to revolt.

The decisive event was an alliance which 'Uthman made with Shaykh al-Tahir al-Tayyib al-Majdhub, the local head of the Sufi order which had its centre at El Damer.[4] By swearing allegiance to the Mahdi and recognizing 'Uthman as his duly accredited representative, Shaykh al-Tahir called from the soil a fanatical and devoted tribal army. Within a few months, the vital line of communication between Suakin and Berber had been cut, and two Egyptian forces had been defeated on the coast near Tokar. Sinkat, the nodal point on the route across the Red Sea Hills, and Tokar both fell in February 1884. Suakin itself was reinforced by British troops, and never fell, although it was frequently threatened by the Ansar under 'Uthman Diqna.

The battle of Shaykan inescapably confronted both the Egyptian and British governments with the problem of the future of the Sudan.

Although the British government was prepared to send troops to Suakin, which was of some strategic importance as a Red Sea port, it was still determined to avoid involvement in the interior, and in January 1884 it insisted that the Egyptians should evacuate their troops and officials. Largely in consequence of a press-campaign in Britain, Gordon was sent out to fulfil a mission which was variously understood by the different parties concerned. The British government believed it had sent him to report on the best method of carrying out the evacuation. Baring,[5] the British agent and consul-general in Cairo, who was the effective ruler of Egypt, thought Gordon was authorized to execute the evacuation. On the way, and after his arrival in the Sudan, Gordon added to the confusions and misunderstandings by communicating the varied schemes which sprouted incessantly in his fertile mind.

He was commissioned by the khedive as governor-general, and provided with two sets of documents; one set speaking of the restoration of good government, the other announcing the policy of evacuation. By a fatal error, Gordon published the second set while passing through Berber on the way to Khartoum. Shortly before this he had written to the Mahdi, offering to recognize him as sultan of Kordofan – an offer which the Mahdi indignantly rejected. These two actions indicated to the Sudanese that the Egyptian government had abdicated its responsibilities. Gordon's authority was now effective only so long as he had physical force to maintain it.

He arrived in Khartoum on 18 February 1884. Having quickly realized that an accommodation with the Mahdi and a peaceful evacuation of the Egyptians were impossible, Gordon swung to the other extreme. He felt himself bound to establish a strong government to check the Mahdi, and demanded the appointment of Zubayr Pasha to succeed him. He went on to propose that Indian troops should be sent to the Sudan to 'smash the Mahdi'. To the inhabitants of Khartoum he announced that British troops would in a few days be at Khartoum – a dangerous piece of bluff. When on 13 March the British government overruled these proposals, which went far beyond the scope of their instructions and intentions, Gordon sombrely resigned himself to remaining at Khartoum until help came or the city fell.

The evacuation of the riverain garrisons was by this time becoming impossible. The telegraph-line to Egypt was cut on 12 March. On 27 April a Mahdist emissary arrived to carry the Holy War into the province of Berber. The provincial capital fell in the middle of May. Khartoum was thus cut off, both from the Egyptian frontier and from Suakin. Meanwhile the Mahdi was preparing to advance on Khartoum. He had left El Obeid in April, and the Mahdist vanguard took up its siege-positions outside the capital in September. The Mahdi himself arrived on 23 October and established his headquarters on the western bank of the White Nile. Khartoum, now strictly besieged, was doomed unless help came.

Under the pressure of public opinion in Britain, Gladstone's government at last agreed to send a relief expedition, but its organization did not get under way until the autumn. The news of its advance, in January 1885, placed the besiegers in a dilemma. They failed to gauge its very limited strength, and some of the Mahdi's advisers counselled a retreat to Kordofan. Finally it was decided to assault the city before the relieving force could arrive. The attack was delivered in the early hours of 26 January 1885. The exhausted garrison was overwhelmed, and Gordon was killed in the fighting. On 28 January the relieving steamers arrived at the junction of the Niles, to learn that they had come too late.

The capture of Khartoum completed the Mahdi's control over a great part of the former Egyptian Sudan, although Suakin, the far north and the equatorial regions were still held for the khedive. The Mahdi disliked the former capital, and transferred his headquarters to a village on the western bank near his old camp. Here in Omdurman were his house, his mosque and, in time, his tomb. The Mahdi and his Ansar had seen the taking of Khartoum as but one in a series of conquests throughout the Muslim world. Their expectations were to be disappointed for after a sudden and short illness, the Mahdi died on 22 June 1885.

He left to his successor a rudimentary administrative system, which reflects both the religious ideology of his movement and the wars which had brought it to power. The Mahdi and his Ansar were dominated by the idea that they were re-enacting the drama of primitive Islam. Hence the Mahdi equated his chief disciples with the Companions of the Prophet.

To three of them he gave titles linking them with three of the four Companions who had succeeded the Prophet as heads of the Muslim community. 'Abdallahi ibn Muhammad was designated *Khalifat al-Siddiq*, the Successor of the Caliph Abu Bakr. 'Ali ibn Muhammad

Hilu, a man of great piety and a disciple of long standing, was entitled *Khalifat al-Faruq*, the Successor of the Caliph 'Umar. The title of Successor of 'Uthman, the third historical caliph, was offered to Muhammad al-Mahdi al-Sanusi, the contemporary head of the Sanusiyya order, but he ignored the proposal, and the place remained vacant. A young relative of the Mahdi, Muhammad Sharif ibn Hamid, was appointed *Khalifat al-Karrar,* the Successor of the Caliph 'Ali the cousin of the Prophet.[6]

These were not empty titles, since each of the three *khalifas*, as they are usually called, commanded a division of the Mahdist army. The Khalifa 'Abdallahi, being of Baqqari origin, commanded the great, if fluctuating, tribal levies of the Baqqara. This division was known from its standard as the Black Flag. The Khalifa 'Ali had a comparatively small tribal force, drawn from his own kinsmen in the southern Gezira: it was called the Green Flag. The Khalifa Muhammad Sharif, being, like the Mahdi, of Dunqulawi origin, commanded the riverain tribes of the main Nile and of the dispersion. His division was probably entitled the Red Flag.

The position of 'Abdallahi was as superior to that of his colleagues as that of Bonaparte to the two other consuls in 1799. He was given the title of Commander of the Armies of the Mahdia, and from the outset controlled the administration as the vizier (although this title was not used) of the Mahdi. His paramountcy excited jealousy, and on various occasions the Mahdi affirmed their implicit mutual reliance. One lengthy proclamation of the Mahdi was in effect a diploma conferring plenary powers on 'Abdallahi. There was a deep significance in his nomination as *Khalifat al-Siddiq*, since his prototype, Abu Bakr, had been the closest to the Prophet of all the Companions, and had succeeded him on his death.

Subordinate to the khalifas were other officers who, in the first place, had often been early adherents to the Mahdi and had raised their districts or tribes in his support. They had thus a dual rôle, as propagandists and, later, as military commanders. These officers are usually called by European, and even by Sudanese, writers the Mahdi's 'emirs', although the title *amir* (commander) was officially superseded in 1883 by that of *'amil* (agent). Such officers, who were commissioned in writing by the Mahdi, might be anything from petty local leaders to military governors of an extensive area, such as 'Uthman Diqna in the east or Muhammad Khalid in Darfur. The rank and file, called by the outside world 'dervishes', a term usually applied to the members of Sufi orders, were from a very early date designated by the Mahdi *Ansar*, 'Helpers'.

Two other great officers of state were appointed during the time of the Mahdi: the treasurer and the chief judge. The Mahdist treasury, which, again following a primitive Islamic precedent, was entitled *Bayt al-mal*, 'the house of wealth', was intended to contain all the material resources of the movement, in both cash and kind. For the elaborate tax-system of the Egyptians, lighter taxes authorized by the Holy Law of Islam were substituted. But throughout the period of the revolutionary war, the treasury was augmented chiefly from the booty acquired in battle. It was no easy task to induce the warriors to hand over their booty to the common treasury, as repeated proclamations by the Mahdi and the Khalifa 'Abdallahi make clear. The treasury was put under Ahmad Sulayman, a man of Nubian origin and a friend of the Mahdi.

The chief judge, entitled *qadi al-Islam*, 'the judge of Islam', was Ahmad 'Ali. He had been a judge under the Turco-Egyptian regime in Darfur. In theory the law of the Mahdist community was the Holy Law of Islam, but the Mahdi in practice exercised extensive powers of legislation. This he did by his proclamations and by his decisions on points of law submitted to him. Although Ahmad 'Ali was the special delegate of the Mahdi's judicial functions, legal cases were also heard and determined by the Mahdi himself, the khalifas and the other chief officers. The Mahdist theocracy was in form a state in which supreme power was held directly from God by the Mahdi, and exercised by other officials only by delegation from him. Yet it is clear that before the Mahdi's death a large part of the substance of power was already held by the Khalifa 'Abdallahi.

The Mahdi was the first Sudanese sovereign to exercise one of the traditional prerogatives of a Muslim ruler: that of striking money. After the sack of Khartoum, gold and silver acquired as booty by the treasury were minted by his orders. The gold pounds of the Mahdi were of an unusually high standard of fineness and, in accordance with Gresham's Law, rapidly vanished from circulation. Dollars, at first of silver, later (in the Khalifa's reign) of increasingly debased metal, continued to be struck throughout the Mahdist period. The coins were modelled on Ottoman currency circulating in Egypt, but with Omdurman as the mint-mark. At no time, however, did foreign specie cease to circulate in the Sudan. The Mahdi ordained that the various types of currency should all pass at their face value. This edict was confirmed by the Khalifa, early in his reign, and gave rise to frauds, practised on the treasury by its own officials. The foreign coins were preferred to the local *maqbul* (i.e. 'acceptable') currency, which was further held in low esteem owing to the prevalence of counterfeiting.

THE REIGN OF THE
KHALIFA 'ABDALLAHI: 1885–98

The death of the Mahdi brought to a head the tensions underlying the revolutionary movement. Although the ideology and organization of the Mahdia reflected the outlook and aims of the pious devotees, and although its later victories would have been impossible without the help of the Baqqara, the fruits of conquest had fallen largely to the riverain tribesmen, especially to the Danaqla and Ja'aliyyin of the dispersion. At the centre of this last group, who are called in the Mahdist documents *Awlad al-balad*, (i.e. villagers, sedentaries) were the Mahdi's own kinsmen, the *Ashraf*. Although many of them were late adherents to the movement, they had claimed a privileged position, and their actions had been disavowed by the Mahdi himself in the last few weeks of his life.

Each of the three groups, whom victory was turning from allies into rivals, had its representative in the upper grades of the Mahdist hierarchy. The leader of the devotees was the Khalifa 'Ali ibn Muhammad Hilu, a truly religious man without political ambitions, who constantly played the part of a mediator and conciliator in the crises which followed the Mahdi's death. The party formed by the *Awlad al-balad* had, as a figurehead rather than an active leader, the Mahdi's young kinsman, the Khalifa Muhammad Sharif ibn Hamid. In so far as the Baqqara were prepared to recognize any authority, it was embodied in neither of these, but in the Khalifa 'Abdallahi ibn Muhammad, himself of Baqqari origin.

At the time of the Mahdi's death, 'Abdallahi headed a strong concentration of military power in Omdurman. A body of *Jihadiyya*, commanded by one of his clients, was garrisoned there, as were also Baqqari tribal levies of the Black Flag division. The forces of the *Awlad al-balad*, belonging to the Red Flag division, his only serious rivals, were, by contrast, scattered in various parts of the Sudan. The Green Flag troops were few in number, and could play no effective military role by themselves.

Thus, when the moment came for the *Ashraf* and *Awlad al-balad* to take control of the nascent Mahdist state, they were in no position to do so, lacking, as they did, both determined leadership and effective military force at the centre. At a council of notables, held immediately after the Mahdi's burial, the intention of the *Ashraf* to designate the Khalifa Muhammad Sharif as the new ruler was frustrated by the rest of the company. While the dispute raged, the Khalifa 'Abdallahi sat silent. His restraint was rewarded. One of the notables at last took him by the hand and swore allegiance to him. The other notables followed suit, last of all the *Ashraf* and Muhammad Sharif himself. Thereupon a public oath-taking followed in the open mosque outside the room in which the Mahdi had died. Proclamations were despatched to inform the provincial governors of the new sovereign, and to empower them to administer the oath of allegiance to their troops.

'Abdallahi now added to his style the new and unique title of *Khalifat al-Mahdi*, 'the successor of the Mahdi': he was now 'the Khalifa' par excellence. He bolstered up his position by skilful propaganda, claiming the sanction of visions for his sovereignty. The *Ashraf* were not yet, however, prepared to abandon the struggle for power. Most of the great provincial commands as well as the chief offices of state were held by them or their sympathizers. A conspiracy was hatched, in accordance with which the military governor of Darfur, Muhammad Khalid, was to march on Omdurman with his very considerable forces. The Khalifa's handling of this crisis is typical of his astute and resourceful policy. He first removed the danger in the capital, by sending a Baqqari officer, Yunus al-Dikaym, to occupy the fertile Gezira, the granary of the capital, which the *Ashraf* intended to allot to the troops of Muhammad Khalid. Next he instructed his representative at Dueim to intercept the mails passing between Omdurman and the western provinces. Thirdly, in April or May of 1886, 'Abdallahi, supported by the Khalifa 'Ali, proposed that the two junior khalifas should relinquish their personal bodyguards and armouries, and that these should be placed under the control of Ya'qub, 'Abdallahi's brother and successor as commander of the Black Flag division.

Meanwhile the army of Darfur had begun a leisurely advance towards the Nile. 'Abdallahi possessed two advantages. First, a large part of the Darfurian army consisted of Baqqari levies, who could not be relied on to support Muhammad Khalid. Secondly, in Kordofan was stationed a powerful Black Flag Army, commanded by Hamdan

Abu 'Anja, whose loyalty to the Khalifa was beyond question. Acting on instructions, which became steadily more uncompromising as 'Abdallahi's position improved in Omdurman, Hamdan intercepted the Darfurian army in April 1886 at Bara. Muhammad Khalid allowed himself to be arrested and deprived of his command without resistance. His forces were incorporated in those loyal to the Khalifa.

For six years after the meeting at Bara, the *Ashraf* and *Awlad al-balad* relapsed into impotence. Chance or policy removed their sympathizers from the chief commands, which 'Abdallahi bestowed on his kinsmen and clients. A year after the Mahdi's death, only two of the great provincial governors whom he had appointed remained in office. One of these, in the Bahr al-Ghazal, was to fall from power in 1887; the other, 'Uthman Diqna, was an indispensable instrument for the control of the Beja, and remained in high office until the overthrow of the Mahdist state. Elsewhere the military governors and other high executive officers were clansmen or clients of 'Abdallahi. In subordinate offices, especially in the bureaucracy, the *Awlad al-balad* could not be superseded by the mostly illiterate and unsophisticated nomads, whom they wryly styled 'Our Lords the Ta'aisha'.

After the ending of the internal threat to his rule, the Khalifa took up an aspect of the Mahdi's work left incomplete at his death – the promotion of the Holy War, to extend the Mahdia (equated by the Ansar with true Islam) throughout the world. There had already been fighting on the frontiers. In December 1885 the Ansar of Dongola had been defeated by Anglo-Egyptian forces, and for a while 'Abdallahi believed an invasion of his territories to be imminent, whereas in fact the battle preceded a withdrawal of Egyptian troops from all posts south of Wadi Halfa. The garrisons of Kasala and Sennar, which had held out with great fortitude and endurance even after the fall of Khartoum, surrendered in July and August 1885 respectively. An Egyptian officer, Sa'd Rif'at, succeeded in evacuating the garrison of Gallabat and bringing the refugees through Ethiopia to safety at Massawa. The intrepidity and resource of this man passed unnoticed by a generation whose deepest emotions had been roused by the failure of Gordon's mission.

The Holy War was fought in three particular areas; in the west, on the Ethiopian marches, and on the Egyptian frontier. The war in the west was in its essential nature a pacification of Darfur. On withdrawing from that province, Muhammad Khalid had appointed as its governor a member of the old royal family, Yusuf Ibrahim. At first Yusuf had acted as a loyal vassal of the Khalifa, but by the summer of 1887 he was obviously aiming to restore the Fur sultanate. Operations against him were entrusted to a young kinsman of the Khalifa, 'Uthman Adam, called Janu, who was governor of Kordofan. 'Uthman advanced into Darfur, defeated the rebels and re-established the Mahdist administration of the province. Yusuf fled, but was shortly afterwards defeated. His brother, Abu'l-Khayrat, succeeded to his claims to be the legitimate sultan of Darfur.

The very success of the Mahdist movement led to the appearance of other messianic figures, aiming to subvert the rule of the Khalifa. One such, commonly known by his nickname of Abu Jummayza, gained a large number of militant adherents on the western frontiers of Darfur. Abu Jummayza sought to legitimatize his movement by claiming that he was the rightful third khalifa, the Successor of 'Uthman. Since it was known that the Mahdi had originally offered this title to Muhammad al-Mahdi al-Sanusi, the intelligence officers in Egypt at first gave credence to the market-rumour that the Sanusiyya were on the march, and that the Khalifa was trembling in Omdurman.

The revolt was indeed serious enough. Abu Jummayza advanced into Darfur, gathering supporters as he went, including the shadow-sultan, Abu'l-Khayrat, and his followers. Two of 'Uthman Adam's subordinates were heavily defeated and the young governor was faced with revolt throughout his province. Yet he did not lose heart, but concentrated his forces in El Fasher. The danger passed away as suddenly as it had arisen. Abu Jummayza died of smallpox, and the heart went out of his followers, who were defeated in a pitched battle outside El Fasher in February 1889. Abu'l-Khayrat fled back to the hill-country of Jabal Marra, where he was murdered two years later. 'Uthman Adam had saved Darfur for the Khalifa, but after his premature death in 1891, his successor, Mahmud Ahmad, was to have considerable difficulty in holding the province.

On the Ethiopian frontier, the Holy War was simply a further phase of the hostilities which had frequently recurred throughout the Turco-Egyptian period, and indeed in earlier times. The absence of a defined frontier, the opportunities for raiding which local war-lords on both sides found irresistible, and the coincidence of bellicose rulers in both Ethiopia and the Mahdist Sudan, made a clash inevitable. Fighting began early in 1887 between the Mahdist commander at

Gallabat and Ras 'Adar, the Ethiopian governor of the contiguous territory. The Ansar were worsted, and their chief killed. This led the Khalifa to send an expeditionary force to Gallabat under Yunus al-Dikaym, who followed a provocative policy. The Ansar were soon afterwards augmented by more troops under Hamdan Abu 'Anja, who was given the chief command.

Abu 'Anja had some difficulty in asserting his authority, not only over Yunus but also over many of the troops, who were on the verge of mutiny under a leader with messianic pretensions. He claimed to be the Prophet Jesus, whose Second Coming is to be expected, according to some Mahdist traditions, after the appearance of the Mahdi. The conspiracy was suppressed, Yunus was recalled to Omdurman, and Abu 'Anja seized the opportunity of his absence to make a large-scale raid into Ethiopia. Ras 'Adar was defeated, and the Mahdist army penetrated as far as Gondar, the ancient capital. Much booty fell into the hands of the Ansar, but the campaign as such was indecisive.

This campaign took place in January 1888. Abu 'Anja made another raid in the summer, but it did not produce the successes of the earlier one. Abu 'Anja then returned to Omdurman, where he was welcomed by the Khalifa. By the end of the year he was back at Gallabat, where he died in January 1889.

The lull in hostilities was soon to end. King John of Ethiopia had sent offers of peace to the Khalifa, and had received a bellicose reply. He prepared for war, and was favoured by conditions in the Mahdist camp. Abu 'Anja's death was followed by a dispute over the command at Gallabat. Recognition was ultimately granted to al-Zaki Tamal, a member of the same servile tribe as Abu 'Anja. In March 1889 the Ethiopian army, commanded by the king in person, drew near to Gallabat. At the first onset, the Ethiopians were victorious, but a chance bullet fatally wounded their king. During the night, the Ethiopians began to withdraw, pursued by the exultant Ansar. Among the booty taken by the Sudanese was the crown of the dead king. It was sent with his head to Omdurman, whence the Khalifa issued lithographed copies of al-Zaki's despatch giving news of the victory. Ethiopia fell into anarchy, from which the Italians, who had occupied Massawa in 1885, profited by establishing control over Eritrea, thereby becoming neighbours to the Mahdist state.

In Darfur, and on the Ethiopian frontier, the Khalifa was grappling with problems of pacification and frontier-disputes such as had faced Gordon and the Turco-Egyptian administrators before him. The Holy War on the southern frontier of Egypt was something new, a legacy of the dream of universal conquest throughout the lands of Islam, which had been frustrated by the Mahdi's death. A campaign against Egypt had been planned by the Mahdi, under the command of 'Abd al-Rahman al-Nujumi, a general of Ja'ali origin who had served with distinction during the campaigns in Kordofan and against Khartoum.

When the Khalifa resumed the Mahdi's schemes, al-Nujumi remained as the designated commander of the expeditionary force. The campaign, however, was slow to get under way. Not until the Anglo-Egyptian forces had been withdrawn from Dongola, and 'Abdallahi had secured his position against his domestic rivals, did an expedition really become feasible. Even then, inordinate delays occurred. These were partly physical, arising from the difficulties of constituting and keeping together a force, mainly of tribal warriors, and provisioning it for an advance through the arid districts of Nubia. There were also difficulties of another kind. Al-Nujumi was the last of the great commanders originating from the *Awlad al-balad*. Although his loyalty appears to have been exemplary, he and his riverain troops were suspect to the Khalifa, who appointed a Baqqari officer, nominally as his lieutenant, but in fact as a standing check on his authority and actions.

The expeditionary force remained at its advanced base in Dongola from November 1886 to May 1889. During this time its morale decayed, its predatory activities antagonized the local people, and its high command was paralysed by the Khalifa's mistrust of al-Nujumi. In February 1889 Yunus al-Dikaym arrived in Dongola to take over the administration. Already in April 1887 the Khalifa had sent messages to invite Khedive Muhammad Tawfiq, Queen Victoria and the Ottoman Sultan 'Abd al-Hamid II, to submit to the Mahdia. Two years later further messages of the same kind were sent, and the Ansar began their march northwards.

Unprovisioned and ill-armed, they struggled desperately on, down the western bank of the Nile. Once across the border, they hoped to receive a welcome and assistance from the Egyptians, whom they were coming to liberate from the English yoke. They were doomed to disappointment. Whatever the secret sympathies of the Nubian villagers, they were aware of the futility of resisting the Anglo-Egyptian military power concentrated around Wadi Halfa. In July, Grenfell, the British commander of these forces, sent al-Nujumi an arrogant demand for surrender. Al-Nujumi replied as arrogantly, asserting his loyalty to the Khalifa, and his trust in the help of God. On 3 August 1889 the two armies met near the village of Tushki.[1] The Mahdist expeditionary force was crushingly defeated, al-Nujumi himself being killed in the battle. The threat to Egypt from the Mahdist state had passed for ever away.

The year 1889 was highly critical for the Khalifa. Although the Anglo-Egyptian victory at Tushki was not, as he had feared, followed by an immediate invasion of his territories, his northern frontier was watched by a vigilant enemy, whose material resources he affected to despise, but whose strength he dimly yet forebodingly apprehended. Elsewhere, also, the expansion of the Mahdist state had attained its limits. The victories of 'Uthman Adam and al-Zaki Tamal had resulted in no acquisitions of territory, but had merely established a temporary and precarious Mahdist supremacy in disputed border-regions. The deaths of Hamdan Abu 'Anja and 'Abd al-Rahman al-Nujumi, both in 1889, soon to be followed in 1891 by that of 'Uthman Adam, deprived him of his ablest generals. 'Uthman Diqna was unable to capture Suakin, even though he remained master of the hinterland. In 1889 old tensions between the Beja and Arabic-speaking Ansar on the Suakin front developed into a quarrel characterized by the rivalry of their commanders, to suppress which the Khalifa had to intervene. The *élan* which had carried the Mahdi's followers to victory in the revolutionary war had passed away.

Besides these military and political difficulties the Khalifa was confronted in 1889 and 1890 with an age-old problem, a devastating sequence of bad harvest, famine and epidemic. These natural calamities had always taxed the resources of rulers in the Nile valley; for the Khalifa they were aggravated by his military dispositions. Three great armies were stationed in Darfur, at Gallabat, and, until the Tushki campaign, at Dongola, consuming unproductively the diminishing supplies of corn. Horrifying tales were told of famished beggars snatching bread in the market-places with the last remains of their strength, of silent villages whose people starved quietly to death behind shut doors. There was nothing new in such stories, which may be paralleled from the chronicles of Egypt in the previous centuries, but European opinion laid upon the Khalifa blame for a catastrophe which he was powerless to avert and could do little to alleviate.

By a fatal mischance, the great famine coincided with one of his major acts of policy, the enforced migration of his tribe, the Ta'aisha, and their Baqqara neighbours from their homelands in Darfur to Omdurman. This act has a dual aspect. From one point of view it was the successful consummation of the policy which the Mahdi and the Khalifa himself had endeavoured to follow from the start; that of attaching the nomads closely and permanently to the regime, and turning them from casual raiders into a standing tribal army. The Khalifa's experiences in the first year of his rule had shown him the desirability of surrounding himself with warriors on whose loyalty he could rely. From another point of view, however, the summons to the Ta'aisha was connected with 'Uthman Adam's pacification of Darfur.

The Baqqara did not respond willingly to their kinsman's call. They were attached to their tribal lands, and the Khalifa, after all, was not their hereditary chief but a parvenu. For long they resisted both threats and promises, until at last, in March 1888, the Khalifa's anger flared out in a proclamation, which is a superb piece of Arabic invective, commanding the Ta'aisha, under pain of destruction and dispersion, to place themselves under the orders of 'Uthman Adam. This command, backed by 'Uthman's military power, was at last effective. The great tribal migration began, and in the early months of 1889 the Ta'aisha contingents reached Omdurman.

The coming-in of the Ta'aisha profoundly affected the future of the Khalifa's rule. They must have depleted the corn-supplies of Kordofan as they made their way to the river. Once arrived in Omdurman, they were a privileged élite, who had to be fed at all costs. The effects of the famine were thus aggravated by this great tribal displacement. The migration also had its political consequences. The settled and sophisticated *Awlad al-balad* had as little liking for these romantic nomads as the lowland Scots had for the Highland clans in the 'Forty-five. The Khalifa's open reliance upon his tribal kin deepened the already existing rift between 'Abdallahi and the most advanced group of his subjects. The Ta'aisha, for their part, proved an ineffective instrument for the purposes of government. They tried to elude the Khalifa's vigilance and slip back to their homelands – on one such occasion their hereditary chief himself was pursued and killed. They were unproductive and overbearing, and as little tolerant of discipline as ever. They rapidly became a liability to the Khalifa, and a stumbling-block in his way when he sought to establish a strong monarchy.

In the early days after Tushki, the Khalifa had sought to conciliate his Sudanese opponents. Muhammad Khalid, who had been brought out of prison some months previously, was sent as a commissioner to investigate the troubles in 'Uthman Diqna's command; then to inquire into conditions in Dongola, and to promote trade there. In April 1890 he actually superseded the Baqqari, Yunus al-Dikaym, as governor of Dongola. Other appointments at this time seemed to betoken a renewed participation of the *Awlad al-balad* in the high offices of state. Commerce was encouraged, both with Upper Egypt and with Suakin.

But there were other, less agreeable, indications. In April 1886 the Khalifa had dismissed from office Ahmad Sulayman, whom the Mahdi had appointed as commissioner of the state treasury, and had replaced him by a certain Ibrahim Muhammad 'Adlan, formerly a merchant. 'Adlan was a first-class administrator, and introduced into the haphazard arrangements for the receipt, storage and disbursement of state resources, both in cash and kind, methods based on Turco-Egyptian practice which survived until the end of the regime. The coming of the Ta'aisha was 'Adlan's downfall. He clashed with Ya'qub, the Khalifa's half-brother, who, as commander of the Black Flag division, had a special responsibility for the Ta'aisha. He toured the Gezira to find corn to provision the troops in Omdurman, but his methods were apparently too lenient to suit the Khalifa. Early in 1890 he was disgraced and executed.

The prospects of an improvement in the political status of the *Awlad al-balad* were soon to be dashed. In Dongola, relations between Muhammad Khalid and his Baqqara subordinates degenerated into an open quarrel and, a year after taking office, he was recalled to Omdurman. Once again, Yunus al-Dikaym took the command in the north. In Omdurman a new conspiracy against the Khalifa developed. As in 1886, its promoters were the *Ashraf*, and its principal supporters were the Danaqla sailors and settlers in the Gezira. Their ostensible complaint was the lack of respect shown towards the Khalifa Muhammad Sharif and the Mahdi's family, but they had also economic grievances of a kind which would affect the *Awlad al-balad* rather than the Baqqara. The revolt seems to have been brought to a head by the recall of Muhammad Khalid from Dongola, and his subsequent imprisonment.

Under the leadership of Muhammad Sharif, the conspirators made their headquarters around the Mahdi's tomb, thus threatening

'Abdallahi, whose house was only a few yards away. On 23 November 1891, the Khalifa assembled his own supporters and tried to cordon off the *Ashraf*. He was in a dilemma, since if fighting broke out the Ta'aisha might get out of control, sack the capital, and flee to Darfur. Hence he was anxious to open negotiations with the *Ashraf*, and in this he was ultimately successful. The Khalifa 'Ali ibn Muhammad Hilu strove for a settlement, and on 25 November the insurgents laid down their arms. They were promised a general pardon; the Khalifa Muhammad Sharif was to be given the full honours and authority due to his position, and the family of the Mahdi were to receive a monthly pension. Having disarmed his opponents, the Khalifa proceeded to reduce them to impotence. A few weeks later, seven notables including the former treasurer, Ahmad Sulayman, were seized and transported up the White Nile to Fashoda, where al-Zaki Tamal put them to death. The Danaqla in the Gezira were rounded up, detained and only released after the confiscation of a third of their goods. In March 1892 the Khalifa Muhammad Sharif was himself arrested and tried before a special body of commissioners. He was deprived of his dignities and flung into prison, where he remained until the eve of the Khalifa 'Abdallahi's own overthrow.

The power of the *Ashraf* and the *Awlad al-balad* was thus finally and completely broken. The next four years display 'Abdallahi as an autocratic monarch. Never had his authority over his subjects seemed to be so firmly established. Organized revolt against him had ceased, and even those Sudanese who disliked his rule were increasingly prepared to acquiesce in it. The transformation of the theocratic state of the early Mahdia into a secular despotism was becoming obvious. One sign of the change was the organization of a new armed force, immediately dependent on the Khalifa, the *Mulazimiyya*, which, from a small corps of orderlies (to which Slatin belonged), was expanded from 1892 onwards into a bodyguard of nine thousand men, commanded by the Khalifa's son, 'Uthman Shaykh al-Din. The *Mulazimiyya* thus superseded the Ta'aisha, as the Ta'aisha had the *Jihadiyya*, as the principal military support of the regime. The *Mulazimiyya* was composed half of slave-troops, half of free Sudanese, but Danaqla and Egyptians were strictly excluded from it. It had its own treasury, to which the Gezira contributed corn and cash.

In the tradition of oriental autocracy, the Khalifa began to

withdraw himself from his people. It had been his custom to attend
the weekly parade of the Ansar, held each Friday outside
Omdurman. Now he appeared, surrounded by his bodyguard, only
on the principal festivals. A great wall was constructed around the
part of Omdurman containing his residence where he and his
bodyguard were housed – a district which until today is known as the
Mulazimiyya quarter. In his councils, two men were prominent, his
half-brother Ya'qub, who from the first had acted as his vizier, and
later his eldest son 'Uthman. Although the two junior khalifas were
perhaps regarded as having a reversionary claim to the succession, on
the analogy of the caliphs, whose 'successors' they were, 'Uthman
was clearly regarded by his father as heir-apparent. He was groomed
in state affairs and, apparently in 1891, married to Ya'qub's
daughter, when he received the honorific title of *Shaykh al-Din*,
indicating his senior standing in the Mahdist hierarchy. Ya'qub
became increasingly jealous of 'Uthman, as the latter's influence
grew, and the political marriage exacerbated their relations. As
'Abdallahi cultivated the manner of a despot, his suspicions of his
servants showed themselves. In 1893, the victor of Gallabat, al-Zaki
Tamal, was arrested and starved to death. The two following years
saw the destitution and death in prison of two successive chief judges,
the first of whom, Ahmad 'Ali, had held office since the time of the
Mahdi.[2]

The Khalifa's temper in these years was no doubt affected by his
growing awareness that the Mahdist state was no longer immune
from the attacks of its external enemies. This was the heyday of the
European scramble for Africa, and the Khalifa's military strength,
which a century earlier would have been adequate to repulse any
likely invader, was set against the superior might and organization of
the European powers. It was ironical that, at the very period when his
rule was least questioned by his subjects, and had been established
internally on elaborate administrative foundations, the Khalifa was
to be overthrown by a foreign invader.

For a time the remoteness of his dominions, the considerable
geographical obstacles to a military conquest, and the very rivalries
of the European powers themselves, deferred a development which in
the circumstances of the time was almost inevitable. There were,
however, ominous portents. In February 1891, an Anglo-Egyptian
expedition from Suakin routed 'Uthman Diqna and captured his

headquarters near Tokar. This was the first decisive defeat of the Ansar on the Red Sea littoral. In December 1893 a Mahdist expedition into Eritrea was heavily defeated by the Italians at the battle of Agordat. This was the prelude to an Italian offensive against Kasala, which fell in July 1894. Slatin has borne witness to the deep impression which this loss made upon the Khalifa. Yet a lethargy of false confidence seemed to overcome him, and he returned a cold reply to the overtures of friendship from Menelik II of Ethiopia, who was also threatened by the Italians.

Further threats to his power were now appearing in the south. The southern Sudan was not effectively part of the Mahdist state. The Bahr al-Ghazal had not had a Mahdist governor since 1886. Emin Pasha, the last khedivial governor of Equatoria, after withdrawing to the south of his province, had maintained a shadow of Egyptian authority on the Upper Nile until he was more or less compelled to evacuate the province by H. M. Stanley's relief expedition in 1889. A Mahdist garrison was established at Rejaf, but the river-line from Fashoda southwards was not permanently held, while away from the river Mahdism was but a name. In 1893 the Khalifa sent an expeditionary force under 'Arabi Dafa'allah to strengthen his hold over the far south, but steamer connections with Omdurman were even more infrequent and hazardous than they had been in the Turco-Egyptian period.

Meanwhile the Belgians had established Leopold II's power in the Congo, and expeditions were beginning to push across the Nile-Congo divide towards the former Egyptian provinces of the Bahr al-Ghazal and the Upper Nile. In 1894 there were clashes between the Belgians and 'Arabi Dafa'allah, while at the same time another Belgian force was contacting the tribal rulers in the Bahr al-Ghazal. In August 1894, however, a Franco-Congolese agreement opened the door to a French advance to the Bahr al-Ghazal and the Upper Nile. In consequence of this, an expedition under the command of Captain Marchand was approved in November 1895 by the French foreign minister.

In March 1896 the British government suddenly and unexpectedly authorized an advance by Egyptian forces into Dongola. The reason for this act is to be sought in the relations of the European great powers: it had no particular relevance to the situation in the Mahdist state, nor was it undertaken primarily for any advantages that might accrue to Egypt from a reconquest of the Sudan, which indeed was not contemplated at this stage. Neither was the advance intended to forestall Marchand's appearance on the Upper Nile, which was at that time regarded as a remote contingency, and in any case could not be affected by military action in Nubia. The event which precipitated the British government's decision was the defeat of the Italians by Menelik at Adowa on 1 March 1896. But the British desire to make a gesture of assistance to Italy, by a move which might distract the Mahdist forces from an attack on the Italian flank at Kasala, was further intended to conciliate Germany and to guard against the dissolution of the Triple Alliance, which at this time were objectives of Lord Salisbury's foreign policy.[3] The expedition was less agreeable to Cromer, Britain's proconsul in Egypt, than to the British officers, who had not forgotten the defeats which troops under their command had suffered at the hands of the Ansar. At home, the British public was allured by the prospect of a long-delayed vengeance for Gordon.

The reconquest took place in two stages. In the first a railway from Wadi Halfa was pushed up the main Nile to support an expeditionary force commanded by Sir Herbert Kitchener.[4] The Mahdist forces in Dongola were defeated in a series of actions, and by September 1896 the whole province had been occupied. Kitchener now began the construction of a new railway line across the Nubian Desert, from Wadi Halfa to Abu Hamad on the main Nile. Abu Hamad fell in July 1897, and the Anglo-Egyptian forces prepared to penetrate to the heart of the Mahdist state.

In this crisis the Khalifa was ill-served by the general to whom he committed the defence of his dominions. He summoned Mahmud Aḥmad from Darfur, and put him in command. Mahmud made his headquarters at Metemma. Its Ja'aliyyin inhabitants refused to obey the Khalifa's order to evacuate their town, vainly appealed to Kitchener for help, and were massacred after an unsuccessful resistance. There for months Mahmud remained, unwilling or unable to move, badgering the Khalifa with a constant flow of despatches, seeking advice on every contingency, and failing to act on the instructions he received. Like al-Nujumi earlier, he found great difficulty in provisioning his army, which began to melt away as the weeks passed.

Meanwhile the enemy was advancing. Berber was evacuated by the Mahdist garrison and fell without resistance to the Anglo-Egyptian forces at the end of August 1897. In February 1898 'Uthman Diqna with his forces arrived in support of Mahmud, but the old fighter and the young general worked badly together. Soon afterwards the Mahdist army left Metemma and advanced to the river Atbara, where it encamped. The Ansar were starving, but, in the hour of their defeat, their old heroic courage returned to them. Kitchener delivered his attack on Good Friday, 8 April 1898. At the end of the day 3,000 Sudanese were dead and 4,000 wounded. 'Uthman Diqna had again escaped, while Mahmud Ahmad was a prisoner, humiliated by his captor. He was taken to Rosetta, where he died in 1906. On the Anglo-Egyptian side, the casualties were 81 killed and 487 wounded.

When the advance on Omdurman began, four months later, the last phase in the campaign opened. On 1 September, the Egyptian and British forces were encamped near an abrupt hill called Jabal Surkab,[5] on the left bank of the Nile, six miles north of Omdurman. The vicinity is known as Karari. Against them the Khalifa threw the considerable reserves he had kept in his capital. Once again, although not without difficulty, Kitchener was victorious. It was estimated that 11,000 Sudanese were killed and 16,000 wounded. The Anglo-Egyptian losses were 49 killed and 382 wounded. Ya'qub died on the field. The Khalifa rode back to his deserted capital and led the remnant of his forces to Kordofan. The battle of Omdurman, more accurately called the battle of Karari, marked the end of the Mahdist state in the Sudan.

The significance of the Khalifa's reign has not always been appreciated either by his countrymen or by foreign observers. A legend, fostered by war-propaganda, grew up around his name, depicting him as a bloodthirsty and barbarous despot, from whose tyranny the Sudanese were released by the Anglo-Egyptian invasion. The reality is rather different. When he came to power, the initial drive of the Mahdia was at an end. The objects of the revolutionary war had largely been attained. The greater part of the Muslim north was under Mahdist rule. His primary problem was to restore order and make administration effective over a vast area in which four years of warfare against the established government had broken down the habits of obedience. His task was complicated by the uncertain loyalty of the *Awlad al-balad*, from whom the Mahdi had drawn the bulk of his ruling élite, and by the insubordination and backwardness of the Baqqara, on whom he himself chiefly relied.

He sought to establish his authority by developing an increasingly elaborate and centralized administration. Although the forms of the Mahdist theocracy were retained, the spirit had, by the middle years of his reign, departed from them. The other two khalifas were in no real sense his colleagues; his closest associate in government was his brother, Ya'qub. The great military commands were held almost exclusively by Baqqara. The simple fiscal system of the Mahdi was abandoned. The revenue was augmented by a whole range of new taxes, dues and confiscations, closely resembling the Turco-Egyptian taxes, which the Mahdi had come to destroy. The development of specialized treasuries, notably the Khalifa's own privy treasury, siphoned off from the original *Bayt al-mal* the cream of its revenue. The judiciary similarly acquired an increasingly complex organization, although no greater independence of the ruler in the performance of its functions.

The reign of the Khalifa, then, is characterized by the passing of the Mahdist theocracy and the creation of a personal rule exercised through a bureaucracy, largely composed of Sudanese civil servants inherited from the Turco-Egyptian regime. 'Abdallahi prevented the northern Sudan from relapsing into anarchy after the Mahdi's death. His success in establishing his control so firmly that it was broken ultimately only by a foreign invader with superior military resources, is a measure of his inherent strength of personality and his administrative talent. Yet the price was high. 'Abdallahi, permanently resident in Omdurman, was never fully in control of his provincial officials, although his system of constant communication with them destroyed their initiative in emergencies. His reliance on the Baqqara opened a rift between himself and the *Awlad al-balad* which weakened the foundations of the state. Finally, the sustained military character of the regime, derived from the revolutionary period, and continued at first in accordance with the policy of the Holy War, and later because of the growing threat from outside, prevented a genuine resettlement of the country. 'Abdallahi was much less a malevolent despot and much more the prisoner of his circumstances than contemporary European writers were willing to perceive.

PART IV

THE ANGLO–EGYPTIAN
CONDOMINIUM
1899–1955

*The cannon which swept away the Dervish hordes at
Omdurman proclaimed to the world that on England – or, to
be more strictly correct, on Egypt under British
guidance – had devolved the solemn and responsible duty of
introducing the light of Western civilization amongst the
sorely tried people of the Soudan.*

Lord Cromer, *Modern Egypt*, 1908.

*At the end of time the English will come to you, whose
soldiers are called police: they will measure the earth even
to the blades of the sedge grass. There will be no deliverance
except through the coming of Jesus.*

Attributed to Shaykh Farah wad Taktuk
(17th century), translated by S. Hillelson.

8

PACIFICATION AND
CONSOLIDATION
1899–1913

The overthrow of the Mahdist state posed the immediate question of the future status and administration of the Sudan. Despite the fact that the Anglo-Egyptian conquest had been undertaken with the stated aim of recovering the lost Sudanese provinces of the khedive, the British, for a number of reasons, were unwilling to accede to the reincorporation of those provinces with Egypt. Opinion in Britain was convinced that the Mahdist revolution had been a reaction to oppressive Turco-Egyptian rule; to reimpose that rule would appear to belie the moral arguments which had justified British intervention. Further, Lord Cromer, the British agent and consul-general in Egypt, who since the British occupation of 1882 had been virtual ruler of the country, sought to avoid for the Sudan the cumbrous international status that had dogged his conduct of Egypt's affairs. The direct administration of the Sudan under the khedivate would, he feared, open the way for the introduction of the capitulations and other international machinery.[1]

An obvious alternative was the administration of the Sudan as a British colony. Yet this too was unfeasible. Egyptian claims had formed the basis for the conquest and gave the British a legal position in the Upper Nile valley which their European rivals, France, Italy and Belgium, could not match. To abrogate the Egyptian claims was therefore impossible. This was borne out at the time of the Fashoda crisis. A French expedition commanded by Captain Marchand occupied Fashoda on the Upper Nile on 10 July 1898. When word of this reached Kitchener he immediately set out for Fashoda, where he told Marchand that 'the presence of a French force at Fashoda and in the valley of the Nile was regarded as a direct infringement of the rights of the Egyptian government and of Great Britain'. It was only after a period of great tension between Britain and France that on 4 November the French government gave way and ordered Marchand to withdraw.

With neither annexation by Britain nor incorporation under the khedivate a suitable solution to the problem of the Sudan's status, Cromer devised a 'hybrid form of government',[2] which appeared both to honour Egyptian claims and to safeguard British interests. This solution was embodied in the Anglo-Egyptian conventions of 1899, which came to be known as the Condominium Agreement since they created a theoretically joint Anglo-Egyptian sovereignty over the Sudan. British claims were openly based on the right of conquest, while Egypt's were defined by reference to 'certain provinces in the Sudan which were in rebellion against the authority of His Highness the Khedive'. The agreement stipulated that the Egyptian and British flags should be flown together in the Sudan, that the appointment and removal of the governor-general should be by khedivial decree, but at the instance of the British government, and that proclamations of the governor-general should be notified to the Egyptian and British governments. The direct authority of the Egyptian government and of its laws, the application of the capitulations and Mixed Tribunals,[3] and any remaining rights of the Ottoman sultan were rejected or omitted altogether in the agreement.

Whereas the agreement recognized Egyptian rights, it reserved almost complete autonomy to the British-nominated governor-general, the ratification of whose appointment was assured by the British occupation of Egypt. Supreme military and civil authority in the Sudan was vested in the governor-general, who could rule by decree. Every governor-general from 1899 until the end of the Condominium in 1955 was a British subject presiding over 'the Sudan Government'. Thus the Condominium was never to be in practice an exercise in joint rule. Although it temporarily placated Egyptian opinion and ensured British dominance, it became increasingly a bone of contention between Britain and Egypt, especially after the First World War, when Egyptian nationalists attacked the agreement as a sham, devised to deny Egyptian rights whilst paying lip service to them. The Sudan Government itself came to view condominium status as a lever by which Britain could manipulate affairs in Egypt, sometimes to the detriment of the Sudan's best interests, and from time to time pressed for a more definitive British control.

The first governor-general to be appointed under the agreement was Lord Kitchener in 1899. He held office until December of that year when he was called to war in South Africa. Kitchener's brief tenure was unsuccessful: a soldier rather than an administrator, he alienated his subordinates and neglected the plight of the exhausted civilian population. His sudden departure left the tasks of pacification and rebuilding to his successor, Sir Reginald Wingate, who had been in charge of the Egyptian Army's military intelligence department since 1887, and was to remain governor-general until 1917.

The first priority of the Anglo-Egyptian regime was perforce the elimination of popular resistance. The battle of Karari had brought about the collapse of the Mahdist state, but the Khalifa 'Abdallahi remained at large with an army and several of the leading Mahdist notables. In November 1899 Wingate, not yet governor-general, met the Mahdists in battle at Umm Diwaykarat in southern Kordofan. The khalifa's army was defeated and 'Abdallahi, the Khalifa 'Ali b. Muhammad Hilu and the Amir Ahmad Fadil were killed. 'Abdallahi's son, 'Uthman Shaykh al-Din, was captured and imprisoned; 'Uthman Diqna escaped but was captured later and died a prisoner at Wadi Halfa in 1926.

The final defeat of organized Mahdist resistance did not, as events were to show, mean the disappearance of the cult of the Mahdi. Despite the deaths of the Khalifa Muhammad Sharif and the two eldest sons of the Mahdi at Shukkaba in 1899,[4] the government had to deal with a number of Mahdist pretenders who appeared from time to time. Indeed, one aspect of Mahdist eschatology indicated the appearance, after the Mahdi, of al-Dajjal, the Anti-Christ, whose coming would herald the second coming of the Prophet Jesus, al-Nabi'Isa. The arrival of this figure was awaited by some, and this, combined with the social upheaval of the time, gave rise to many claimants to the title of Nabi'Isa and, indeed, to the Mahdiship. None of these 'false prophets' suppressed during the Wingate years was able to attract much popular support and all were dealt with harshly by the insecure new government. Despite their insignificance, as viewed today, these risings became a preoccupation of the government and were influential in determining its policies towards Islam in general.

Pacification of the southern provinces was hampered by the inaccessibility of the region and by shortages of staff and funds. Communications were poor. The obstruction of the Sudd, barriers of accumulated vegetation which rendered the rivers impassable, had to be cleared. With almost super-human efforts the Bahr al-Jabal was opened up in 1904, but the Bahr al-Ghazal required regular Sudd-clearing expeditions which were facilitated after the First World War by the introduction of mechanical dredgers. Despite improved river navigation, however, the government was able only slowly to bring the vast region and its heterogeneous, non-Arab, non-Muslim population under control. Posts were established and manned by northern troops under British officers, but beyond these posts the process of pacification was to continue well into the 1920s. Military patrols as a means of bringing the hinterland under control were abandoned only gradually, when it was realized that these alienated as well as subdued, and were in any case expensive and without lasting results.

Indicative of the comprehensive task facing the new government was the need to delimit the Sudan's international boundaries. Cromer in 1899 was careful not to define the Condominium as extending over all the territory which formerly belonged to Egypt. The Nile-Congo watershed was accepted in March 1899 as the line of demarcation between French and British control. To the north of this line lay the sultanate of Darfur, autonomous once again, but tributary to Khartoum. The boundary with Eritrea was fixed between 1898 and 1902. A treaty between Ethiopia and Great Britain in 1902 determined a frontier which, as in the past, was to cause constant trouble to the authorities in the Sudan. The boundary with the Congo Free State was agreed in 1906. The Lado Enclave, which had been leased for life to King Leopold II of the Belgians, reverted at his death in 1910 to the Sudan. The frontier with Uganda was agreed in 1913, and in 1914 the Sudan received a further stretch of the Upper Nile in exchange for part of the former Lado Enclave.

The administrative structure of the Condominium was erected during Wingate's governor-generalship. The British relied upon the arrangements of the Turco-Egyptian and Mahdist regimes, on their experience in Egypt and India, and upon methods adopted through trial and error for the particular circumstances of the Sudan.

Dominating the administration was the governor-general who, as sirdar or commander-in-chief of the Egyptian Army (until 1924 when the positions were separated) combined absolute civil and military authority. In theory responsible to the co-domini, the governor-general in fact reported to London through the British representative in Cairo. Since the Sudan was not a colony, its affairs were dealt with by the Foreign Office rather than by the Colonial Office in London. This, and its unique status, combined with the extraordinary powers granted the governor-general in the Condominium Agreement, allowed him considerably more independence than was usually enjoyed by a colonial governor. Disagreements as to British policy could have a trilateral aspect, with British officials in Khartoum, Cairo and London holding widely different views. The British occupation of Egypt meant that many such disagreements were therefore intra-mural, the formal conditions of the Condominium Agreement being of less importance than considerations of British policy and the personal relations between the governor-general and the British representative and advisers to ministries in Cairo. Whereas the Foreign Office insisted that the Sudan Government was responsible to the British representative in Cairo, in practice his control over Sudan affairs was limited to questions affecting Egyptian or British interests, and decreased as time went on. A Sudan Agent, resident in Cairo, acted as spokesman for the governor-general.

The governor-general was thus not completely independent. In financial affairs he was limited by the *Regulations for the Financial Administration of the Sudan* appended to the Condominium Agreement, by which the Sudan's annual budget had to be approved by the Egyptian Council of Ministers, and by subsequent financial arrangements. Further, the agreed political necessity of low taxation in the Sudan meant that funds must be obtained to offset the budget deficit. These funds came from the Egyptian Treasury until 1913, when the budget balanced. Yet even after that date the Sudan depended financially on Egypt in two important ways: the capital already invested by Egypt, on which no interest was being paid; and the maintenance of the Egyptian army in the Sudan, which was charged entirely to Egypt. To Egyptian objections that financial support should entail some political control, the British responded that Egyptian subventions were in fact a long-term investment, and that the quiescence of her southern border more than adequately compensated Egypt for the cost of maintaining the army.

Within the Sudan, the central government was divided into three major and several minor departments. Dominating this structure were 'the three secretaries', civil, legal and financial. The financial secretary, responsible for drawing up, controlling and administering the budget, and for disposing of financial questions, had great latitude, which allowed his hand to be felt in other areas of administration. The legal secretary was the governor-general's chief legal adviser, responsible for framing the laws and ordinances promulgated by the governor-general and for supervising the courts. Eventually the most important of the three, the civil secretary headed the civil service and acted as liaison between central and provincial governments. As in the conduct of the governor-general's relations with Cairo, the influence of the secretaries often depended more on the relative forcefulness of personalities than on exact definitions of duties. In 1909 a governor-general's council was established, consisting of the three secretaries, the inspector-general, and between two and four other members nominated by the governor-general, as a purely advisory body. During Wingate's term the council had little independent influence, but under his successors functioned unofficially as a cabinet.

The importance during the early Condominium of personal relations is best exemplified by the unique position of the inspector-general, Slatin Pasha, *vis-à-vis* the secretaries and provincial governors. After his escape from Omdurman in 1895 he had helped Wingate in preparing the Anglo-Egyptian advance. On assuming the governor-generalship, Wingate created the office of inspector-general for Slatin who, as an Austrian national, had to resign at the outbreak of the First World War, when the post ceased to exist. Slatin's responsibilities extended over the whole range of tribal and religious affairs. This and his intimacy with Wingate made him second in importance only to the governor-general, and brought him frequently into conflict with other officials. Slatin had a deleterious effect on the intelligence department which suffered from his highly personal methods. These survived his departure and minimized the effectiveness of the department during episodes of revolt in the 1920s.

The country was divided into provinces, the number and boundaries of which were altered through the years. Each was headed by a governor (*mudir*) responsible to the governor-general through the various departments. Provincial districts (sing. *markaz*) were in the charge of British inspectors (sing. *mufattish*), who from 1922 were called district commissioners. A district comprised a number of sub-districts, over each of which presided a *mamur*. This class of official was largely made up of Egyptians, though a policy of sudanization gradually introduced educated Sudanese, as sub-*mamurs* from 1915 and as *mamurs* shortly thereafter. Thus provincial and central administration was British in the higher ranks, and Egyptian (and eventually Sudanese) in the lower.

The first three governors-general, Kitchener, Wingate and Sir Lee

Stack, were all soldiers. This, the unsettled state of the country and the priority of establishing law and order, resulted in the first generation of British officials being drawn overwhelmingly from officers of the Egyptian army, who were seconded for service in the Sudan. The case for soldier-administrators was strongest in the south, where they were often employed on a contract basis. In the north, however, it was early felt by Cromer that a special service of carefully chosen British civilians was needed. Civilians were therefore employed as early as 1901 in administration, and in 1905 a system of recruitment was established by which British university graduates endowed, in Cromer's words, 'with good health, high character and fair abilities' were brought out. These civilians composed what became known as the Sudan Political Service.

The political service produced the ruling élite of the British-dominated administration. Isolated from the world at large and from the practice of administration elsewhere in Britain's empire, the political service was largely immune to outside criticism. The structure of the government, which often interposed an Egyptian official between a British officer and the Sudanese; the officer's independence of action and absolute local authority; and a paternal attitude that could approach condescension, were deficiencies of the service which created the image of 'father of the people', especially in the south. These were balanced by dedication, hard work and incorruptibility. Paternalism was more amenable to petitions than to demands, more to tribal instincts than to anything symptomatic of 'individualism'. A government composed, in the words of a British newspaper, of 'athletic public school boys accustomed to hard work rather than to hard thinking', more than adequately met the needs of administration in the difficult early years of the Condominium. The service did, in fact, embody what its founders had envisaged. When, however, after the First World War, the first stirrings were felt of a Sudanese national consciousness, a degree of sophistication and far-sightedness was required which was, with few exceptions, lacking.

That paternalism was so soon questioned was the result in part of a limited educational advance during Wingate's governor-generalship. In the words of (Sir) James Currie, who was appointed as first director of education in 1900, a system was required to enable the masses 'to understand the elements of the system of government', to train 'a small class of competent artisans', and 'to produce a small administrative class for entry to the government service'. Insufficient budgetary provisions and a feeling on the part of some British officials that 'over-education' posed a greater threat to the country than did no education at all, were reflected in a policy that considered education an adjunct to administration and a necessity for technical progress, but never as of value in itself. The opening in 1902 of the Gordon Memorial College, for which subscriptions had been raised in Britain, provided the venue for the first intermediate and secondary schools. The system established was highly selective, politically affected, and reflected both the needs of government departments for graduates and the prevailing administrative policy.

Religious policy during the Wingate years was determined largely by considerations of political security. Mahdism was suppressed, insofar as it was within the power of the government to do so: the Mahdi's *Ratib*, the devotional work used by his followers, was proscribed; surviving members of the Mahdist hierarchy and their families remained in prison or were closely watched, a policy seemingly justified by the series of petty Mahdist-style risings. The *tariqas*, long the focal points of popular Islam, were viewed with suspicion and were not officially recognized, although the Khatmiyya *tariqa* and its hereditary leaders, the Mirghani family, received special consideration in consequence of their long record of loyalty. To combat the influence of popular Islam, Wingate created in 1901 a Board of Ulema, consisting of members of the recently re-established hierarchy of orthodox-cult officials: the *mufti,* the grand *qadi*, and other notables. To this board were referred for opinions all government proposals affecting Islam, but in practice the board's lack of popular influence limited its effectiveness. Further steps to cultivate orthodox Islam included government financing of mosque construction, facilitating the pilgrimage, and the encouragement of *kuttabs* in which the Qur'an was taught. Risking controversy in Britain, the government strongly opposed Christian missionary activity in the northern Sudan.

A careful concern for Muslim opinion was also shown in the government's judicial policies. The *Sudan Penal Code* and *Code of Criminal Procedure* were based on Indian models. But matters of personal status came under the jurisdiction of the Shari'a, which was administered by Muslim courts at the district, provincial and central levels, supervised by the grand *qadi* at Khartoum. *The Mohammedan Law Courts Ordinance and Procedure Regulations* of 1915 allowed the grand *qadi* discretion to depart from usual Hanafi practice. This resulted in a reform of family law, in accordance with the modernizing views of 'Abduh and Qasim Amin, which pre-dated that of Egypt.[5] In addition to the government codes and the Shari'a, the force of tribal law was recognized as necessary and expedient, especially with reference to the lightly-administered and far-flung nomadic tribes.

Religious policy in the south differed markedly from that pursued in the Muslim north. Obsessed with the dangers posed to internal security by 'fanatical' Islam, Wingate and his subordinates sought to exclude Muslim influence altogether from the southern provinces. Christian missionary organizations, frustrated by government policy in the north, were allotted spheres for proselytization in the south. Education, in the English language, was entrusted to them. Efforts were made to discourage the learning and use of Arabic, and even the wearing of 'Arab' dress. To halt the spread of Islam resulting from the presence of northern troops and *jallaba*, an Equatorial Corps, recruited locally, was established in Mongalla Province. Other territorial companies were soon added, and northern troops gradually removed. *Jallaba* were increasingly excluded by British officials. Some modern writers have discerned in these steps the conscious beginnings of a 'Southern Policy' aiming at the political separation of the southern provinces from the Sudan. In these early years, however, the tendency towards a separate policy was uncoordinated and was based, as was policy in the north, on a consuming fear of Islam as a threat to government control as was apparent in recurrent Mahdist or pseudo-Mahdist risings.

Wingate's governor-generalship witnessed a steady improvement in the Sudan's economy. A cardinal principal of economic policy was light taxation. The systems enforced during the Turco-Egyptian and Mahdist periods were largely retained. A land tax and *'ushur* (a percentage of crop value), date tax and herd tax were levied on the settled population, and were frequently paid in kind. A herd tax levied on nomads was replaced in 1901 with an annual 'tribute' paid by a tribe as a whole. Revenue from all these sources was minimized by the difficulties of assessment and collection. Property taxes, market dues, and tolls were also introduced. The major burden of taxation fell inevitably on the settled agricultural population.

Revenue and expenditure increased respectively from £E156,888 and £E331,918 in 1900 to £E1,654,149 and £E1,614,007 in 1913, when the annual Egyptian subvention ended. By that time Egypt had advanced £E5,353,215 to cover the Sudan's budget deficits. In the same period Egypt had loaned, without interest, £E5,365,680 for development projects, largely in the area of railway construction. The railway built by Kitchener to facilitate the Anglo-Egyptian conquest was adapted for civilian use and was extended as far as the Blue Nile, opposite Khartoum, in 1899. A spur from the Nile to the Red Sea was opened in 1906, terminating at the newly-constructed Port Sudan, which was opened in 1909 to replace the inadequate old port of Suakin. The main railway line was extended south across the Blue Nile to Khartoum, railhead reaching Sennar in 1909 and westward to El Obeid in 1911. Railway extension resulted in the establishment of new towns: Khartoum North, Atbara at the western end of the spur to Port Sudan, and Kosti where the railway crossed the White Nile south of Khartoum. From Kosti a steamer service connected the north with the southern Sudan, where railway construction was impractical. Road construction lagged far behind.

Development, especially of agriculture, was hindered by a chronic labour shortage. The government's policy towards slavery came to reflect the economic and potential political consequences of this shortage. The slave-trade itself was prohibited by the Condominium Agreement. In one respect the new government was more fortunately placed than Khedive Isma'il and Gordon had been in the 1870s: contrary to assertions which are still sometimes uncritically retailed, the trade seems to have declined sharply during the Mahdia. Its previous expansion had been, as we have seen, a corollary of the penetration of the Upper Nile and the Bahr al-Ghazal, but these areas which, with the Nuba Mountains, had been the principal hunting-grounds for slaves in the Turco-Egyptian period, had been virtually outside the range of Mahdist control during the reign of the khalifa. The closing of slave markets in the areas under Ottoman or British control was another factor in the decline of the slave-trade. Domestic slavery, however, was subject to different considerations during the early years of the Condominium. Agricultural production was seen to be adversely affected by the high wages paid to casual labourers at government construction sites, since cultivators left the land. Various recruitment schemes were attempted with little success. A central labour bureau sought to impose a maximum daily wage and to control the domestic slave population. Encouragement was given to immigrants, especially West Africans passing over the pilgrimage route to Mecca, to settle in the Sudan. The government's fear of the political effects of a sudden curtailment of domestic slavery, and the economic consequences of such action, meant that the eradication of the institution would be gradual, and instances of slave-trading, especially along the Ethiopian border, continued well into the 1920s.

Of all the development projects undertaken during Wingate's governor-generalship, the most ambitious and significant was the scheme to irrigate part of the Gezira plain for the production of cotton. Experimental planting began as early as 1900, but it was recognized that the Gezira's potential could be realized only by the construction of a vast irrigation project, which received its initial funding when a loan of £3,000,000 was guaranteed by the British government in 1913. The completion of the Gezira Scheme, however, had to be postponed until the conclusion of the First World War, when it became, as did many aspects of Sudan Government policy, embroiled in the increasingly hostile relationship of the co-domini.

9

WAR AND REVOLT: 1914–24

The Sudan played no direct part in the First World War, yet the effects of the war were considerable in economic and political terms, and were felt also in the evolution of administrative policy. A minor campaign in 1916 against the autonomous sultanate of Darfur had its origins in the deteriorating relations between the sultan, 'Ali Dinar, and the Sudan Government prior to the war, and in Anglo-French rivalry. 'Ali Dinar had ruled his ancestral kingdom since the overthrow of the Mahdist state, but increasingly felt the pressure of French expansion to the west, against which he felt the Sudan Government should, but would not, assist him. In 1909 the French had conquered the sultanate of Wadai, and in 1911 had seized a part of Dar Masalit. These annexations worried Khartoum because no delimitation of borders between French and British controlled territories had been agreed, nor was any possible so long as 'Ali Dinar maintained his independence. With the Anglo-French alliance in the First World War, 'Ali Dinar's posture towards the Sudan Government became more belligerent, and the entry of the Ottoman Empire into the war and the consequent deposition by the British of the Egyptian khedive, convinced 'Ali Dinar that he must join the *jihad* against the infidel Europeans. While the Sudan Government had decided as early as August 1915 to move against 'Ali Dinar, favourable circumstances were presented only in February 1916, when the sultan reinforced a border garrison, thus providing the Sudan Government with the pretext for a war which had become inevitable.[1]

A force of between two and three thousand troops, supported by three aeroplanes, was concentrated in Kordofan and advanced with difficulty, owing to the extreme heat and a shortage of water, to a point about twelve miles from the sultan's capital at El Fasher. After a battle the Fur army withdrew, and El Fasher was occupied on 23 May 1916. 'Ali Dinar escaped, but on 6 November was surprised in his camp and killed. A boundary agreement with the French was

128

reached in 1919 whereby Dar Masalit remained part of Darfur, while the sultanates of Tama and Sila came under French control. The frontier was finally delimited in 1924.

The annexation of Darfur eliminated whatever threat was posed to the government's authority from that quarter. Of more concern to Wingate at the outbreak of the World War had been an apprehended sympathetic reaction of the Muslim Sudanese to the Ottoman Empire's entry on the side of the Central Powers. The resignation of Slatin deprived Wingate of his adviser on native affairs, and the departure of British officers for the war stretched the already under-manned administration. Wingate's insecurity was reflected in the government's abandoning of its hostile policy towards the Ansar and the *tariqas*, which were correctly seen as the only objects of supra-tribal loyalty. An attempt was made to influence the population through their leadership. Accordingly, Sayyid 'Abd al-Rahman, the Mahdi's son, was freed from many of the restrictions which had been imposed upon him by Slatin, and was encouraged to tour areas of traditional Mahdist strength to urge loyalty to the government. The apparent success of this collaboration in maintaining calm seemed indicative of Mahdist acquiescence in the sayyid's leadership, and marked the beginning of 'Abd al-Rahman's remarkable rise to prominence in the post-war period. Renewed competition among the sects ensued, with serious and unforeseen consequences for the political evolution of the country.

A less appreciated but probably more significant factor in ensuring the population's loyalty was the war's positive effect on the Sudan's economy. The Sudan Government rejected suggestions that Sudanese should be recruited as manual labourers for the war effort in the Middle East, but the demands of the Egyptian Expeditionary Force for provisions fuelled an increase in the value of external trade from £E3,056,530 in 1914 to £E6,889,443 in 1919. Government revenue increased from £E1,857,856 in 1916 to £E4,425,340 in 1920. Price inflation was offset by a rapid rise in wage scales, and the demand for luxury goods evidenced a general prosperity.

The conquest of Darfur was the last major event of Wingate's long and important governor-generalship. In December 1916 he became British high commissioner for Egypt,[2] and was succeeded as sirdar and governor-general[3] by his civil secretary, Sir Lee Stack. Stack's term of office witnessed a steady increase in tension between the co-domini, the first stirrings of a Sudanese national consciousness, and the questioning or abandonment of established patterns of political relations within the Sudan.

So long as the British controlled Egypt, the essentially improvised status of the Sudan, as determined in the Condominium Agreement, was not an issue in Anglo-Egyptian relations. The inherent flaws of that status became increasingly evident after the war, when the full force of Egyptian nationalism erupted. Initial Egyptian sympathy towards the Allied cause had been dissipated by the material hardships suffered during the war. The British declaration of a protectorate over Egypt in 1914 had been explained and accepted as a step towards independence at the war's conclusion, and expectancy was heightened by the announced Anglo-French intentions towards the Ottoman Empire's Arab possessions and by President Wilson's Fourteen Points. Wingate's advice that the Foreign Office should follow a constructive line with the nationalists led by Sa'd Zaghlul was rejected. Wingate himself was recalled, to be replaced by Lord Allenby, the British victor in Palestine. It had become clear that Britain planned no substantial alteration of her relationship with Egypt, and the consequent violent disturbances throughout Egypt in 1919 brought matters to a head. Order was restored, and a special mission, headed by Viscount Milner, went to Egypt to recommend the basis for the country's future constitutional development. But the British object of maintaining control and the nationalists' demand for complete independence were basically incompatible, and a series of abortive negotiations served only to harden positions. As an earnest of British good faith Allenby demanded, and in February 1922 the British government issued, a declaration of Egypt's independence. Independence, however, was qualified by the reservation for settlement in future negotiations of four fundamental issues, one of which was the Sudan.

The Egyptian revolution of 1919 and the subsequent negotiations reinforced Britain's strategic interest in the Sudan. It was considered imperative to minimize Egyptian participation in the Sudan's administration and, indeed, to remove from the Sudan as many as possible of the Egyptians serving there. To do this effectively, however, would necessitate the replacement of Egyptian army units with an all-Sudanese force, which would involve costs which the Sudan Government was unable to incur and which Britain refused to assume. In 1920 the British foreign secretary, Lord Curzon, suggested that the cost should be borne by Egypt, as payment 'for the water she enjoys'. He concluded that 'the ulterior motive which British interests demand' was the 'complete political and military independence' of the Sudan from Egypt. In other words, the British objective was not only to eliminate Egyptian involvement in the Sudan, but also to ensure that Egypt should bear the costs of such a breach.

The British position was not a reaction simply to Egyptian nationalists' demands for independence, but took on added urgency with the assumption that Egyptians stationed in the Sudan would 'infect' the educated Sudanese with nationalist ideas of their own. As early as 1919 Milner had looked towards 'a system like that prevailing in Northern Nigeria' as a means of obviating the 'necessity of creating an effendi class' of Western-educated Sudanese imbued with nationalist sentiments in dissonance with British interests. The 'system' to which he referred was Indirect Rule, under which administrative and judicial functions would be barred to the growing class of Sudanese officials which the government, through its education policy, had created with precisely those functions in mind, to be left instead to agents of traditional tribal authority. The efficacy of Indirect Rule not only as an attractive and economical administrative alternative but as a political necessity was greatly enhanced by the appearance of vague but real indications of Sudanese 'national' feelings.

There had been little overt reaction among the Sudanese to the Egyptian revolution. Indeed, Stack felt that a 'spirit of national consciousness' could be used to the advantage of the government, since that spirit might be expected to express itself as desirous of ending Egyptian participation in the Sudan's affairs. But the first of a series of Sudanese political organizations to appear after the war was the League of Sudan Union in 1920, which in its anonymous circulars took a decidedly anti-British position. In 1922 an ex-Army officer of Dinka origins, 'Ali 'Abd al-Latif, was arrested and imprisoned for submitting to the *Hadara* newspaper an article calling for 'self-determination for the Sudanese'. By the time of his release in 1923 he had become a celebrity. With several associates, drawn, significantly, from the ranks of government employees, he founded the White Flag League, apparently with Egyptian encouragement and financial backing. The League's ostensible aim was the political 'unity of the Nile Valley', although the tactical value of espousing this goal as a way to win Egyptian support could not have been lost on the League members. The British authorities refused to admit that 'Ali 'Abd al-Latif and like-minded individuals were anything but half-civilized dupes of Egyptian politicians, yet this maligning attitude masked the reluctance of the government to admit any grievances as legitimate. To do so would imply a failure of the British mission in the Sudan and weaken the British position in negotiations with Egypt. It was easier, though unrealistic, to tar with one brush, and without distinction, pro-Egyptian and genuinely concerned Sudanese.

Yet a distinction could have been drawn. The White Flag League and its shadowy counterparts had a very limited appeal, and were composed mainly of minor officials and ex-officers, notably clerks in the Posts and Telegraphs Department. A prominent part was played by Muslim southerners. There was no tribal basis to any of these organizations, and they therefore lacked mass support. But apart from these activists was a more moderate group of government officials, officers and merchants, of more prominent social origins, who, while rejecting a pro-Egyptian position, were unwilling to place their future unrestrictedly in the hands of the British. Although supporting the continuation of the Condominium, they wanted the government to announce a definite plan for the eventual independence of the Sudan, and a definition of the British and Egyptian roles in that plan. Their concern had developed since the end of the war and gained strength with the government's initial efforts to implement the recommendations of the Milner Report. They interpreted the regulation and extension of authority of tribal shaykhs, as provided for in 1922,[4] as being directed against them. A precipitate government reaction to Egyptian intrigues and the noisy opposition of the White Flag League would bring down radical and moderate alike and, they feared, put an end to the aspirations of those law-abiding Sudanese who were working their way up in the government departments. The moderates, however, were soon isolated by events.

The British authorities were not alone in their alarm at the appearance of secular opposition. We have seen how, in the early days of the war, the government had turned to the leaders of the *tariqas* and Ansar for help in maintaining order. The outbreak of the Egyptian revolution made the support of these influential men even more imperative. In 1919 a delegation of Sudanese religious and tribal notables, led by Sayyid 'Ali al-Mirghani, head of the Khatmiyya, went to London ostensibly to congratulate King George v on the successful conclusion of the war. But by this time the disposition of the Sudanese towards the Condominium partners had become an important element in the diplomatic struggle between them. It was therefore of value for the British to show that the traditional Sudanese leadership supported them and rejected Egyptian 'pretensions'. This collaboration was equally important for the notables, and for none more than Sayyid 'Abd al-Rahman al-Mahdi.

Following the war the influence of the Mahdi's son had continued to grow, especially among the tribes of the western Sudan. An acrimonious debate within the government over how to deal with this 'recrudescence' of Mahdism produced no definite policy, and the consequent 'drift' embittered the sayyid's relations with the administration while at the same time failing to check the spread of his appeal. In 1921 an attack by disgruntled tribesmen on the government post at Nyala in Darfur had been blamed, with little justification, on his agents in the area, and unsuccessful attempts were made to limit their activities. To reimpose the old restrictions, however, involved the risk of alienating his large and volatile following; to do nothing risked making him irresistible. The government realized too late that 'Abd al-Rahman's prestige depended less on their favour than the government itself depended on his support. This was made clear in 1924. The White Flag League agitators threatened not only British dominance in the Sudan, but also the established religious and tribal notables. 'Ali 'Abd al-Latif was viewed as a dangerous upstart who seemed to challenge the established pattern of authority. In the summer of 1924 the traditional leaders were afforded the opportunity to strengthen their claims as the true representatives of the Sudanese, to dispose of a new and discordant rival, and to place the government in their debt. As in 1914 when the historic antipathy between the Mahdists and the British had been submerged by a shared hostility to the Turks, so in 1924 the two united in a common fear of the Egyptians. By rallying to the British position Sayyid 'Abd al-Rahman precluded the possibility that a pro-Egyptian agitation could win mass support.

Political developments in the Sudan were reflected in deteriorating Anglo-Egyptian relations. The framing of Egypt's constitution in 1923 occasioned a new crisis when Britain intervened to prevent a constitutional reference to the king of Egypt[4] as 'sovereign of the Sudan'. In January 1924 the first parliamentary elections returned the Wafd under Zaghlul as prime minister. In September discussions began in London between Zaghlul and the new Labour government of Ramsay MacDonald. For the first time in Anglo-Egyptian negotiations, the Sudan Government played a decisive part. Stack and the financial secretary, (Sir) George Schuster, did everything in their power to prevent a compromise between the co-domini which would allow a continued Egyptian role in the Sudan's administration. Events in the Sudan added weight to their manoeuvres. Throughout the spring and summer anti-British demonstrations occurred with alarming frequency and increasing seriousness. In July 'Ali 'Abd al-Latif was arrested and imprisoned. In August the Egyptian army Railway Battalion at Atbara rose in a revolt which was put down by British troops. Simultaneously the cadets of the Military School in Khartoum marched through the streets in defiance of orders; their leaders were jailed. The Sudan Government, fearful of being 'sold out' by a British government eager to achieve a rapprochement with Egypt, insisted that any compromise would be fatal to British authority in Khartoum. Gradually, as the negotiations with Zaghlul deadlocked, the British government came to agree with Stack's assessment. What was needed, in Stack's words, was an 'excuse for drastic action'.

That excuse was provided on 19 November when Stack was shot and fatally wounded by an Egyptian in Cairo. Allenby, without awaiting the approval of the new Conservative government in London, issued an ultimatum to Zaghlul requiring, among other things, the immediate evacuation of the purely Egyptian army units from the Sudan, and putting on record that the Sudan would increase the area to be irrigated in the Gezira Scheme from the previously agreed limit of 300,000 feddans[6] to 'an unlimited figure as need may arise'. Although this second provision was later disavowed by the British government, it shocked Egypt into the realization of how far the British might go to maintain their position in the Sudan, and made painfully obvious the vulnerability of Egypt's vital Nile waters. Unable to accede to the ultimatum, Zaghlul resigned, and Allenby instructed Khartoum to commence evacuation of the Egyptian troops, a move which had been meticulously planned well in advance of the crisis.

The evacuation was not carried out without incident. The Egyptian artillery and other units stationed in Khartoum North refused to entrain without direct orders from Cairo. In deference to their commanding position these were arranged. In the meantime, elements of the XIth Sudanese battalion marched through the streets of Khartoum, determined to join the recalcitrant Egyptian units. Events suggest that the rebellious Sudanese had experienced a crisis of conscience, whether to take orders from their British superiors or to honour their oath of allegiance to the Egyptian king, which seemed to demand refusing those orders. A British force opposed them in the streets, and after twice refusing orders the Sudanese were fired upon. They took refuge in the military hospital, where they were bombarded by British artillery, and fought to the last man. The remaining Egyptian troops were evacuated, and three Sudanese officers were later executed for their parts in the revolt.

A PERIOD OF REACTION
1925–36

The tension which had been building up since 1919 was at last relieved by the crisis of 1924. The Egyptian troops had been forcibly removed, and Egyptian civilian officials were soon to follow. British control had been assured, but the form of the Condominium was retained, against the opposition of the Sudan Government itself, as an inducement to future Egyptian co-operation. A Sudan Defence Force consisting solely of Sudanese troops and financed by an Egyptian subvention, willingly granted as a vestigial token of Egypt's joint rule, was established under a British commander, the sirdarship and governor-generalship having finally been separated. Quiet was restored to the towns. The complex political alignments of recent years were clarified, as the radicals all but disappeared, the traditional élite emerged triumphant and the moderates were increasingly isolated, tainted by association and made irrelevant by their exposed impotence to influence events. A government debate as to the future course of administration was resolved: it now embarked on a headlong rush towards implementing fully a system of Indirect Rule.

The adoption of the Nigerian model, with modifications, was, as we have seen, not a reaction solely to the dangers of an 'effendi class', which had in British eyes proved to be an instrument of Egyptian designs, but was also considered as an antidote to the growing power of Sayyid 'Abd al-Rahman. His obviously de-tribalizing appeal would be limited by the stabilizing effects of reinforced tribal authority. Thus, to 'counteract the preponderating influence of religious leaders' and to minimize the numbers and influence of the educated urban class, Indirect Rule was considered imperative. Its statutory beginnings in 1922, in the form of the *Powers of Nomad Sheikhs Ordinance*, had by 1923 regularized the traditional judicial functions of about three hundred tribal shaykhs. But Stack had considered this as only one aspect of a comprehensive system of devolution, necessitated by attention as much to financial circumstances as to administrative policy, another part of which was the gradual promotion of educated Sudanese to ever more responsible posts in the government. The *Khartoum, Khartoum North and Omdurman Council Proclamation* of 1921 had established a 'consultative and advisory' council to discuss relevant urban affairs, and Stack had envisaged similar councils at the district, provincial and central levels. This progressive idea died with him. The balance of Stack's policy was abandoned, as evidenced by a statement by Sir John Maffey when he became governor-general in 1927:

Advisory Councils cropped up as a possible means to our end. . . . Later on in certain intelligensia areas, when we have made the Sudan safe for autocracy, such Councils would be in keeping with the broad principle. Otherwise Advisory Councils contain the seeds of grave danger and eventually present a free platform for capture by a pushful intelligensia.[1]

In order to function, Indirect Rule required tribal cohesion and strong tribal leadership. The centralizing impact of the Turco-Egyptian and Mahdist regimes and, indeed, of the direct methods employed since the Anglo-Egyptian conquest, had, however, weakened or destroyed both of these prerequisites, with a few exceptions such as among the Kababish. The government nonetheless embarked on a course resolutely undeterred by the realities of the social structure. This was described by Currie, the former director of education, after a visit to the Sudan, as a 'spectacle' in which administrators searched enthusiastically for 'lost tribes and vanished chiefs'. He later put his criticism more bluntly:

The time has long passed when it was possible to gull the Native demanding equality of economic opportunity with patter about indirect rule, or fob him off with a social scheme in which a subsidized ruler – too frequently an obsolete antiquity – dances to the pipes of young gentlemen whose sole idea is that things shall 'stay put'. They cannot, by a hard fate, be squires in England, but to ape the part in Africa is fascinating.[2]

The principal architects of Indirect Rule in the Sudan were Maffey, governor-general from 1926 until 1933, whose views were based on his Indian experience, and (Sir) Harold MacMichael, who, as assistant civil secretary from 1919 to 1925 and civil secretary from 1925 to 1934, had a dominant part in determining administrative policy. In 1927 the *Powers of Sheikhs Ordinance* extended the authority, previously recognized in shaykhs of nomadic tribes, to the sedentary population, thus impinging on the jurisdiction of territorially based officials.

The government's fear of the educated class, noted by Currie, was also reflected in a radical alteration of education policy. Whereas that policy had always been linked to administrative requirements, by the mid-twenties it was dominated by a dogmatic subservience to Indirect Rule. Modern education, it was felt, had led to the creation of a discontented class of de-tribalized individuals who had, in 1924, bitten the hand that fed them. In 1927 the governor of Darfur stressed the importance of limiting this class:

It may be argued that the progress of education and general enlightenment is merely bringing about natural evolution, and that the present individualism is but a step or phase in the process. Such an argument is . . . not only fallacious but dangerous. Tribal customs and organizations have been evolved through the ages; they have enabled tribes to survive as entities the stress of war and civil commotion; these customs and traditions are . . . cherished and obeyed to a degree which is almost incredible by such tribes as remain today uncontaminated by modern progress.[3]

Native *khalwas* were therefore substituted in increasing numbers for government-sponsored *kuttabs*.[4] The number of subsidized *khalwas* increased from six in 1918 to 768 in 1930. In 1920 there had been eighty elementary schools; not another was opened in the north before 1929. The amount of government expenditure earmarked for education fell from a high of 3.9 per cent in 1915 to 1.9 per cent in 1926. The Military School in Khartoum was closed, as was the small school for training Sudanese sub-*mamurs*.

The adoption of Indirect Rule had an even greater significance in the southern Sudan than in the north. We have seen that the government, from the early days of the Condominium, had sought to limit the spread of Islam in the south, and that certain steps had been taken to achieve this. After the war this object was pursued with greater urgency, imbued now with the dogmatic dictates of Indirect Rule. The southern governors' meeting in 1922 proposed leaving administration 'in the hands of native authorities . . . under British supervision'. But often such authorities did not exist. Where tribal organization no longer existed, it might 'still be possible to re-create it'. Under the provisions of the *Passports and Permits Ordinance* of 1922, the south was classified as 'closed districts', resulting in the progressive exclusion of northern traders and the limitation of southerners travelling to the north to find work. Everything possible was to be done to encourage 'tribal consciousness'. Beginning in 1922, chiefs' courts (*lukikos*) were established under the guidance of

British officials. The exclusion of northerners and the requirements of Indirect Rule composed the administrative aspect of what came to be called 'Southern Policy'. An equally important element of that policy was southern education, which had always been the province of the various missionary societies. From 1926 grants-in-aid were made to their schools. A language conference held at Rejaf in 1928 led to the selection of six languages to be employed in instruction, and appropriate textbooks were as a result prepared. English was promoted as a lingua franca and a necessary skill for advancement in government service. Arabic, and even the use of common Arabic terms, were to be discouraged. Whereas in 1926 there existed only four elementary boys' schools employing vernacular instruction, by 1930 there were thirty-two, and in the same period intermediate schools using English increased from one, with thirty-five students, to three, with 177.

The combination of the closed district system, Indirect Rule and education policy encouraged and increased the differentiation of north from south which had already existed. Thus Southern Policy entailed both the progressive separation of the south and the fostering of particularism within it. As in the north, the aim of policy was the cessation or reversal of trends towards homogeneity. There has been seen in Southern Policy as early as 1919 a British design for the eventual political independence of the south from the north. A document prepared for the Milner mission in 1920 had suggested that 'the possibility of the Southern (black) portion of the Soudan being . . . linked up with some central African system' was 'borne in mind'. But this and subsequent similar remarks were visionary and were neither reflected in, nor influential on, the development of administrative policy for the south, as events were to show.

The mid-1920s were years of prosperity for the Sudan. The Gezira Scheme was officially opened in 1926. Its completion, postponed by the war, had been jeopardized by huge cost-overruns, but the political and economic effects of abandoning the project persuaded the British government to rescue it with guaranteed loans totalling £14,920,000 by 1924. The limitation of the project to the irrigation of 300,000 feddans, which had been undertaken by Allenby in 1920 to ease Egyptian misgivings, would have entailed a recurrent loss, and it was to this problem that the Gezira clause of Allenby's 1924 ultimatum to Egypt had been addressed. Thus in 1925 an Anglo-Egyptian committee reviewed the basis of the allocation of Nile waters as between Egypt and the Sudan. The resulting Anglo-Egyptian Nile Waters Agreement of 1929 imposed a quota system by which consumption rather than acreage to be irrigated determined the respective allocations.

The Gezira Scheme itself was a remarkable experiment in co-operative farming, a tribute to the vision of those British officials who conceived and executed it. The partners in the enterprise were the government, the Sudan Plantations Syndicate and the tenant farmers who worked the land. Each tenancy was forty feddans. Absentee landlordism and the sale or rental of land were controlled. Profits were divided in the proportion of forty per cent each to the government and the tenants, and twenty per cent to the syndicate. Of a forty-feddan tenancy, ten feddans were devoted to cotton, five each to millet and fodder, and twenty left fallow. Grain and fodder were, like the cotton, irrigated free of charge, and were designated for the use of the tenant. Marketing of the cotton crop was the responsibility of the syndicate. As a result of the agreement with Egypt over water allocation, the irrigated area was increased in 1929 to over 500,000 feddans. The Gezira Scheme served as a model for later agricultural developments.

Other cotton-growing schemes had been begun before the First World War in the Gash and Baraka deltas, where streams arising in Eritrea finally lose themselves in the deserts of the eastern Sudan. These also were developed after the war, the Gash Scheme (organized on a tripartite basis similar to that in the Gezira) being conceded to the Kassala Cotton Company, which was linked financially with the Sudan Plantations Syndicate. A consequence of the rise of cotton production in the Gash region was the construction in 1924 of a railway between Kasala and Port Sudan. This was subsequently extended to Sennar, so that by 1929 the Gezira was directly linked with the Red Sea coast.

The years of the Great Depression were particularly difficult for the Sudan. The dangers of over-reliance on a single cash-crop, cotton, were made obvious when simultaneously the world demand slumped and local production fell disastrously owing to a series of crop diseases and locust invasions. Government revenue fell from £E6,981,590 in 1929 to £E3,653,394 in 1932, and a substantial percentage of revenue was committed to servicing the Gezira debt. Financial retrenchment was inevitable, as were complaints from those upon whom this seemed to fall with greatest severity. In 1931 the starting salaries of 'graduates'[5] in the government's employ were cut by thirty per cent, a move which those affected interpreted as a further deliberate blow to their class. A strike by Gordon College students ensued, which was eventually settled when the government compromised in the matter of starting rates, but deep suspicion remained, as did the reinforced awareness of the graduates' vulnerability. The unity established over this issue was short-lived. Immediately after the resolution of the pay dispute the graduates' ranks were broadly split, ominously along sectarian lines, reflecting the continuing rivalry of Sayyid 'Abd al-Rahman and Sayyid 'Ali al-Mirghani.

Despite the tensions brought on by the depression and the government's administrative policy, the decade following the troubles of 1924 was a quiet one politically. The shock of 1924 and the consequent rush towards Indirect Rule had isolated the politically-active educated class. The British settlement of the crisis had removed the Egyptian factor from Sudan politics, further obviating the necessity to the government of the educated class's allegiance. Although the Condominium remained, in name only, there seemed little possibility that Egypt would ever again have an active voice in Sudan affairs. Against this background it is not surprising that the radical activities, demonstrations and strikes of 1924 were displaced as the dominant form of political expression by a quieter, more introspective mood. This was exhibited in study groups and literary societies which stressed education and a greater degree of political sophistication as requisites for effective political progress. Literary newspapers were founded, usually to disappear soon afterwards, which, however, served to ventilate views and to buoy the confidence of the educated class. The most influential of these was *al-Fajr* (*The Dawn*), published between 1934 and 1937. The easing of government censorship in 1935 allowed a more open exposition of opinion, and educational and administrative policies, especially Indirect Rule, were attacked. The attitude towards Egypt remained uncertain. The apparently meek surrender to the British in 1924, and its consequences, coupled with the Nile Waters Agreement of 1929, which took no notice of Sudanese public opinion and awarded the lion's share of water to Egypt, were the cause of great disillusionment. But, just as in 1924 when the Egyptian presence had been viewed by the moderates as a restraint on the Sudan Government, so in the decade after 1924 the educated class continued to see the idea of 'the

Sudan for the Sudanese' as a code-phrase for British hegemony. Thus Egypt continued to be viewed as the only potential ally of the beleaguered nationalist cause.

A rapidly changing international situation, culminating in the Italian invasion of Abyssinia in 1935, created a coincidence of Anglo-Egyptian interests with far-reaching consequences for the Sudan. In 1936 a treaty of alliance between the two countries secured British strategic aims in Egypt. The status of the Sudan, which had complicated relations since the war, remained that resulting from the 1899 agreements, although it was agreed that 'nothing in this article prejudices the question of sovereignty over the Sudan'. Egyptian troops, barred since 1924, were again to be 'placed at the disposal' of the governor-general, and Egyptian immigration was to be unlimited 'except for reasons of public order and health'. In deference to the Sudanese who, as in previous negotiations, were unrepresented, the two governments pledged that 'the primary aim of their administration in the Sudan must be the welfare of the Sudanese', a phrase considered patronizing by politically-minded Sudanese.

The treaty was poorly received in the Sudan. The government itself feared the consequences of increased Egyptian influence which might well lead to another crisis like that of 1924. Those intellectuals who had looked to Egypt for support felt betrayed by the apparent Egyptian eagerness to participate more fully in the existing administration. Moderate opinion was incensed that yet again the Sudanese had been left unconsulted about their own future. The Ansar leadership disliked the shelving of the sovereignty issue, since this implied the possibility of a future assertion of Egyptian sovereignty. The result of these various misgivings was the determination, on the part of the educated class, that self-reliance must be the rule in efforts towards their political goals, and, on the government's part, that an acceleration in the re-thinking of administrative policy, already under way, would be necessary to channel those efforts along a moderate course.

THE DEVELOPMENT OF SUDANESE NATIONALISM: 1937–52

The appointment of Sir Stewart Symes to the governor-generalship in 1934 heralded a significant change in government attitudes towards the educated class and towards administrative policy generally. Symes had previously served in the Sudan under Wingate, and was a man of definite views, which were not, however, always shared by his British subordinates. While praising the benefits of Indirect Rule, he nonetheless planned and executed a number of reforms aimed at developing 'an administration working first and foremost in collaboration not with tribal authorities but with the Sudanese intelligentsia'. As the reaction in the post-1924 era had been felt primarily in the related areas of educational and administrative policy, so in the mid-thirties those areas witnessed the most wide-ranging reforms.

As a result of the Gordon College strike of 1931 a committee of inquiry had been set up, which was persuaded to extend its terms of reference to the lower levels of education. One of the committee's recommendations was the transfer of the Training College for elementary teachers from Khartoum into rural surroundings. The principalship of the new institution, opened in 1934, was given to V. L. Griffiths, who had been appointed as an inspector of education in 1931, after teaching experience in India. Griffiths hoped that by giving teacher-training a fresh start, in surroundings similar to those in which the school-masters would have to work, the next generation of teachers would develop initiative and a sense of profession which at that time they lacked. The site he selected for his college, in open country near Dueim, was unpopular owing to its isolation. The college at Bakht er Ruda, as the site was called, later became the Institute of Education. In due course the institute took on a major reform of teaching methods, and produced a large number of textbooks. A general reform of intermediate education, undertaken in 1939, was hampered by staff shortages and other exigencies of the Second World War, and by a lack of interest on the part of Sudanese teachers who saw greater opportunity in other branches of education and in the government service.

To the law school which had been established in Khartoum in 1931 were added, in 1936, schools of engineering, veterinary science and agriculture, in order that the requirements of government departments for technical personnel might increasingly be filled from among Sudanese graduates. The Kitchener School of Medicine, opened in 1924, continued to turn out qualified Sudanese doctors. The technical schools were fused into a single institution, to which the name of the Gordon Memorial College was transferred in 1945. This new college was combined with the Kitchener School in 1951 to form the University College of Khartoum, affiliated with the University of London, and became, shortly after independence, Khartoum University.

Although important reforms were instigated by Symes and his civil secretary, (Sir) Angus Gillan, in the area of administration, it was an underlying change in attitude that was most significant. Indirect Rule (which by the 1930s had evolved into 'Native Administration') was to be replaced by 'local government', under which the basis of administration in all but the most remote nomadic domains was to be territorial rather than tribal, a return in theory to the position of 1922. The three *Local Government Ordinances* of 1937 affected the administration of municipalities, townships and rural areas. In the cities and towns, existing laws were consolidated. In the rural areas the demise of inflexible Indirect Rule was signalled by the abandonment of tribalism as the basis for local administration. The process of reform led eventually to a comprehensive *Local Government Ordinance* in 1951.

The abandonment of strict adherence to the principles of Indirect Rule, while born of the realization that maintenance of tribal authority tended towards its ossification, and that in any case sudanization of the bureaucracy could not and should not be curtailed, was accelerated by the domestic political consequences of the 1936 Anglo-Egyptian treaty. Whereas in the decade following 1924 the educated class, which was effectively identical to the class of minor Sudanese officials, had been left in the wilderness without influence on government policy, the return to a nominal Anglo-Egyptian partnership meant a revival of the pre-1924 rivalry of the co-domini for the support of the Sudanese. But past disappointments with Egyptian policy, and the ignominy felt on the conclusion of the treaty without reference to Sudanese opinion, underlined the importance to the educated class of presenting to the government a united front which could claim the role of spokesman for the Sudanese. Several years of discussion culminated in February 1938 with the founding of such an organization, the Graduates' General Congress.

The original 1,080 members of the Congress were, as defined in the organization's rules, former pupils in post-elementary schools and, by special permission, 'Sudanese educated elsewhere.' The Congress's internal structure consisted of an elected council of sixty, who in turn elected an executive committee of fifteen. The first general secretary was Isma'il al-Azhari, a descendant of a family of religious notables and a mathematics teacher at the Gordon College, who had studied at the American University of Beirut. The nature of the Congress's membership, primarily drawn as it was from the ranks of government employees, made it implicitly a trade union. This was reflected in its constitution, notified to the government in March, which stated the purpose of the Congress as serving 'the public interest of the country and of the graduates'. In a letter to the government, Azhari outlined the interests of the Congress as philanthropic and social on the one hand, and in 'matters of public interest involving the Government or lying within the scope of its policy and concern' on the other. Azhari recognized that 'most of us are Government officials and are fully conscious of our obligations as such, but we feel that the Government is aware of our peculiar position as the only educated element in this country, and of the duties which we, in this peculiar position, feel to be ours'. The government, having encouraged the formation of the Congress, welcomed it as a charitable and social organization representing the views of its own members, just as it had welcomed the Sudan Schools Club in Omdurman, the Congress's predecessor, but warned that the organization was not recognized as a political body.

The government's acceptance and, indeed, encouragement of the Congress was dictated by the prevailing political climate. The Congress's leaders were the successors of the moderates of 1924 rather than of the pro-Egyptian radicals, and as such were seen as a bulwark not only against a revival of Egyptian influence after the signing of the 1936 treaty, but also against the growing power of Sayyid 'Abd al-Rahman al-Mahdi. But the claim of the Congress to 'a peculiar position' as spokesman for the Sudanese was to lead, predictably, to serious clashes with the government. Further, the belief that the graduates could forge a strong and truly secular political movement indicated the government's misappraisal of sectarian strength. Just as sectarianism had brought about the collapse of the graduates' unity in 1931, so it would spell the downfall of the Congress a decade later. A parting of the ways with the government was not long in coming. In 1940 the Egyptian prime minister, 'Ali Mahir Pasha, visited the Sudan, and was approached by the Congress with a request for Egyptian financial support for various charitable schemes. Whereas the Congress had seemed, both to the government and to the Egyptians, a potential ally of the British cause, it now became evident that the organization could as well be of value to Egyptian interests. This was in fact a reflection of the weakness of the graduates, whose hopes seemed now, as in 1924, tied to a continuing Anglo-Egyptian rivalry.

The Sudan was much more directly involved in the Second World War than it had been in the First, since Italy was an enemy power. Kasala was occupied by the Italians for a few months in 1940, and afterwards an army of British, Indian and Sudanese troops, under General Platt, invaded Eritrea and won the decisive battle of Keren on 15 March 1941. This ended the danger on the Sudanese border, but a greater danger remained in the north, until Montgomery's victory at El Alamein in November 1942 destroyed the prospect of a German occupation of the Nile valley. As during the First World War, the government service was seriously depleted, and domestic programmes were necessarily curtailed. While there was considerably less concern over the loyalties of the Sudanese than there had been in 1914–18, the prejudices and fears of British officials were revived by what they considered to be an attempt by the Congress to exploit for political gain the government's preoccupation with the war. Nor should this suspicion be deprecated, for the serious breach between the Congress and the government occurred at a time when the outcome of the war in North Africa was in doubt. That the government should consider domestic politics of secondary concern, and expect the Congress to do the same, was only natural.

In 1940 followers of Sayyid 'Abd al-Rahman al-Mahdi had gained control of the Congress organization. This pre-eminence was short-lived, however, owing to splits in the ranks of the Ansar, some of whom rejected the subservience of the Congress to Sayyid 'Abd al-Rahman's personal ambitions. The opposition to Sayyid 'Abd al-Rahman, led by Azhari, pressured the Congress executive to issue to the government, on 3 April 1942, a memorandum of twelve demands which went obviously and provocatively beyond the limits to the Congress's activities which had been tacitly agreed. Most of these demands dealt with administrative and judicial reforms and with educational and economic development. The primary demand was for

the issue, on the first possible opportunity, by the British and Egyptian governments, of a joint declaration granting the Sudan, in its geographical boundaries, the right of self-determination, directly after this war; this right to be safeguarded by guarantees assuring full liberty of expression in connection therewith; as well as guarantees assuring the Sudanese the right of determining their natural rights with Egypt in a special agreement between the Egyptian and Sudanese nations.

The response of the government, in a letter from the civil secretary, Sir Douglas Newbold, to the president of the Congress, was harsh and unyielding. By the submission of the memorandum and by its wording the Congress had 'forfeited the confidence of Government'. Newbold warned that that confidence could not be restored, nor could the prospects of the educated class be enhanced, unless the Congress confined itself 'to the internal and domestic affairs of the Sudanese and [renounced] any claim, real or implied, to be the mouthpiece of the whole country'.

Following the government's refusal of the memorandum, the Congress's constitution was amended at the instigation of Azhari's group, the Ashigga [*Ashiqqa'*] (literally 'brothers by the same father and mother'), to allow the membership of elementary-school graduates. The executive of the now greatly-expanded Congress was won in the ensuing elections by the Ashigga. Thus the potential value to the government of the Congress as a moderating force was lost, and further co-operation was eschewed. It appears that the Ashigga had engineered the issue of the twelve demands in order to discredit the moderate Ansari control of the Congress and to replace it with a more radical, independent leadership.

In 1943 the Ashigga under Azhari emerged as the first genuine political party in the Sudan, favouring union with Egypt. In 1944 it gained the tacit support of Sayyid 'Ali al-Mirghani. The head of the Khatmiyya, whose dynastic history was so closely bound up with that of Egyptian influence in the Sudan, was naturally perturbed at the rapid rise of his rival, Sayyid 'Abd al-Rahman, whose family had in the past triumphed at the expense of his own. He feared that 'Abd al-Rahman would succeed in establishing, with British support, a Mahdist monarchy in the Sudan. Although Sayyid 'Ali stood ostentatiously aloof from politics he exerted great influence behind the scenes, and his followers were less restrained. Only in an alliance with Egypt, however limited to reasons of tactical gain, could they see a safeguard against a revival of the Mahdist state. And only with the support of the Khatmiyya could Azhari, for his part, see any hope for the future of the narrowly based Ashigga.

As a response to this development, moderate supporters of Sayyid 'Abd al-Rahman established in 1945 the *Umma*[1] under his patronage, as a political party favouring the complete independence of the Sudan, and ostensibly separated from the Ansar. It might seem that a party claiming total independence would have more appeal than one advocating union with Egypt, but two considerations militated against the general acceptance of nationalism of the Umma type. First, its leaders were known to be prepared, as the Ashigga were not, to co-operate with the existing administration in the progressive realization of independence: hence it was easy to represent them as tools of British imperialism. Secondly, the patronage of Sayyid 'Abd al-Rahman made it difficult for non-Ansari moderates to separate the cause of complete independence from the personal ambitions of the Mahdi's son. Thus, as in 1924, the two wings of the politically minded class were broadly identified as favouring either an independent Sudan to be achieved with British co-operation ('the Sudan for the Sudanese'), or union with Egypt ('the unity of the Nile valley'). The events surrounding the factionalization of the Congress, which had shown promise as a secular body, illustrated the fundamental if much-deprecated fact that the sectarian leaders retained the keys to political strength.

The timing of the Congress memorandum of 1942 was unfortunate not only for the reasons already given, but because the government was then more than ever before amenable to suggestions of further associating the Sudanese in the administration of the country. The idea of provincial and central advisory councils, first mooted in the early twenties but lost in the flood-tide of Indirect Rule, was revived by Sir Douglas Newbold shortly after he became civil secretary in 1939. The falling-out with the Congress after April 1942 hastened this development and provided a new impetus as the government sought to create a body more broadly-based than the Congress, and therefore, it was hoped, able to siphon off Congress support. But the body created under the *Advisory Council for the Northern Sudan Order* of 1943 seemed rather a response to public pressure than the act of a strong government sure of public support. The Advisory Council's presidency was held by the governor-general, its vice-presidency and effective leadership by the civil secretary. Twenty-eight ordinary members were provided for, eighteen to be chosen from provincial advisory councils (also established in 1943), and ten others to be selected by the governor-general to represent social and economic interests. The Advisory Council met eight times between 1945 and 1948, when it ceased to exist.

The establishment of the Advisory Council was a promising development, an attempt by the government to come to terms with Sudanese nationalism, but was, however, severely criticized on several grounds. The Council was purely advisory. Responsibility for determining its agenda and the length of its sessions and debates rested with the government. These restrictions, although recognized by Newbold as detracting from the Council's appeal, were defended by him as necessary safeguards of a first step towards developing representative institutions. The provincial members were almost all tribal leaders, and the ten appointed by the governor-general were almost all government officials. The council debates, while focusing at times on subjects of importance, were nonetheless criticized, against a background of rising political tension, as trivial and meaningless. Opponents argued that the Council created the impression of government accountability but was in reality a mere debating society of yes-men and ignorant provincials, without power. A further point of criticism was the limitation of the Council to the northern Sudan, which the government explained as necessary because of the politically undeveloped state of the south and its lack of qualified representatives, but which was taken by suspicious northerners as an indication of the government's desire to separate the two regions. For these reasons the Congress boycotted the Council, the representative quality of which was further dissipated.

With the end of the war the status of the Sudan again became a serious irritant to Anglo-Egyptian relations. The Sudanese were determined that in any new round of negotiations their opinions should carry weight. In November 1945 the governor-general, Sir Hubert Huddleston, told the Advisory Council that its views and those of 'other representative bodies' would be solicited if the Sudan question were discussed by the co-domini. In December the Egyptian government formally requested the renegotiation of the 1936 treaty, and the British agreed to this. For the first time it seemed that the Sudanese themselves might be influential in determining the course of negotiations, provided the political parties could agree on a line of approach. A group of independent members of the Congress worked out a formula to reconcile the two nationalist groups, and in March 1946 an all-party Sudanese delegation went to Cairo to contact the negotiators. There the delegation rapidly broke up, since the Egyptians insisted that any settlement of the Sudan question must include recognition of the union of Egypt and the Sudan under the Egyptian crown. The Umma and their allies therefore returned to the Sudan, while the unionists, under Azhari, remained in Cairo and received from the Egyptians sole recognition as spokesmen of the Sudanese.

Negotiations went ahead between Sidqi Pasha, the Egyptian prime minister, and Ernest Bevin, the British foreign secretary, in London. A draft treaty was agreed upon, the Sudan question being treated in a separate protocol, which stated:

> The policy which the High Contracting Parties undertake to follow in the Sudan within the framework of unity between the Sudan and Egypt under the common Crown of Egypt, will have for its essential objective to secure the well-being of the Sudan ... the development of self-government, and consequently the right to choose the future status of the Sudan. Until the High Contracting Parties, in full common agreement, realize the latter objective, after consultation with the Sudanese, the Agreement of 1899 will continue and Article 11 of the Treaty of 1936 ... will remain in force.

This vague formula, designed to please everyone, pleased no one. The governor-general threatened resignation, the British prime minister, Attlee, was obliged to state that 'no change in the existing administration of the Sudan is contemplated', and Sidqi thereupon resigned from office. In January 1947 the British and Egyptian governments announced that negotiations had been broken off. In July Egypt brought its case to the United Nations. After prolonged debate, in which Egypt appeared, by its demands for union, to be arguing against the Sudanese right to self-determination, the question was set aside without resolution. The maladroit wording of the Sidqi-Bevin protocol had, however, embarrassed the Sudan Government, and the negotiations had accelerated its plans for wider

Sudanese participation in the administration. The Umma viewed the protocol as a betrayal, and threatened to boycott the Advisory Council. Riots occurred involving supporters of the rival parties.

Anticipating events, the government had announced in April 1946 that it was 'aiming at a free independent Sudan which will be able as soon as independence has been achieved to define for itself its relations with Great Britain and Egypt'. A committee had been set up in March to recommend ways of speeding up the sudanization of the government services. On 22 April an administrative conference was called to discuss and recommend the 'next steps in associating the Sudanese more closely with the administration of their country'. The participants were drawn from the government, the Advisory Council, and the pro-independence parties; the Graduates' Congress and other political parties refused to participate. The conference's first report, issued on 31 March 1947, called for the establishment of a legislative assembly, representing the whole country, to replace the Advisory Council, and an executive council, at least half of whose members should be Sudanese, to supplant the governor-general's council.

The unanimous recommendation of the administrative conference that a legislative assembly should not be limited, as the Advisory Council was, to the northern Sudan but should represent the entire country, necessitated the government's reconsideration of its policy towards the south. We have seen that the southern provinces had been dealt with separately since the Anglo-Egyptian conquest. The basis for a broad cultural unity, provided throughout the north by Islam and Arabic, was lacking in the southern Sudan. Pacification and the establishment of administration in the south had been much more slowly accomplished than in the north, where the Sudan Government was heir to a well-rooted tradition of centralized government derived from its Turco-Egyptian and Mahdist predecessors. The backwardness of the southern tribes, as compared with the sophistication of the riverain and urban Sudanese, was an impediment to the rapid integration of the two regions. The economic stringency which beset the government until the end of the First World War, and the concentration of finance in the Gezira Scheme after the war, made impossible any costly schemes for the development of the south and its peoples.

The post-First World War period saw a continuation and refinement of this distinct pace of development, largely as a response to the requirements of Indirect Rule which, as in the north, appealed to British officials for practical, political and philosophical reasons. Theoretically, Indirect Rule was inexpensive and required few trained personnel; it would isolate the south from the dangerous and unpredictable nationalist currents then appearing in the north; it would allow the development of the south along lines peculiar to itself, influenced by British and Christian ideals and safe from Muslim penetration. British administrators and Christian missionaries shared an interest in the success of Indirect Rule. The record of both groups, especially in the early years of the Condominium, is impressive in its selflessness and devotion to duty in the face of great obstacles. But the proprietary instincts of the British in administration, and of the missionaries with regard to education and to culture generally, were allowed too free a rein by the advent of Indirect Rule. The elimination of northern administrative personnel and traders, and of the use of Arabic wherever possible, artificially insulated not only the southern peoples but the missionaries and officials themselves from political, economic and social forces with which, if a unified Sudanese state were to be maintained, the region would eventually have to contend. The allotment of 'spheres of influence' to the missionary societies transferred to Africa the anachronistic sectarian rivalries of Europe. If this period had been used to prepare the south for integration, criticism by northern Sudanese and others would have been blunted and the future faced with more equanimity. But when, in the late 1940s, integration was in fact adopted hastily as government policy, it was far too late for a period of thoughtful transition.

The precipitate change was the result not only of nationalist pressures but also of a realization of no feasible alternative. The vague notion of separateness, based on the obviously different characteristics of the south, enhanced by the poor communications and general backwardness of the region, exacerbated by a lack of staff and funds and, finally, legitimized in the 1920s by the adoption of Indirect Rule was in the 1930s first tacitly and later explicitly admitted as constituting a 'Southern Policy'. Like Indirect Rule itself, of which the policy was not an extension but the most notable example, this succeeded in its subsidiary aims and, indeed, managed to stabilize the state of the tribal system, but failed in its political application. When it was realized that, as in the north, tribalism whether decadent or revivified was an inadequate base for future administration, a return to 'direct' rule was unavoidable. Yet as late as 1946 the government's policy remained the 'separate development' of the south, and the option was retained, though as always in an unconsidered and nebulous way, of one day linking the south to some East African configuration.

In June 1947, in response to the recommendations of the administrative conference, (Sir) James Robertson, who had succeeded to the civil secretaryship on the death of Newbold in 1944, held a conference at Juba to discuss the future status of the south and its role in the proposed legislative assembly. In a decisive statement of policy Robertson indicated that the south was 'inextricably bound for future development to the Middle East and Arabia and Northern Sudan' and that the southern peoples should therefore 'be equipped to take their places in the future as socially and economically the equals of their partners of the Northern Sudan in the Sudan of the future'. Ironically, it fell to the southern representatives at the conference to argue for the newly-abandoned 'Southern Policy' and to opt for a slow and cautious advance of their people who, it was said, were not yet 'grown up'. The northern representatives argued that the best way to learn the art of government was to participate in it, while the British officials present sought safeguards for the southern Sudanese in the proposed legislative assembly. A telling exchange of views concerned southern memories of the slave-trade. While it was absurd to suggest that a trade which had flourished at a time when administrative control was either weak or totally absent could revive under the strong and honest rule established by the Condominium, it was nonetheless true that memories of that trade had been fostered and retained, and contributed to the suspicion with which the north was viewed and to the feeling of trusteeship with which many southerners and their British administrators viewed each other.

The recommendations of the administrative conference were accepted by the governor-general's council in July 1947, and it was agreed that safeguards should be included in the ensuing legislation to 'ensure the healthy and steady development of the Southern people'. No such safeguards were explicit, however, in the draft ordinance which was submitted to the British and Egyptian governments in August. While accepting the principle of the legislative assembly, the Egyptians rejected the ordinance as not going far enough and excluding Egyptian participation in the new regime. The British government accepted the draft which was, despite the Egyptian objections, promulgated as *The Executive Council and Legislative Assembly Ordinance.* Under its provisions the governor-general's council was replaced by an executive council of twelve to eighteen members, at least half of whom had to be Sudanese. The three secretaries and the British commander of the Defence Force were *ex-officio* members. The assembly consisted of up to ten nominated members, thirteen southerners, and fifty-two northerners, of whom ten were to be elected directly and forty-two indirectly by electoral colleges. *Ex-officio* members would represent the executive. The assembly was to choose one of its members as leader. The executive council was responsible for initiating and proposing government legislation. Private members' bills were allowed, but had to be submitted first to the executive council if they concerned defence, coinage and currency, or 'the status of religious or racial minorities'. The governor-general retained veto power over all legislation. The assembly was barred from legislating on matters dealing with the ordinance itself, relations with the co-domini and with other foreign governments, and the question of Sudanese nationality. Elections to the assembly took place on 15 November 1948, and were boycotted by the unionists. The Umma and its allies therefore gained control of the assembly, which named that party's secretary-general, 'Abdallah Bey Khalil, as its leader at the first session which opened on 15 December.

The impasse in Anglo-Egyptian negotiations, which had been resumed in 1950, ironically speeded up political developments in the Sudan. Pressure from the United States on the British government to reach an agreement with Egypt which would safeguard Western interests in the Suez Canal, kept alive among the Umma leadership the fears raised by the abortive Sidqi-Bevin protocol that the British might abandon their position in the Sudan to reach a favourable settlement of the Canal question. The Umma therefore increased their demands for immediate self-government with a view towards early independence. Meanwhile a new political party was established, the National Front, which while unionist like the Ashigga, favoured dominion status under the Egyptian crown rather than complete unification. This party had the support of Sayyid 'Ali al-Mirghani and many of his followers. The British therefore tried to persuade the Khatmiyya to participate in the Legislative Assembly as a counter to the Umma, while the Umma itself sought Khatmiyya participation as a way of checking the extreme unionists. These attempts at conciliation failed. In the Egyptian king's speech from the throne to parliament on 16 November 1950 the intention was declared to abrogate the 1899 and 1936 Anglo-Egyptian agreements. This spurred the Umma-dominated assembly in Khartoum to pass a resolution on 15 December requesting of the co-domini self-government in 1951. The close vote on this motion (thirty-nine to thirty-eight), however, allowed the governor-general to ignore it and instead to adopt a motion passed earlier which called for a commission to recommend constitutional changes. The Constitutional Amendment Commission, as it was called, was boycotted by the Ashigga and Khatmiyya but supported by the Umma. Composed of thirteen Sudanese and chaired by a British expert, the commission convened on 29 March 1951.

On 8 October the Egyptian government abrogated the 1899 agreement and the 1936 Anglo-Egyptian treaty and announced a constitution for the Sudan. Although this unilateral act was rejected by the British and Sudan governments, and the new 'constitution' was rejected by all Sudanese parties except the Ashigga, it nonetheless threw open the long-standing sovereignty question. Arguing that the Sudan was now left without a legal government, six of the Constitutional Amendment Commission's members voted to replace the governor-general with an international commission. The government thereupon dissolved the commission, but its British chairman proceeded to prepare a report based on the recommendations previously discussed by the commission. These formed the basis of the *Self-Government Statute* which was enacted by the Legislative Assembly on 23 April 1952. This provided for an all-Sudanese council of ministers responsible to a bicameral parliament: a chamber of deputies of eighty-one elected members, and a senate of fifty, twenty to be appointed by the governor-general and thirty to be elected by provincial electoral colleges. The governor-general was to retain special responsibility for the public service and external affairs, and had the right to veto any legislation affecting the south. The sovereignty question was side-stepped by reference to the governor-general as the 'Supreme Constitutional Authority' in the Sudan. The British government approved the draft statute in October. In the meantime the Egyptian government, which, having abrogated the 1899 agreement, was in no position to approve or reject a proposal dealing with it, had attempted to reconcile

Sudanese opinion by agreeing to withdraw its proposed constitution for the Sudan. This manoeuvre was rejected by the Umma and became irrelevant with the overthrow of King Faruq in July 1952.

Before turning to the final stage of the movement towards self-determination, economic and social developments of the period under review can usefully be summarized. The Sudanese economy continued in this period to be firmly based upon agriculture, and depended on cotton as its major cash-crop. In 1944 it was decided that the Sudan Plantations Syndicate's concession to operate the Gezira Scheme would not be renewed when it expired in 1950. In July 1949 an ordinance provided for a Gezira Board to assume the management function, and the twenty per cent share of profits previously allotted the syndicate was to be channelled into research, schemes for social development in the Gezira, and the costs of management. The sudanization of the inspecting and engineering staff, hitherto British, had already been recommended by the Legislative Assembly in 1948, and proceeded rapidly after the nationalization of the Scheme. Agricultural projects were undertaken in other areas. Experimental work on mechanized grain production was begun in 1945 on the Ghadambaliyya plains near Gedaref. Cotton production here gave less satisfactory results.

Cotton had been grown on a small scale since 1931 in the Zande district of Equatoria province, but further development had been hindered by the reluctance of the Azande as cultivators, the government's desire to postpone action until a comprehensive programme for the entire south could be devised, and by the war. An ambitious and potentially revolutionary project was conceived during the war by the director of agriculture and forests, Dr J. D. Tothill, who had held a similar post in Uganda. He proposed 'An Experiment in the Social Emergence of Indigenous Races in Remote Regions', for which he chose Zande district, and aimed at nothing less than 'the complete social emergence and social and economic stability of the Zande people'. Improved communications, education and social services, and a manufacturing capability in addition to the development of agriculture, were planned to lead to self-sufficiency. Financed by the central government and administered by an Equatoria Projects Board, the Zande Scheme, as it was called, had by 1952 improved communications and transport and established a power station and oil, soap and cloth mills. By 1954, 175,000 acres were under cotton, with a yield of 6,370,000 pounds.

Tothill's proposals were gradually and fundamentally altered, however, and the scheme never achieved his aims. Poor wages necessitated using forced labour and although wages were raised they remained very low. The social dislocation resulting from the implementation of the scheme and a deterioration in relations between chiefs and people contributed to dissatisfaction. Finally, the failure of British administrators to abandon in practice the paternalism of Southern Policy despite its official abandonment in 1946, and distrust among local people of their northern Sudanese successors resulted in only modest success for a scheme which might have contributed to the mitigation of southern fears of what independence might bring.[2]

The Second World War, like the First, was a boom period for the Sudan economy generally. The value of imports rose from £E8,060,849 in 1941 to £E41,966,091 in 1951. In the same period exports increased in value from £E8,895,157 to £E62,177,529, largely owing to the profitability of cotton. Budget surpluses allowed greater attention to development, and a special development budget of £E13,750,000 was adopted for the period 1946–51. For the 1951–6 period a second development budget of £E34,000,000 was adopted, and concentrated on the improvement of communications, production schemes, social services and public utilities. Serious difficulties attended these economic advances. While the agricultural population – the vast majority of the people – benefited from the increased value of their products, the small but important urban working classes suffered as wages failed to meet the increased cost of living. From 1938 to 1947 this had risen by over a hundred per cent. Dura, the staple food grain, had doubled in price from 1939 to 1945 and the 1948 price was triple that of 1946.

This imbalance inevitably produced tensions which, combined with political developments, contributed to the growth of a Sudanese labour movement after the war. Labour relations in the period 1946–53 were characterized by workers' mistrust of the government – the country's largest employer – by militancy culminating in frequent strikes, and by an increasing politicization and association of the movement with the drive towards self-determination. The labour movement had its origins in Atbara, where ninety per cent of the inhabitants were Sudan Railways employees and their dependents. In June 1946 a Workers' Affairs Association of railway artisans was formed, but government recognition was withheld pending consideration of the whole question of trade unions. A government plan to establish works committees was interpreted as an attempt to control the embryonic movement, just as its plans in the political sphere were seen as tactics of delay and disruption of the nationalist cause. A demonstration of railway workers was held in July, during which leaders of the WAA were arrested. A strike followed which, after the mediation of Sudanese politicians, resulted in government recognition of the WAA. A pattern was thus established by which the strike became, not the ultimate recourse but the first weapon to enforce workers' demands.

Between 1948 and 1952 a body of labour legislation was enacted, based on British and colonial precedents. The most important instrument, the *Trade Union Ordinance* of 1948, provided for the registration and legal operation of unions. By 1952 nearly one hundred unions had registered, many of which were insignificant and short-lived. The most important union remained the Sudan Railway Workers' Union (SRWU) which by 1951 had 17,000 members. By 1953 it was estimated that some 100,000 Sudanese were unionized. Steps were taken early to associate the various unions under an umbrella organization, which came into being as the Workers' Congress in 1949. This was superseded in November 1950 by the Sudan Workers' Trade Union Federation. The SWTUF soon adopted overt political aims when in 1951 it proclaimed its intention of defeating British imperialism and achieving self-determination for the Sudan. With the Ashigga and other groups the SWTUF formed the United Front for the Liberation of the Sudan, generally seen as a communist front organization.[3] The SWTUF played an important part in the final phase of the nationalist movement, but its position was weakened by its inability to mobilize member unions in general strikes. Thus in 1952 a general strike was called off when some member unions refused to co-operate, and a severe rebuff was suffered when the SWTUF called a three-day general strike to protest the Anglo-Egyptian agreement of 1953. The early connection between the labour and nationalist movements was unfortunate in that the former became prey to the same party political and sectarian influences that had bedevilled the Graduates' Congress and subsequent attempts to achieve associations of Sudanese free from tribal and religious bonds.[4]

SELF-GOVERNMENT AND
SELF-DETERMINATION: 1953–6

The period between the Egyptian revolution in July 1952 and the formal independence of the Sudan on 1 January 1956 was clouded by the same fundamental issue that had dominated the history of the Condominium since its inception: the ultimate sovereignty of the Sudan. British control of Egypt had rendered the question academic until 1922 when Egypt's independence and the nationalist movement began to concentrate attention on the status of the Sudan and future control of the Suez Canal. The disturbances of 1924 had provided an opportunity for Britain unilaterally to end the Condominium, but the British government continued to view the sovereignty of the Sudan as a point of leverage in its negotiations with Egypt, and the opportunity was passed over. After 1924 Egyptian participation in the administration of the Sudan was negligible, and the question seemed dormant. The Anglo-Egyptian agreement of 1936, however, and especially the rise of Sudanese nationalism during the war, once again brought the sovereignty issue to the fore, at a time when Britain's independence of action was limited. Forced to compete with Egypt for the support of the Sudanese, the Sudan Government entered a phase familiar in colonial history, wherein the government proposed reforms by which the Sudanese would eventually become masters of their own country, while the nationalists maintained pressure for speedier attention to their demands. The pressure was at times lessened by the divisions that plagued the nationalist movement, and was at other times increased by the continuing Anglo-Egyptian struggle. The greatest weapon in the British arsenal was the demand of successive Egyptian governments that Egypt and the Sudan must be united under the Egyptian crown: so long as that demand was made the British could depend upon a large measure of popular support in the Sudan. The Egyptian revolution finally broke the impasse.

Even before the overthrow of King Faruq, the Egyptian government had announced a willingness to accede to the self-determination of the Sudanese, but this was seen as just another tactic in the old Egyptian strategy. The revolutionary government headed by General Neguib, who was himself half-Sudanese, had been educated in the Sudan and was popular there, decided to call the bluff of the British. He opened negotiations with the Umma party, which had never regained its confidence in the British after the shock of the Sidqi-Bevin protocol, and on 12 October 1952 an agreement was reached. This called for Sudanese self-determination, to be preceded by a transitional period of self-government during which the governor-general would act in concert with an international commission while a similar commission would prepare for elections. This agreement was followed by another, signed on 10 January 1953 by all leading Sudanese parties, which endorsed the Egyptian proposals. Faced with an unprecedented unanimity of Sudanese political parties and the Egyptian government, the British had run out of room to manoeuvre, and a new Anglo-Egyptian Agreement was consequently reached in short order.[1]

The new Agreement, signed on 12 February 1953, adopted most of the proposals agreed by Egypt and the political parties. A transitional period, during which sovereignty was to be 'kept in reserve' until self-determination was achieved, was not to exceed three years. The governor-general, who remained 'supreme constitutional authority', was to exercise his powers with the assistance of a five-member 'governor-general's commission' consisting of two Sudanese, one Egyptian, one Briton and one Pakistani. He retained direct responsibility to the British and Egyptian governments for the conduct of foreign affairs and the supervision of the *Self-Government Statute*, which was to be amended in accordance with the agreement. An international electoral commission was to prepare for elections to a Sudanese parliament. The transitional period would end, and all foreign troops would be evacuated within three months of the parliament's resolution that arrangements for self-determination should be set in motion. Provision was made for a Constituent Assembly to draw up a constitution and to decide whether the Sudan was to be linked with Egypt or should be completely independent.

The electoral commission, composed of one Egyptian, one Briton, one American and three Sudanese representing the Umma, the unionists and the south, made important modifications in the electoral rules. Whereas the *Self-Government Statute* had provided for direct elections in at least thirty-five constituencies, the commission, in accordance with a principle enunciated in the agreement between the political parties and the Egyptians, raised the number to sixty-eight (of a total of ninety-seven seats). Qualifications for voting were determined, and a special graduates' constituency, in which an added qualification, completion of an educational course of secondary standard, was imposed, had its representation increased from three to five. Elections had to be delayed until after the rainy season, and were held in November and December 1953.

The unionists had, as we have seen, boycotted previous representative assemblies. Their participation in the 1953 election thus marked the first direct confrontation of the major political views. The Ashigga, after a period of internal divisions and consequent decline, had re-emerged as the leading element in a National Unionist Party (NUP) led by Isma'il al-Azhari. Its principal rival was the Umma under the patronage of Sayyid 'Abd al-Rahman al-Mahdi and led by his son, Sayyid Siddiq. A third party, the Socialist Republicans, was, despite its name, a grouping of conservative, predominantly Ansari tribal chiefs who supported the Umma goal of complete independence but feared and resented Sayyid 'Abd al-Rahman's alleged personal ambitions. This party, established in 1951, was therefore regarded favourably by the British as an alternative both to the unionists and to the Umma, whose recent agreements with Egypt had isolated the British. A Southern Party, organized in 1951 and established formally in 1953, contested the twenty-two southern constituencies. A number of independent candidates, of various motivations and sympathies, also stood for election.

The election resulted in a decisive NUP majority. Of the ninety-seven seats at stake in the lower house, the NUP took fifty, and the Umma a disappointing twenty-three. The Socialist Republican Party won a mere three seats and soon disintegrated. Independent candidates, including a communist returned in the graduates' constituency, won twelve seats, and the Southern Party won nine. The NUP also dominated the Senate, where its twenty-one elected and ten nominated members gave the party a clear majority. The voting had shown that the NUP drew most of its support from the towns, the settled riverain areas, and areas of Khatmiyya strength. The Umma, on the other hand, won all but one of its seats in Darfur, Kordofan and the Blue Nile Provinces where Mahdism was strong. The weak Umma showing came as a shock to the British, an apparent rejection of the incalculable British contribution to the Sudan. But subsequent events suggested that rather than a rejection of the 'complete independence' advocated by the Umma and the British, the electorate was voicing its mistrust of the Umma's long association with the government, and a desire to have done with the existing regime. Similarly, the NUP victory was less a mandate for union than for change, which the NUP, by its policy of non-cooperation and the important role played by its leaders in the nationalist cause, had come to represent. Advocacy of union had itself by 1953 been seen as an avenue towards independence which would circumscribe a potential Mahdist supremacy. Indeed, even had the NUP followed up its election victory with steps towards effecting union with Egypt, events both inside and outside of the country presented impediments to such a course.

The Sudanese parliament opened in January 1954 with Azhari, the country's first prime minister, naming an all-NUP cabinet. The Umma, bristling in the unaccustomed role of opposition, showed the full force of its hostility to union on the occasion of the parliament's ceremonial opening on 1 March. A crowd of some 40,000 Ansar, many of whom had come in from the countryside, gathered in Khartoum to demonstrate at the arrival of General Neguib, who was to attend the inaugural ceremonies. Riots broke out, resulting in several fatalities (including the British commandant of the Khartoum police), and the opening had to be postponed. Disaffection with extreme unionism was increased by subsequent events in Egypt. Colonel Nasser's ousting of the personally popular Neguib in November 1954 caused disenchantment in the Sudan, as did the suppression by Nasser of both the Egyptian communists and the Muslim Brotherhood, organizations to which young Sudanese especially were attracted.[2]

Further evidence of the limitations on the new government in Khartoum was given by developments in the south. There disenchantment was increased by the rapid progress of sudanization. This had been official government policy for years, but its pace was quickened by the rush towards self-determination after the conclusion of the Anglo-Egyptian Agreement in 1953. Under the terms of that agreement a Sudanization Committee was established by Azhari's government in February 1954 with the aim of completing the transfer of the administration to Sudanese hands as soon as possible, 'to provide the free and neutral atmosphere requisite for

Self-Determination'. The argument of the British member, that sudanization should not be achieved at the expense of administrative efficiency, had necessarily to give way in the face of the Sudanese members' determination. British administrative officials were dismissed, a delicate process eased by generous government compensation. But of some eight hundred posts sudanized, a mere six went to southerners. The political decision taken at the time of the Juba Conference, that the south was 'inextricably bound' to the north, seemed, with sudanization, to be confirmed as the British abandonment feared by southern leaders. Following months of unrest during which, in July 1955, striking southern workers on the Zande Scheme were shot down by northern troops attempting to disperse them, the Equatoria Corps of the Sudan Defence Force refused orders in August. Hopes that the British would intervene on their behalf were abandoned when the new governor-general, Sir Alexander Knox Helm, ordered the mutineers to lay down their arms. With this they complied, but disorder had by then spread throughout the south, with great loss of life, especially among resident northerners. Although order was eventually restored, these events were an ominous advent to independence.[3]

Whereas the Umma Party's determination and strength in the wake of electoral defeat had been amply demonstrated in March 1954, it was ironic that the victory of the NUP did nothing to unify its various factions. While the ostensible goal of the Umma had been and remained the complete independence of the Sudan, supporters of the NUP were divided as to the extent of the relationship with Egypt they envisioned. Further, while the Umma was the political arm of the Ansar, the more amorphous NUP had never been assured the support of the Khatmiyya. As NUP leader, Azhari had therefore to rely for influence on his personal reputation as an opponent of the British, and to manage party affairs by a series of political manoeuvres. Irreconcilable opposition in the country to union, and Azhari's own more subtle view, probably shared by Sayyid 'Ali al-Mirghani, that unionism had always been essentially a tactic employed to exploit the Anglo-Egyptian rivalry – subsidiary to the grand strategy for independence – led him gradually to abandon the pro-Egyptian stance. Whether or not this about-face was occasioned more by opportunism than by principle, it robbed the NUP of its ideological content and brought about a degeneration of the party into personal factions. In December 1954 three members of the NUP cabinet were dismissed by Azhari; within days they formed, with the approval of Sayyid 'Ali, the Republican Independence Party, with the professed aim of independence but in close co-operation with Egypt. In June 1955 Muhammad Nur al-Din, the vice-president of the NUP, was dismissed from the cabinet, and charges were exchanged between him and the prime minister as to whose faction constituted the official party. Political union with Egypt having by now been largely abandoned, these and other intra-party disputes were essentially little more than unedifying personal conflicts on the eve of independence.

With the major political leaders agreed on the fundamental question of the country's future status, Azhari sought to bypass the procedures requisite for self-determination which had been laid down in the 1953 Anglo-Egyptian agreement, while his opponents manoeuvred for a share of the limelight when independence came. In August 1955 the parliament passed a resolution demanding the evacuation of British and Egyptian forces, and by mid-November the troops had been withdrawn. On 29 August another resolution called for a plebiscite to determine the constitutional status of the country. On 8 October the Umma Party proposed a coalition government, a suggestion rejected by Azhari, whose control of events was, however, perceptibly weakening as his moment of glory approached. On 10 November he lost a vote of confidence by four votes and resigned, only to be reinstated on the 15th by a two-vote margin. On 3 December Sayyid 'Abd al-Rahman and Sayyid 'Ali, meeting publicly for the first time in almost a decade, united in calling for a coalition government immediately after independence, a call to which Azhari felt compelled to agree. Meanwhile it had been realized that a plebiscite would be a time-consuming and unnecessary exercise, potentially disruptive, and on 19 December the lower house resolved unanimously to declare the independence of the Sudan, a motion adopted by the senate on the 22nd. A Transitional Constitution, under which the parliamentary regime would continue to govern a 'Sovereign, Democratic Republic', and the powers of the governor-general would be vested in a five-man Supreme Commission, was enacted by the parliament on 31 December. The last governor-general had departed on leave two weeks earlier, and did not return. On 1 January 1956 the rush to independence, which only a decade before had seemed a legacy for some future generation, was completed when the flags of the co-domini, the last symbols of Cromer's 'hybrid form of government', were lowered in Khartoum.

PART V

THE INDEPENDENT
SUDAN

We, under democracy, are placing the people's powers in the hands of the people by every means. Additional elections . . . are not the only means. There are other means. I believe that the most successful way to place the people's powers in the hands of the people is revolution.

> Babikr 'Awadallah in a radio address following the May 1969 coup.

The Sudanese People's Forces have decided unanimously – in order to save the country and its independence, to avoid bloodshed and support the people and their choice – to yield to the wishes of the people and assume power.

> General 'Abd al-Rahman Muhammad Hassan Siwar al-Dahab in a radio address on 6 April 1985.

13

THE FIRST PARLIAMENTARY
AND MILITARY REGIMES: 1956–64

The inception of the Republic could not fail to remind many Sudanese of the foundation, over seventy years before, of the Mahdist state. Yet there was little real similarity between the two. The ideology of the Mahdia was purely religious: any compromise between it and the khedivial administration in the Sudan was out of the question. The Mahdist state was born out of the devastation of a revolutionary war, in which the established administrative system had been subverted, and the precarious economic development of the Turco-Egyptian period arrested. The nationalists who had founded the Republic, on the other hand, were deeply affected by Western culture and political ideas. They sought not to destroy, but to control the administration which had been built up under the Condominium. They professed, with varying degrees of sincerity and understanding, attachment to parliamentary democracy. Hence the Republic was essentially not the supplanter but the successor of the Condominium government. New Year's Day 1956 marks only in a formal and conventional sense a new era in Sudanese history. The real line of demarcation must be placed either earlier, on the 'appointed day' of 9 January 1954, when the essential transfer of power from British to Sudanese hands took place; or, less aptly, on 17 November 1958, when the Army coup d'état ended the first phase of parliamentary government.

The curious sense of anti-climax which attended the formal independence of the Sudan[1] was a reflection of the continuity not only of the system of government, but also of the tenor of politics. It was only with great difficulty that Azhari was able to maintain his position as prime minister after independence. On 18 January 1956 his government was defeated in the lower house on a budget vote, but was maintained in office when he won a confidence motion the next day. At the end of the month the resignation of three ministers forced Azhari to form a coalition government. The new cabinet, sworn in on 2 February, included Mirghani Hamza and Muhammad Nur al-Din, as well as two prominent Umma politicians, 'Abdallah Khalil, the former leader of the Legislative Assembly, and Ibrahim Ahmad. Azhari's decline was completed when in June twenty-one members of his parliamentary party formed, with the support of Sayyid 'Ali al-Mirghani, the People's Democratic Party (PDP). On 5 July 'Abdallah Khalil, secretary-general of the Umma, was elected prime minister against Azhari by a vote of sixty to thirty-two. On the 7th a new coalition cabinet, including prominent ex-NUP members of the PDP but excluding Azhari, assumed office.

Superficially, the new government, by bringing together the supporters of the rival religious leaders, appeared finally to recognize the priority of national over sectarian loyalties. In fact, however, the opposite was true: the trappings of power had been handed to those who actually held it, the sectarian leaders. This paper alliance of the rival sects' supporters was reminiscent of the efforts, some thirty years before, of the two sayyids to crush the nascent secular nationalism of 'Ali 'Abd al-Latif. The alliance of 1956 was if anything more artificial and tactical: the coalition partners had divergent views on even the most fundamental questions of policy, and united only for the purpose of defeating Azhari. The brief history of the first parliamentary period was to be characterized from this unpromising start by petty rivalries and the crippling mutual suspicions of coalition partners. The Western-oriented Umma was seen to be manoeuvring for the appointment of Sayyid 'Abd al-Rahman as life-president of the Sudan under a constitution as yet unwritten; the PDP, one wing of which looked to revolutionary Egypt for inspiration, was vigilant of the interests of Sayyid 'Ali. The depressing resiliency of this sectarian rivalry robbed the new republic of even a brief period of political vitality.

During the 1956–8 parliamentary period the characteristics of sovereignty were assumed. The new republic was recognized by foreign governments, and in January 1956 became a member of the Arab League. On 6 February the Sudan was admitted to the ranks of the United Nations. Membership of international financial bodies followed. A diplomatic corps was established, presided over by Mohammed Ahmed Mahgoub, the Umma foreign minister, who represented the Sudan on the world stage. In 1957 steps were taken to initiate a Sudanese currency,[2] the first since the days of the Mahdist state. The results of the first scientific census of the Sudan, announced in January 1957, put the population at 10,200,000. On this basis parliamentary constituencies were redrawn and their number was increased from ninety-seven to 173 in preparation for elections which, after a postponement, were scheduled for 1958.

Economic policy during the first parliamentary period concentrated on enlarging the country's agricultural capacity and improving communications. The Managil Extension to the Gezira Scheme, to add 800,000 acres of irrigated land and increase the area under cotton to almost 500,000 acres, was well under way in 1956, with completion planned for 1961–2. A new five-year plan beginning in 1957 was estimated to cost £S137 million. But the concentration of capital resources in cotton-growing schemes, a cause for anxiety since the inception of the Gezira Scheme, was to prove disastrous in the late 1950s. The 1957 and 1958 cotton crops were poor, and a falling world market combined with the government's insistence on maintaining a fixed minimum price for cotton resulted in a monumental stock of unsold cotton and a serious depletion in the country's currency reserves, largely dependent on income from cotton sales.

Related to the economic downturn as a cause of the coalition government's failure was the conduct of the Sudan's foreign affairs. Two questions were prominent in the 1956–8 period. As before independence, the Sudan's dealings with the outside world were dominated by the bilateral relationship with Egypt. The Suez crisis in 1956 strained relations with Britain and produced strong Sudanese support for Egypt. But serious tension nonetheless arose over the question of the allocation of Nile waters. The Sudan had ignored provisions of the 1929 Nile Waters Agreement when implementing its new irrigation projects. Egyptian plans to construct the High Dam at Aswan made a settlement of the issue more urgent. The Sudan government demanded that a revision of the 1929 Agreement must precede a dam construction which would have serious economic and demographic repercussions in the Sudan. The groundwork for agreement was laid by the government of 'Abdallah Khalil, but its conclusion fell to the successor regime. A gratuitous irritant to Sudanese-Egyptian relations was the provocative Egyptian claim, in February 1958, to two areas, one on the Nile, the other on the Red Sea coast, on the grounds that these lay north of latitude 22°, which had been specified as the Sudan's northern boundary in the Condominium Agreement. Egypt sent troops to occupy the areas, which since the beginning of the Condominium had been administered by Khartoum and which had participated in the 1953 elections. The resulting crisis was resolved without formal agreement when Egypt withdrew her troops.

A second important area of foreign relations concerned the Sudan's acceptance of aid from the United States. Conversations between the two governments began in mid-1957. The deteriorating economic position and ambitious development plans of the Sudan gave force to the government's readiness to accept American aid. But a political backdrop of growing Arab hostility to the West, and the United States' moves to counter this with the Eisenhower Doctrine, created serious tension between the coalition partners. The increasingly pro-Egyptian PDP, despite assurances from the Umma leadership, saw the proposed aid agreement as necessarily strengthening US (and anti-Egyptian) influence in the Sudan. Resolution of this internal rift awaited the convening of a new parliament after the 1958 elections.

The alliance of the Umma and PDP continued through the 1958 election campaign, as the coalition partners agreed not to oppose each other in the constituencies. This, the consequent conservation of their financial resources, the redistribution of seats noted above and the naturalization of large numbers of pro-Umma Fallata, resulted in a victory at the polls for the coalition.[3] The new parliament consisted of sixty-three Umma, twenty-six PDP, forty Southern Liberal, and forty-four NUP members. The NUP won the highest number of votes. A new coalition government was agreed by the Umma and the PDP, with 'Abdallah Khalil retaining the premiership.

The Southern Liberal Party had been founded shortly after the 1953 elections. Educated southerners' grave suspicions of northern politicians, exacerbated by events since 1954, had found expression in their support for the granting of federal status to the south.[4] Their unity on this single issue, however, was insufficient to overcome traditional tribal and personal differences and the cynical opportunism of some of their own members. The mask of southern solidarity was torn away after the 1958 elections, when Liberal MPs voted with either the ruling coalition or the NUP opposition in parliament. Liberal support for the government was uncertain at best, and following ratification of the US Aid Agreement in July 1958 parliament was adjourned to avoid a government defeat on a confidence motion.

By mid-1958 the position of the government was fast becoming intolerable. Deteriorating economic conditions were underlined by the obvious incapacity of the political parties to cope with them. Serious national issues were seen to be subordinated to increasingly hectic manoeuvres necessitated by the unworkable Umma-PDP coalition. Political machinations reached a finale in the late summer when the Umma leadership began actively to explore the possibility of coalition with Azhari's NUP. This was complicated by reports of a possible NUP-PDP alliance which, if consummated, would remove the Umma from power in yet another bizarre manoeuvre. Before any of these plans could be fulfilled, however, the army had stepped in and swept away parties, politicians and the parliamentary regime itself.

On the morning of 17 November 1958, only a few hours before parliament was to reconvene, the army took control of key installations in the Three Towns. The commander-in-chief, Major-General Ibrahim Abboud, announcing the military's assumption of power, claimed in a radio address that the army had no alternative but to save the country from the chaotic regime of the politicians. A state of emergency was declared. The five-man Supreme Commission, which since independence had replaced the governor-general, was dismissed. The transitional constitution was suspended, government ministers were (briefly) placed under arrest, political parties were dissolved, and trade unions were abolished. The Sudan was proclaimed a 'democratic republic' with popular sovereignty. Power was invested in a thirteen-member Supreme Council of the Armed Forces which in turn delegated 'full legislative, executive and judicial powers' to Abboud. A council of ministers was named, seven of whom also sat on the Supreme Council, while five were civilians. Two ministers of the last coalition government were also included. Abboud himself was named prime minister and minister of defence. A statement by the civilian minister of foreign affairs, Ahmed Kheir, promised that the government would honour the international commitments made by its predecessors, pledged to strengthen ties with African and Arab states, placed special emphasis on improving relations with Egypt and Ethiopia, and gave diplomatic recognition to the People's Republic of China.

An intriguing aspect of the coup had been the extent of 'Abdallah Khalil's involvement in it. Rumours of a coup had circulated for some weeks before 17 November. Evidence suggests that 'Abdallah Khalil, who before entering politics had a long and distinguished military career, had discussed with Abboud a temporary army

171

takeover, to be followed by a government in which he, Abboud and Azhari would play leading parts, supported by the army. The possibility of a new coalition government, excluding him from office, may have figured prominently in the prime minister's thinking. In any case, events were to show that whatever 'Abdallah Khalil's expectations were of the army takeover, Abboud and his colleagues had ideas of their own. As former prime ministers, 'Abdallah Khalil and Azhari were granted annual pensions of £S1,200 and receded from view.

The bloodless coup triggered feelings neither of euphoria nor of great regret at the passing of parliamentary government. On the international level the coup was but the latest in a series in the Muslim world, beginning with Egypt in 1952 and continuing in Iraq and Pakistan in 1958. Within the Sudan public opinion was more relieved than jubilant, less excited than exhausted after three years of increasingly cynical and sterile party politics. Support was forthcoming from the still undisputedly pre-eminent religious leaders. Sayyid 'Ali welcomed the coup, among the leaders of which were prominent members of the Khatmiyya; Sayyid 'Abd al-Rahman's response was more guarded, and foreshadowed eventual Umma hostility towards the military regime.

The view that the military takeover had originally been planned as a temporary measure gained force from the events of the regime's first year in power. While the coup itself had gone smoothly, struggles within the army ensued, as factions and personalities competed for dominance. Abboud himself was a benevolent figure, seemingly removed from and indifferent to these internal disputes, and to this may be laid the fact that he survived them. On 2 March 1959 Brigadier Muhyi al-Din Ahmad 'Abdallah, the commander of the Eastern Area who had not been included in the Supreme Council, and Brigadier 'Abd al-Rahim Shannan, commander of the Northern Area, moved troops into the capital. General 'Abd al-Wahhab and two other members of the Supreme Council were arrested. The intervention of 'Abdallah Khalil and the two sayyids resulted in the freeing of 'Abd al-Wahhab and the withdrawal of the troops. But two days later they reappeared in Khartoum in greater strength. The disgruntled commanders demanded and got the resignation of the Supreme Council. Abboud appointed a new Supreme Council of ten members, including Muhyi al-Din and Shannan. On 9 March General 'Abd al-Wahhab was removed from all his posts and retired with a grant of three thousand acres of government land.

The ousting of 'Abd al-Wahhab by the area commanders clarified the factional dispute, in that they were now left to contend directly with the real strong man of the regime, General Hassan Beshir Nasr, who with 'Abd al-Wahhab had planned the November coup. In May another crisis occurred when supporters of Shannan again led their troops into Khartoum. Hassan Beshir had the chief plotters arrested at Shendi, and the troops returned to headquarters. In June Muhyi al-Din and Shannan were arrested and brought before a court martial. They were sentenced to death on a charge of incitement to mutiny, but on 22 September the sentences were commuted to life imprisonment. Both were released from prison after the revolution of October 1964.

One further abortive coup took place in 1959. This, which occurred on 9 November, originated in the Infantry School at Omdurman, and was led by a number of young officers. The rising was suppressed without difficulty, and the leaders were brought to trial and sentenced to death. They were hanged on 2 December, an event which shocked public opinion, and which indicated that the regime would tolerate no further dissension in the ranks. Any initial notion that the new government was sure of its own power base had, however, within a year of its inauguration been destroyed.

The death on 24 March 1959 of Sayyid 'Abd al-Rahman al-Mahdi was a notable event. The great sectarian and nationalist leader had dominated politics in the Sudan since the re-emergence of the Ansar during the First World War. The modern Mahdist sect is largely his creation, while the independence of the Sudan in 1956 was seen as the culmination of his life's work. He was succeeded as head of the Ansar by his son, Sayyid Siddiq.

Contributing to the impression of the military regime's establishment of authority was a new Nile Waters Agreement concluded with Egypt on the day before the young officers' coup attempt. In 1955 the Sudan, while opposing in principle the Aswan Dam project, had put forward three principles on which a settlement of the waters question must be based: that the Sudan's share of the Nile waters should be determined before work began on the High Dam; that the resettlement and 'adequate alternative livelihood' of the people of Wadi Halfa town and district, whose removal the new dam would necessitate, must be provided for at Egypt's expense; and that the Sudan should have the right in future to build whatever works she deemed necessary for the use of her share in the Nile

173

waters.[5] The parliamentary government's attempts to reach an agreement on this basis had failed. Negotiations were resumed in October 1959 and a new Nile Waters Agreement was concluded on 8 November. The Sudan was to receive £E15 million to cover the losses to be incurred at Wadi Halfa, a figure which was, however, to fall far short of the £S26 million finally spent on compensation and resettlement.[6] Upon completion of the High Dam, the Sudan was to be allocated 18,500,000,000 cubic metres of water per year as against 55,500,000,000 for Egypt, with a margin of 10,000,000,000 cubic metres for evaporation losses. Work on the dam began in 1960.

The foreign policy pursued by the military regime was one of non-alignment and support for African independence movements. The perceived Western orientation of the previous government was balanced by a sense of pragmatism. The Nile Waters Agreement opened a new period in Sudanese-Egyptian relations, symbolized by the visit of President Nasser in November 1960. Abboud made state visits to important non-aligned countries, as well as to the USA and USSR, and these were reciprocated, notably by the visits of President Brezhnev, Premier Chou En Lai, and President Tito. Military equipment was accepted from Britain, and Food for Peace from the USA. On a visit to the UNO headquarters in 1961, Abboud argued for the membership in the world body of the People's Republic of China. Diplomatic and economic boycotts of South Africa and Portugal were instituted in 1963. In the same year the establishment of the first African Development Bank was agreed in a meeting of African finance ministers at Khartoum.

While the signing of a Nile Waters Agreement lent prestige to the military regime, the resettlement of the people of Wadi Halfa developed into a serious political issue, with long-term repercussions. The government presented them with five alternative sites for resettlement, four on the Nile and one on the Atbara. As early as 1955 the previous government had determined that the displaced population should be settled on the Atbara, and despite their near-unanimous opposition, this site, near Khashm al-Qirba, was chosen for them. Widespread demonstrations began at once in the Wadi Halfa area, to be followed by others in Khartoum and elsewhere. The grievances of the Nubians formed a rallying-point for opposition to the regime; students, schoolboys, and trade unionists playing a prominent part. Coming as they did in the wake of the November coup attempt, these demonstrations took on a political character distinct from the resettlement issue, and the government dealt harshly with them.

Civilian opposition to the regime, which had been sparked by the demonstrations of the people of Wadi Halfa, steadily mounted in 1960–1. The regime was dominated by members of the Shayqiyya tribe (Abboud, Hassan Beshir, Abu Rannat, the Chief Justice, and Ahmed Kheir) with strong Khatmiyya connections. Further evidence of its orientation were the retirement of General 'Abd al-Wahhab, an Umma supporter, and the favourable attitude towards the regime adopted by the PDP. The leaders of the outlawed political parties (with the notable exception of the PDP) petitioned the government on 29 November 1960 to return the country to civilian rule with a new parliament operating under a permanent constitution. This petition was without effect. The dissolution in June 1961 of the newly-reconstituted railway workers' union, which had called a crippling strike for higher wages; the closure of the University owing to student demonstrations; and the detention of a lawyer who had alleged in court that a witness had been tortured, preceded another petition by Azhari and 'Abdallah Khalil. This resulted in their being placed in detention at Juba, along with Mahgoub, two communists, and leaders of the other political parties except the PDP. The detained leaders were released in January 1962. A further blow to civilian political leadership was the death, in September 1961, of Sayyid Siddiq al-Mahdi, who was succeeded as religious leader [Imam] of the Ansar by his brother, Sayyid al-Hadi, while political leadership of the movement was taken up by Siddiq's son, Sayyid Sadiq.

The period of military rule saw the further development of two extremist political groups, the communists and the Muslim Brotherhood. The origins of the Communist Party in the Sudan are to be found in Egypt, where in 1944 its predecessor was launched by Sudanese students connected with the Democratic Movement for National Liberation, an arm of the Egyptian Communist Party. The party was established in the Sudan in 1946 by students and intellectuals as the Sudanese Movement for National Liberation. Between 1946 and 1951 the party was riven by internal disputes. Declared illegal by the Condominium government and its parliamentary and military successors, the party was organized behind a number of fronts, and found its chief support among three sections of the population: western-educated students and members of the intelligentsia, trade unionists, and tenant farmer associations. Leadership of the first railway workers' union, the WAA, was in communist hands from 1947, as was leadership of the umbrella organization of unions, the SWTUF, from 1952. The party's fortunes declined when it condemned the Anglo-Egyptian Agreement of 1953, and its subsequent strike calls were unsuccessful. The party contested the 1953 elections as the Anti-Imperialist Front, winning one seat in the House of Representatives. In January 1957 the Anti-Imperialist Front joined with Azhari's NUP and the students' union in forming the National Front in opposition to the Western tendencies of the Umma-dominated coalition government. Thus, when the military regime upon its assumption of power banned political parties, the communists, under 'Abd al-Khaliq Mahjub, already had considerable experience in underground organization, and managed, despite the government's imprisonment of many communists, to survive. In 1964 the election of Shaykh al-Amin Muhammad al-Amin, an avowed communist, as president of the Gezira Tenants' Association, indicated the viability of the movement. From 1962 the communists, working through various front organizations, were active in kindling opposition to the military regime.[7]

Parallel to the development of communism in the Sudan was the increasing attraction of the Muslim Brothers. Founded in Egypt in 1928, the Brotherhood is a militant organization with a fundamentalist Islamic ideology. Like the communists, it was suppressed in Egypt after the 1952 revolution. During the closing days of the Abboud regime the Brotherhood was led in Khartoum by Dr Hasan al-Turabi, a lecturer in the University, where much of the most active support for the movement has been found. From the 1950s the student body of the University tended towards polarization between the Brotherhood and the communists, a phenomenon which has continued.

In its administrative policy the military regime bore a curious resemblance to its Condominium predecessor. Following the recommendations of a commission appointed in August 1959 under the chairmanship of Abu Rannat to consider the association of the people in the governing of the country, the regime promulgated three ordinances, the *Province Administration Act* of 1960, the *Central Council Act* of 1962, and the *Local Government Act* of 1962. These established local, provincial and central councils to advise the government. Thus the regime sought, as had the British in the 1940s, to circumvent the political parties and to rely for legitimacy on politically safe and innocuous council members. The Central Council, equivalent to a parliament, was without independent authority and had little impact.

In the economic field the military regime achieved mixed results. The minimum reserve price for cotton, which under the previous government had combined with a falling world demand to create a huge supply of unsold cotton, was abandoned in January 1959. This resulted in the diminution of the backlog, but at prices close to the cost of production. The government's budget showed a slight surplus in 1958–9, and the 1959–60 figures provided a surplus of £S22.6 million. Figures for subsequent years were of a similar order. In February 1960 the Central Bank of the Sudan was formally inaugurated. An Agricultural Bank was established in 1959 with capital of £S5 million to provide credit facilities for farmers, and in August 1962 the Industrial Bank of the Sudan began its operations of granting credit for the promotion and expansion of private industry. In June 1960 the International Bank for Reconstruction and Development (IBRD) granted a loan of fifteen million dollars to finance completion of the Managil Extension, and arrangements were made in 1961 with the IBRD and West Germany for financing construction by an Italian group of the Roseires Dam. In March 1962 a railway line was extended from southern Kordofan to Wau in the Bahr al-Ghazal. Trade agreements were concluded with the Soviet Union and other Eastern European states, as well as with Britain, the USA and other countries. Bilateral economic relations with Yugoslavia and West Germany were particularly active.

In October 1962 a 'Ten-Year Plan for economic and social development' was announced. Investment over the period covered by the plan was to total £S512 million, of which £S285 million was to be provided in special Development Budgets for major projects. The plan concentrated on agricultural and irrigation schemes; improving transport and communications; and lessening the Sudan's dependence on the agricultural sector generally, and especially on cotton. The Ten-Year Plan proved over-ambitious, however, as the government, like its predecessors, failed to take account of the essential dependence of the Sudan, for surplus revenue, on the dominant agricultural sector, which remained prey to world market and local conditions. As budget surpluses failed to reach the level necessary to fund the special development budgets, projects were trimmed and confidence eroded, while the country's indebtedness rose alarmingly.

A problem potentially more serious for the regime than its economic difficulties had been developing in the southern Sudan. In the wake of the 1955 disturbances the southern provinces had been quiet, and the wrangling of southern politicians in Khartoum had few repercussions for their constituents. The policies of the military regime, however, escalated the level of tension between the two regions beyond the point of political debate and eventually, or so it seemed to the government, beyond the point of political solution. A large body of southern opinion became convinced that, whatever its pronounced intentions, the government in Khartoum was not to be trusted.

In its southern administrative policy the regime, free from the political restrictions that parliamentary government had imposed on its predecessor, was tactless to the point of provocation in its appointment to provincial and district positions of northern officials. Southerners were, as before, bypassed or transferred to the north. But it was in the related areas of educational and religious affairs that the Abboud government showed its political ineptness. We have seen that southern education had, under the Condominium, been in the hands of foreign missionaries whose schools were, after 1927, subsidized, and, after the Second World War, supplemented by government institutions. In 1954 an International Commission on Secondary Education recommended that the missionary schools should be taken over by the government and that Arabic, not English, should be the universal language of instruction in the south. These suggestions evidenced a recognition of education's importance in nation-building, but betrayed an ignorance of southern sensitivities. Subsequently, in February 1957 the government of 'Abdallah Khalil had announced its intention of nationalizing the missionary schools, and these were integrated into a national educational system. The Abboud regime took stronger action. The gradual progress of arabization and islamization, to which the policies of the Condominium government had served as a partial barrier, was to be hastened through an aggressive government policy. Six intermediate Islamic Institutes were opened, mosques were constructed and subsidized, missions were prohibited from opening new schools, and the day of rest was changed from Sunday to Friday.

Missionaries going on leave were denied re-entry to the Sudan. Religious activities of missionaries outside church were prohibited.

Thus a policy which, had it been instituted gradually in the early days of Condominium rule, would have served to produce a broader national character, appeared under the heavy hand of the military to be aimed at suppressing an emerging though still unclearly articulated southern identity. As missionary activities had been seen, in Condominium days, as part of the Southern Policy designed to provide a separate evolution of southern society, their curtailment was viewed, especially by Southern intellectuals, as a thinly-veiled political provocation. The government in turn blamed the missionaries for inciting southern hostility towards the regime. In 1962 *The Missionary Societies Act*, an attempt 'to regulate, by means of a system of licences, the activities of Missionary Societies in the Sudan', was a crude device to allow unlimited interference with missionaries. The intention foreshadowed in this Act was clarified on 22 February 1964 when the government ordered the expulsion of all foreign missionaries engaged in the southern Sudan. An attempt in July 1964 by the foreign minister of Lebanon to mediate between the Sudan and the Vatican was unsuccessful, and was followed by the expulsion of several missionaries from the north.

Rising discontent in the south was further revealed by political developments. Leading southern intellectuals and politicians fled the country. In February 1962 Father Saturnino Lahure, Joseph Oduho and William Deng established in Leopoldville (Kinshasa) the Sudan African Closed Districts National Union (SACDNU), which took its name from the fact that the government had reimposed the old closed-districts system. In the following year this organization became the Sudan African National Union (SANU) with headquarters at Kampala. From its inception SANU, like the earlier southern political parties, was hampered by internal splits and personal differences within its leadership. It provided, however, evidence to the world at large of events in the south, and acted as spokesman for the growing number of southern refugees who, as security in the south broke down, had fled to neighbouring countries. It was estimated in 1964 that some sixty thousand refugees were in Uganda alone and in May of that year the Ugandan government announced that some seven thousand refugees had crossed its borders in one ten-day period. In response to SANU's appeals, the UN began to provide funds for the relief of refugees. The conclusion of extradition agreements between the Sudan and Ethiopia and Uganda failed to stop the emigration.

A more disturbing symptom of the burgeoning crisis was the establishment in 1963 of the Anya Nya, a loosely-knit guerrilla army deriving its name from that of a poison concocted in Madi country from snakes and rotten beams. The Anya Nya had as its nucleus veterans of the 1955 mutiny who had eluded capture by taking to the bush. In January 1964 a force of Anya Nya attacked Wau. Although this failed, it served together with government measures to suppress the Anya Nya, to publicize the guerrilla movement and make it a rallying-point for southern opposition. The emergence of the Anya Nya also signalled the spread of the conflict to the rural population. The increasing intractability of the southern problem and the obvious inability of the government to deal with it led indirectly to the fall of the Abboud regime.

THE TRANSITIONAL GOVERNMENT AND THE SECOND PARLIAMENTARY REGIME: 1964–9

Popular acceptance of the Abboud coup in November 1958 had been based not on attraction to any policy the military promised to implement, but simply on the ousting of the politically bankrupt parliamentary regime. During the six years of its existence, however, the military regime itself proved incapable not only of solving basic political and economic problems, but also of providing the internal stability which had been expected from the army. The demonstrations of the people of Wadi Halfa in 1960, the strike of the railway workers in 1961, the unrest of the students in the University, and a strike by tenants of the Gezira Scheme in 1963, revealed that even a military government could be opposed and in certain circumstances forced to give way. Poor participation in elections to the new system of councils had shown popular lack of interest in the government's administrative plans. Difficulties of insufficient funds and official corruption encountered in the implementation of the Ten-Year Plan had dissipated the optimism engendered by the government's early economic successes. The worsening position in the south, where even a government of soldiers, freed from parliamentary restraints, could not impose its will but was in fact seen to have no policy more imaginative than repression, argued powerfully against the efficacy of the regime. Opposition to the Abboud regime was therefore broadly based, but with little other than antipathy to the generals to unite it. While the opposition's consolidation in October 1964 proved potent enough to overthrow the government, its fundamental differences soon thereafter brought about the failure of the second parliamentary regime.

The demise of Abboud's government came swiftly and unexpectedly. Tacitly admitting its bewilderment with the southern problem, the government appointed in September 1964 a commission of enquiry to investigate the causes of southern unrest and to propose solutions. This commission, which was immediately disavowed by SANU, invited public discussion of the southern problem. The students' union of the university, long a centre of opposition to the regime, concluded in a meeting that no solution was possible so long as the military regime remained in power. The ministry of education, under the jurisdiction of which the university had been placed, banned further meetings. On 22 October, however, this order was defied, and in the course of police attempts to disperse the meeting a student was shot and fatally wounded. On the next day a funeral procession of some thirty thousand people quickly spawned demonstrations and riots which the police could not control. The army stepped in but was itself unable to restore order.

On 25 October a group of teachers, students and members of the bar established the Professionals' Front, which was soon joined by other professional associations, trade unions and the Gezira tenants. The front's executive council, dominated by communists, called for a general strike, and this was taken up by workers and civil servants, paralysing the capital. Demonstrations spread to provincial centres. In Omdurman the leaders of the banned political parties met and formed a United Front. The position of the government, though gravely damaged, was still tenable, and order might still have been restored had it not been for dissension within the army itself. Brigadier Hassan Beshir Nasr, second in command of the army, urged strong measures and saw himself as a potential successor to Abboud, but plots by junior officers to stage a coup against the army leadership convinced Abboud that there was no alternative to the resignation of the government.

On 26 October General Abboud announced the dissolution of the Supreme Council and the resignation of the cabinet. Negotiations for the formation of a new government were begun between the army and the Professionals' and United Fronts. An incident, during which some twenty demonstrators were killed after troops opened fire on them, lent urgency to the discussions and heightened popular feelings against the army. The two Fronts agreed to the formation of a Transitional Government, which was announced on 30 October. Abboud stayed on as president, and Sirr al-Khatim al-Khalifa, a civil servant unaffiliated with a political party, was named prime minister. The new cabinet was composed of seven representatives of the Professionals' Front, two southerners, and one representative of each of the five main political parties (Umma, NUP, PDP, the Muslim Brothers and the communists). Through their strong position in the Professionals' Front the communists emerged with three cabinet seats. Abboud's position as president was anomalous, and on 14 November he was forced to resign, to be replaced as head of state by a five-man commission, as before the 1958 coup. Abboud was given a pension and retired. Other members of the Supreme Council were arrested and imprisoned in Darfur.

The fall of the Abboud regime, in contrast to the overthrow of its predecessor, was the occasion for public celebration. Popular excitement could not, however, mask the difficulties facing the improvised Transitional Government, a coalition of mutually antagonistic groups. Certain reforms were nonetheless agreed in order to erase the statutory vestiges of the military regime. The provisional constitution was reinstated. The council system imposed by the Abboud government was dismantled. Political prisoners were released and censorship lifted. Political parties were legalized, and the autonomy of the university was restored, and steps were taken to check corruption.

Internal difficulties of the Transitional Government were inherent in its composition. The Professionals' Front, formed in the revolutionary atmosphere of October and influenced by the strong communist element in the leadership of its member associations, favoured radical alterations of the country's political and economic systems. Most of the established political parties, painfully aware of their own quiescence under the military government and their insignificant part in bringing about its downfall, chafed at being outnumbered in the cabinet by the Professionals' Front, and insisted on national elections at the earliest possible time. The Professionals' Front, the communists and the PDP argued that the continuing state of emergency in the south precluded immediate elections, which the traditional parties could be expected to win easily, thus re-establishing their legitimacy. Their sense of urgency was the greater owing to a number of administrative and other reforms mooted by the Professionals' Front itself and its constituent organizations. The radicalism of these proposals, one of which would have replaced the territorial basis of constituencies with a 'professional' basis along the lines of the old graduates' constituency, brought about the secession from the Front of a number of its member associations. The deadlock caused by the polarization of the cabinet was broken when in February 1965 thousands of Ansar demonstrated in Khartoum against the government. Following a lull in political activity occasioned by the visit of Queen Elizabeth, the cabinet resigned on

18 February. A series of unsuccessful attempts to form a new government ensued. The Council of State thereupon asked Sirr al-Khatim al-Khalifa to organize a new coalition, and this was accomplished on the 23rd. This cabinet was dominated by the Umma, NUP and Muslim Brothers, with the PDP and communists refusing to participate. The Professionals' Front broke up, although its representatives retained a voice in the cabinet. On 1 April the PDP and communists, in the hope of postponing elections, agreed to occupy the cabinet seats reserved for them, but on the 6th the Council of State decided to hold elections at the end of the month, which the PDP determined to boycott.

Meanwhile the government was taking steps to solve the increasingly serious and confused southern problem. On 6 December 1964 a shocking incident in Khartoum underlined the urgency of a settlement. A demonstration of southerners resident in Khartoum was organized to welcome Clement Mboro, the minister of the interior, on his return from a southern tour. When his arrival was delayed, wild rumours circulated, and the crowd, uncontrolled by the police, rushed into the city, where clashes with groups of northerners left scores dead. The resulting panic induced many to leave for the south. For the first time the full impact of the southern problem had been felt in the capital itself, and while the events of 'Black Sunday' raised further doubts about the possibility of reconciliation, they also reinforced the necessity of a settlement.

Immediately after the fall of the Abboud regime, representatives of SANU had written to the Transitional Government proposing a conference to negotiate a settlement.[1] A number of conditions were attached to this offer, among them that an amnesty be declared for southern refugees, that the *Closed Districts Ordinance* and *Missionary Societies Act* be repealed, and that SANU be recognized as a political party for the purpose of contesting the coming elections. On 10 December the prime minister granted a general amnesty to all Sudanese who had left the country since January 1955. A Sudanese delegation headed by 'Abdin Isma'il and Ezbon Mondiri went to Kampala and negotiated a draft agreement with Uganda providing for the resettlement of refugees in the Sudan. The leaders of SANU refused to return before an agreement was reached on the future status of the south, and therefore insisted that any conference should be held outside the Sudan, in the full light of world opinion. Further negotiations in Kampala between SANU and Da'ud 'Abd al-Latif, the ex-governor of Equatoria, resulted in SANU's agreement to attend a conference in Juba in February. Prior to that, SANU would appeal to all southerners to cease fighting, and the government of the Sudan would ensure the safety of the SANU delegates and lift the state of emergency in the south as soon as the fighting abated. It was further agreed that the international press would be allowed to report the proceedings, at which Uganda was to have observer status.

The conference was delayed by the political crisis in the north, by an intensification of fighting around Juba, and by a split among the southern political leaders. A moderate faction, headed by William Deng and espousing federal status for the south, agreed that the conference could take place in Khartoum. Another faction, led by Aggrey Jaden and demanding independence, rejected Khartoum as the site for a conference. A third group, resembling in its composition the Professionals' Front, had been organized in Khartoum as the Southern Front under the leadership of Gordon Abiei following the October revolution. It initially opposed Deng's conciliatory stance since this encouraged the government to negotiate with him alone, without reference to the Front or to SANU leaders in exile.

The Round Table Conference opened in Khartoum on 16 March 1965. Representatives of all the major political parties, of the Professionals' Front, SANU, and other leading southerners attended, with observers from Uganda, Kenya, Nigeria, Tanzania, Algeria, Egypt and Ghana. The conference was chaired by the vice-chancellor of Khartoum University, Professor el-Nazir Dafa'allah. An opening address by the prime minister placed the blame for the southern problem on 'natural geographical and sociological factors' and especially on the 'evil colonial policies' of the British and the 'hypocritical European missionaries'. The northern political parties, mindful of the impending elections, eschewed both intransigent insistence on northern supremacy and imaginative concessions to the southern demands. They rejected both unitary and federal systems, and proposed a regional government for the south which would effectively devolve control of education, public health, commerce, agricultural policy and internal security to a regional democratic council under an executive council. Sovereignty would be retained by the national government, and national legislation would take precedence over decisions of the regional council. The SANU and Southern Front delegates responded with a call for a plebiscite in the south to decide among the alternatives of federation, union and independence. They proposed southern control of finance, foreign affairs and the armed forces within the south, a customs union with the north, and other reforms falling just short of independence. In its final resolutions the conference was able to agree on principles to guide policy in the south, but admitted that it 'could not reach a unanimous resolution' on the question of the south's constitutional status. A twelve-man committee was appointed to consider plans for constitutional and administrative reform. The committee reported in late 1966, without appreciable effect.

Meanwhile, preparations went ahead for parliamentary elections. The upper house had been abolished, and the franchise extended to all of eighteen years of age and above, including women. Failure to solve the southern problem precluded elections in the south. Superficially, the choice facing voters was complicated by the fact that some fifteen parties and a large number of independents were contesting the elections. Most of these parties were ephemeral vehicles for personal candidatures. The fundamental positions of the major parties were little different from those espoused in 1958. The Umma still depended largely on support from areas where the Ansar were numerous, while the NUP maintained its hold in the towns and settled regions along the main Nile. The results of polling, which took place in late April and early May, gave the Umma seventy-six seats, the NUP fifty-four, the Islamic Charter Front (dominated by the Muslim Brothers) five, and the communists eight, one of whom was the Sudan's first woman MP. All of the communist victories were in the special graduates' constituency, which had been revived with fifteen seats. Twenty-four independents were elected, including ten members of the Beja Congress and seven of the Nuba Mountains Federation of Independents, both of which were purely regional interest groups. The PDP, still the focus of Khatmiyya political support, won three seats despite its boycott of the elections, and suffered an internal split between its traditional majority and the faction of the party leader, 'Ali 'Abd al-Rahman, who had allied the party with the communists under the Transitional Government. Despite the postponement of elections in the south, the region was represented by twenty new MPs, mostly northern merchants who, it was ruled by the Supreme Court, had fulfilled the requirements for nomination and were thus elected unopposed.

The way was now clear for the Umma and the NUP to form a coalition government which, after predictable argument over which party should provide the premier, was organized under the Umma's Mohammed Ahmed Mahgoub, the former foreign minister. This was, superficially, a 'national' government in that the coalition partners between them commanded a vast majority in parliament. Strong leadership and a unity of purpose could have provided unprecedented stability. But personal ambitions, especially of the vainglorious Mahgoub and the cynical Azhari, the NUP's veteran leader, were too strong to be subordinated, and party differences made nonsense of the coalition. Tinkering with the still-provisional constitution was by now habitual, and an amendment allowed Azhari's election as permanent president of the five-man Supreme Council of State, thereby politicizing that institution. Each coalition partner took six seats in the cabinet, while the traditional reservation of three ministerial appointments for southerners was initially maintained. Andrew Wieu and Alfred Wol of SANU were named to the cabinet, but soon resigned over the appointment of Buth Diu of the recently revived but insignificant Liberal Party.

The history of the second parliamentary regime is dominated by two problems: the continuing disturbances in the south, which during this period assumed the proportions of a civil war; and the often bitter relations between (and especially within) the political parties. These combined with the resulting lack of direction in economic affairs to destroy the second, as they had the first, parliamentary regime.

In its conduct of southern affairs the civilian government of Mahgoub seemed to have learned little from the failures of its military predecessor. Within a month of the new government's taking office, two incidents of shocking violence in the south raised the southern problem to an even more disastrous level. On 8 July 1965 northern troops at Juba went on a rampage that left hundreds of southern residents dead and whole sections of the town in ashes. On 11 July at Wau a further mass killing of southerners occurred. While the government reacted by restating its policy that lawlessness must be crushed and order restored before constitutional reforms could be discussed, SANU in exile demanded the intervention of the United Nations to bring a halt to atrocities. The Juba and Wau incidents sparked a new exodus of southerners into neighbouring states, where tens of thousands were settled in refugee camps. The Anya Nya, with arms acquired through the Congo and from other foreign sources, responded to the new government offensive with atrocities of their own. A pattern developed, sickeningly familiar, in which the civilian population was caught up in the heightening spiral of violence. Villages spared the torch by one side were burnt by the other. Government control was soon limited to the major towns and heavily fortified posts; elsewhere it ceased to exist, and in some areas was replaced by a rudimentary Anya Nya administration.

The rapid deterioration in the south was reflected in a confusing evolution of political groupings both within and outside of the Sudan. In Khartoum the Southern Front, which had remained since the overthrow of Abboud a loosely-knit group of intellectuals with ties to SANU in exile, became in June 1965 an official political party under the presidency of Clement Mboro. The Front supported the south's right to decide its own future status as part of the Sudan or as an independent state, and was influential among southerners in Khartoum through its newspaper, *The Vigilant*. William Deng's SANU faction, which itself took on the trappings of a political party in 1965, remained committed to a federal solution. The influence of these parties was limited largely to southerners in Khartoum and in the government-held towns of the south. Neither could claim to speak for the southerners in exile or, more importantly, for the Anya Nya.

The southern political organizations outside of the Sudan continued to be weakened by internal rifts. The personal differences between Aggrey Jaden and Joseph Oduho, who led factions of SANU in exile, were briefly reconciled in December 1965 when the latter's newly-established Azanian Liberation Front was joined by Jaden's faction of SANU. Espousing complete independence for the south, the ALF failed both to win the support of the Anya Nya and to unify the leadership, which was becoming increasingly irrelevant without Anya Nya allegiance, of the exiles. The ALF should be seen, therefore, as an attempt by that leadership to coordinate the political activities of the exiles with the Anya Nya campaign. But the ALF was unable even to maintain the unity of its own executive. Aggrey Jaden was dismissed from his position as vice-president, and in August 1967 established the Southern Sudan Provisional Government. Thus the intensification of the struggle in the south after the accession of the Mahgoub government in June 1965 had two important results. Southerners were convinced that the north was intent on a military solution, which increased the sense of legitimacy and therefore the attraction of the Anya Nya. Secondly, the southern political leaders in exile, while still incapable of putting aside their personal differences and uniting the political and military arms of the struggle, nonetheless were hardened in their conviction to win independence for the south. Both of these developments detracted from the positions of the southern parties in Khartoum. The situation was further complicated by the deaths of two important southern leaders. In January 1967 Father Saturnino Lahure was killed near the Ugandan border, and in May 1968 William Deng, the president of SANU, was ambushed with six associates and killed, probably by a government patrol, in the Bahr al-Ghazal.

The theme of personal antagonism is evident as well in northern political developments during this period. Whereas Mahgoub, as prime minister, was the head of government, he was not the leader of the Umma. That position was held by Sadiq al-Mahdi, who at the time of the 1965 elections was too young to run for parliament. When he turned thirty the ambitions of the Oxford-educated heir to the leadership of the Mahdi's family clashed inevitably with those of the pompous but ineffective Mahgoub. Sadiq al-Mahdi's desire to assume the premiership met with the opposition of his uncle, the Imam al-Hadi, who on the death of Sayyid Siddiq in 1961 had taken up the religious leadership of the Ansar. The deepening rift in the Umma was deftly exploited by the party's old rival, Azhari. The NUP leader tested his strength *vis-à-vis* Mahgoub in a dispute over which of them should represent the Sudan at summit meetings. The constitutional implications of this question took second place to an unedifying and childish rivalry, and the frailty of the ruling coalition was revealed as the NUP members of the cabinet supported Azhari by resigning, only to rejoin the government when it was decided that Azhari would in future represent the Sudan at international conferences.

A more serious indication of the coalition's deeper attachment to traditional and personal politics than to the principles of democracy it had vaunted after the October revolution was its attitude towards the Communist Party. In November 1965 a speech in Omdurman by a Syrian communist in which Islam was ridiculed provoked demonstrations by the Muslim Brothers who demanded that the CP be banned. A resolution to this effect was passed by a huge majority in parliament, and on 24 November the constitution was amended to outlaw communism. In December the CP was summarily disbanded, its property confiscated, and its members in parliament unseated. Arrests of party officials followed. The matter was taken to the

Supreme Court, which eventually ruled the banning illegal, but its judgement was disregarded. Political expediency rather than popular demand was the reason for the government's action, a fact not lost on the public, especially after the resignation, in protest, of the Chief Justice, Babikr 'Awadallah. The communists responded with the simple device of establishing, in January 1967, the Socialist Party, the executive of which included leading communists.

Sadiq al-Mahdi's anomalous position was resolved after he reached the age of thirty and won a by-election for parliament. Whether or not it had been previously agreed with Mahgoub that this should precipitate the prime minister's replacement by Sadiq is unclear, but Mahgoub resisted demands that he step down. Despite the support of the Imam al-Hadi for Mahgoub, a motion of no-confidence in the prime minister was introduced on 25 July 1966. Mahgoub's fate was sealed when Azhari, perhaps still annoyed by his confrontation with Mahgoub, but more likely exploiting this opportunity to widen the rift in the Umma, threw the support of the NUP behind the motion, which carried by 126 votes to thirty. On 27 July Sadiq al-Mahdi became prime minister and a new cabinet was formed.

The brief premiership of Sadiq al-Mahdi, from July 1966 to May 1967, witnessed attempts at constructing a permanent constitution for the Sudan. The ability of parliament to act as a constituent assembly was obviously hampered so long as regular elections could not be held in the South. In March 1967 the government therefore went ahead with elections in thirty-six southern constituencies. The elections were boycotted by the Southern Front but contested by William Deng's faction of SANU. The volatile conditions obtaining in the region resulted in a small poll. The Umma emerged with fifteen seats, SANU with ten, and the NUP with five, while the remaining seats were won by the Unity and Liberal Parties and by independents. The government established a Constitutional Draft Committee, only seven of whose forty-two members were southerners, and SANU and the Front therefore refused to participate. Sadiq himself favoured an Islamic constitution, which perhaps his weakening position in the Umma demanded, but which could only undermine initial hopes that he would break with the bankrupt Southern policies of his predecessors.

On taking office Sadiq had attempted to abandon the sectarian basis of Sudanese politics which had been revived after the October

190

revolution. He advocated reforms in agrarian and social policy which were, however, unacceptable to his conservative uncle. Sadiq's apparent ability to attract popular support across traditional lines provoked an alliance in parliament between the Imam's supporters and Azhari's NUP. Thus in May 1967 Azhari, for the second time in less than a year, abandoned the parliamentary leader of his nominal coalition partner and brought down the government. The Umma was now effectively split, and a ramshackle coalition of the NUP, the Imam's wing of the Umma, and various other groupings was formed, with Mahgoub returning as prime minister. Sadiq and his faction of the Umma went into opposition. General elections were set for 1968, and Mahgoub was left to preside over what was, in effect, a caretaker government.

The interim period witnessed further political manoeuvres, orchestrated by Azhari. In December 1967 he merged the NUP with the PDP to form the Democratic Unionist Party (DUP). Even when faced with this formidable alliance, which returned the Khatmiyya to active politics, the Umma factions were unable to heal the rift in their leadership, and they approached the elections as rival parties vying for the traditional Umma support.

The 1968 elections were contested by a multiplicity of parties and front groups, most of which had no identifiable organizations or programmes. The graduates' constituency, the existence of which seemed a barometer of government orientation, was again abolished. The DUP emerged with 101 seats in the new parliament. The disastrous consequences of the Umma's internal split became evident as Sadiq's wing won thirty-six seats and the Imam's wing thirty. Sadiq himself and several of his leading supporters failed to win re-election. Six independent Umma members were returned, and SANU and the Southern Front won fifteen and ten seats respectively. The smaller parties and independents won a total of twenty seats. A coalition of the DUP and the Imam's wing of the Umma was formed, and Mahgoub retained the premiership. Azhari was re-elected president of the Supreme Council of State. Ten ministries in the new cabinet went to the DUP, five to the Imam's wing, and two to the Southern Front. Thus, while the coalition commanded a huge majority in parliament, its composition was nonetheless too diverse and mutually suspicious, and its leader, Mahgoub, was too weakened, to provide much hope of stable government.

The Sudan's foreign relations during the second parliamentary regime were dominated by Middle Eastern and African affairs. A pattern, which was to continue under the succeeding military regime, was established by which the Sudan, because of its geographical position, Afro-Arab population, and lack of ideological commitment, was increasingly to mediate in international disputes. The successful adoption of this role was complicated, however, by the continuing unrest in the southern Sudan and the government's attempts to quiet it. In a decade which witnessed the independence of most of Europe's remaining African possessions, the founding of the Organization of African Unity, and the establishment of a vocal Afro-Asian presence in the UN, the Sudan was continually embarrassed by the international repercussions of the southern crisis. Critics of the government, both within and outside of the Sudan, could not fail to notice the apparent contradiction of policy towards the south, on the one hand, and support for various African secessionist movements on the other. This support led inevitably to disputes with neighbouring states. Thus in 1966 the mediation of President Diori of Niger was needed to restore relations with Chad after troublesome border clashes. A similar dispute with Ethiopia was worsened by the passage of arms for the Anya Nya through that country, and by support in the Sudan for Eritrean secessionists. Relations with the Central African Republic and the Congo (Kinshasa), both of which sheltered large numbers of southern refugees, were likewise strained, and revolutionaries in the Congo were openly aided by the Sudan. At the same time, the government sought to effect solidarity with pan-African aims, and severed diplomatic relations with Britain in 1965 over the handling of the Rhodesian unilateral declaration of independence. These were restored in April 1966.

In Arab affairs the Sudan played a more positive part, largely owing to the interest in international relations generally taken by Mahgoub, both as foreign minister under the Transitional Government, and as prime minister. Relations with Egypt remained close. The Six Day War in 1967 resulted in strong Sudanese support of Egypt and the severance of relations with Britain and the US after Egypt charged those governments with actively supporting Israel. Relations with Britain were restored early in 1968, but were resumed with the US only in July 1972. Western support for Israel led to a new era of closer military and economic co-operation with the Soviet Union, which was to continue until the coup of 1971. The Sudan's position as honest broker in the Arab world was underscored by the convening of the Arab foreign ministers and heads of state in Khartoum in August 1967. The Sudan was also active in mediating in the dispute between Egypt and Saudi Arabia over the Yemen.

Mahgoub's preoccupation with external affairs and in the debilitating rifts between and within the political parties, especially his own, was reflected in an apparent inattention to the state of the Sudan's economy.[2] Although gross domestic product increased in the 1960s by some 44.6 per cent, and the agricultural sector's share of the GDP decreased from 47.7 per cent in 1965 to 35.6 per cent in 1969, agricultural production in 1969 contributed no less than 97.2 per cent of the country's export earnings. Thus, while the economy was diversifying, its reliance on agriculture, especially cotton, for foreign exchange actually increased. An Industrial Development Corporation was established in 1965 to manage public investment, and in 1967 the *Organization and Promotion of Industrial Investment Act* was designed to encourage private investment. In 1968 an Agricultural Reform Corporation was established to manage the private cotton schemes which from that year the government began to nationalize. The Sudan's balance of payments during the second parliamentary period showed a surplus only in 1969, and in no year did the value of exports exceed that of imports. While government revenue increased from £S73.7 million in 1964–5 to £S91.9 million in 1967–8, indebtedness increased alarmingly from £S3.9 million in 1965 to £S46 million in 1969. Reliance on indirect taxes, always contingent on world-wide and local fluctuations in demand, continued, with direct taxation accounting in 1967–8 for only 4.4 per cent of total government revenue.

Economic growth was prejudiced by the instability of successive coalition governments and the volatile nature of the trade-union movement. Following the October revolution a rapid development of unionism had occurred. The restraints imposed by the military regime were removed, only to be reimposed in inept fashion by its parliamentary successor. The imbalance of this development may be seen in reference to the number of new unions which appeared and the increase in union membership. In 1964 there were seventy-four unions with a total membership of 124,842. By 1968 there were 357 unions, but membership had risen to only 162,286. In that year some 263 unions had fewer than two hundred members each, while only one, the railway workers, had more than twenty-five thousand.

Concerted industrial action thus became more difficult, but damaging localized strikes, often with political overtones, increased. The government's inability to control labour disputes, like its maladroit handling of student unrest, was a symptom of an underlying political malaise.

The crisis of the second parliamentary regime was therefore not basically economic, but political. Strong action in Khartoum was necessary not simply to deal with day-to-day affairs, but to restore public confidence in the parliamentary system. But that confidence, had it existed even after the ousting of the Abboud regime, was gradually eroded by the continuing personal rivalries which, so it seemed, had dominated political life since independence. Each new manoeuvre therefore contributed to exasperation with the politicians and to contempt for parliamentary life itself. In February 1968 Sayyid 'Ali al-Mirghani who, with Sayyid 'Abd al-Rahman al-Mahdi had been a pillar of traditionalist politics, died at the age of eighty-eight. In November Mahgoub suffered a stroke and was absent from the country for a three months' convalescence. On 11 April 1969 the Umma split was finally healed and the factions merged, leading quickly to the deposition of the Mahgoub government. Mahgoub stayed on in a familiar caretaker role, while elections were planned for early in 1970. The revitalized Umma and the DUP entered into negotiations over the nature of a new constitution, and announced agreement in early May. This was by now irrelevant, however, for the discredited politicians had, as in 1958, allowed for too long the subversion of the parliamentary system to personal advantage. When the army returned to power at the end of May 1969 the second parliamentary regime was to have as few defenders as the first.

THE REGIME OF
JAAFAR NIMEIRI[1]

The composition of the officers' group which seized power in May 1969 bore only a superficial resemblance to that which overthrew the government in 1958. Yet the circumstances leading to the coups were similar. As in 1958, so in 1969, the prestige of the politicians and of parliamentary institutions had reached a low ebb, as they drifted from one crisis to another. The economy had suffered from mismanagement and neglect. The situation in the south showed no sign of improvement and was damaging the Sudan's foreign relations. Broad agreement between the Umma and al-Azhari on the establishment of a presidential system seemed destined, as had their agreement to form a coalition in 1958, only to prepare the way for another showdown. The 1969 coup was thus, in its origins, not simply a bid for power by disgruntled officers determined to undermine the system inherited from the co-domini, but a reaction to the collapse of that system under the weight of its own failures.

The coup was led by a 'Free Officers' movement within the army under the leadership of Colonel Jaafar Nimeiri, who had on two previous occasions, in 1957 and 1966, been suspected of plotting against the government. Swift and bloodless, the takeover provoked no immediate overt opposition. The provisional constitution, the five-man Supreme Council of State, the constituent assembly, the public service commission and the electoral commission were all dissolved, public meetings were banned, and newspapers temporarily closed down, to re-open soon afterwards under strict censorship. The political parties were outlawed and their property confiscated, while leading politicians, including al-Azhari and Mahgoub, were placed under arrest. Twenty-two senior army officers were retired, and Nimeiri himself was promoted to the rank of major-general. The country was renamed as the Democratic Republic of the Sudan. As in 1958, two institutions were established to conduct the government. A Revolutionary Command Council of ten, nine of whom were young army officers, was formed under

Nimeiri's presidency. The sole civilian member was the ex-chief justice, Babikr 'Awadallah, who was also named prime minister. A cabinet of twenty-three, responsible to the RCC, was announced on 26 May. Four of the RCC's members and at least eight of the cabinet ministers were communists or leftists. Several members of the 1964–5 Transitional Government, two southerners, and repre-sentatives of the intelligentsia and of business were included in the cabinet. A statement by the prime minister, that the new govern-ment would be 'leftist, socialist but not extremist or fanatic', was thus borne out in its composition. While the balance of power reposed in the RCC, and the strength of left-wing elements as measured by their prominence in the new establishment was soon to prove misleading, the 'May Revolution' nonetheless represented a real shift to the left and away from the traditional style of Sudanese politics, contingent as that was on sectarian and personal loyalties.

In the immediate aftermath of the coup, the relative strengths of Nimeiri and Awadallah, the officers and the civilians, and the communists and more moderate members of the government were all unclear. It was apparent, however, that the new government considered itself the successor not to the previous military regime of Abboud, but to the combined forces of junior officers and the Professionals' Front which had toppled Abboud's government in 1964. The fact that the Communist Party was, despite its strong representation in the government, not exempted from the order to disband all political parties was an indication of Nimeiri's essentially centrist position, and an omen of the struggle for control which was to dominate the first two years of the regime. The period witnessed the elimination of challenges from the right and the left, and ended in the consolidation of Nimeiri's power.

From the traditional political parties the new government had little to fear. With their leaders under house arrest or in jail, and their main weapon, an appeal for the defence of parliamentary democracy, blunted by their own transparent self-interest, the par-ties were powerless to mount organized resistance. On 25 August 1969 Isma'il al-Azhari died at the age of sixty-nine. The nationalist leader who had from the late 1930s fought for, and in 1956 presided over, the demise of British rule, had been forced at independence largely to abandon the hope of forging a secular government of the centre. This failure had been partly the effect, but more importantly a cause, of the unattractive role of power-broker he assumed during

the two parliamentary periods. At his death the Sudanese generously recalled his earlier role. The real threat to the new regime came
in any case not from the former NUP, some of whose members were
amenable to the pronounced aims of the government, but from the
Mahdists. Discussions with Sadiq al-Mahdi, to win the support of
his faction of the Umma, broke down over his objection to communists in the government, and he was arrested on 6 June. The
Imam's wing of the Umma, based on the Ansar, thus remained the
only serious threat to the government from the ranks of the right.
The Imam al-Hadi made no attempt even to appear conciliatory,
but withdrew with his lieutenants to Aba Island, the cradle of
Mahdism and stronghold of his family.

In March 1970 relations between the Ansar leader and the government reached a climax. Riots in Omdurman, resulting in heavy
loss of life, were followed by a direct test of strength. Nimeiri
embarked on a provocative journey up the White Nile, ignoring the
Imam's warnings that a visit would be dangerous and that, in any
case, Aba Island would be closed to him. Violent clashes accompanied the general's tour. On 27 March the government launched an
air attack on Aba, which was followed by the invasion of the island
by government troops. Resistance, though hopeless, was fierce, and
subsequent estimates of fatalities among the Ansar were as high as
12,000. The Imam al-Hadi, grandson of the Mahdi, was himself
killed, during an apparent attempt to escape across the Ethiopian
border. Aba was occupied, and the extensive holdings of the
Mahdi's family were confiscated. On 3 April Sadiq al-Mahdi went
into exile. This assertion of the regime's authority removed, at least
for the foreseeable future, the danger of organized Ansar resistance, and served as a warning to disestablished political parties
generally. But the violent nature of the assertion, unparalleled in
the history of the independent Sudan, ensured the permanent disaffection of a large and powerful element of the population.

While the removal of the threat posed by the Ansar may have
seemed to consolidate Nimeiri's power over a perceptibly leftist
government, it in fact paved the way for a confrontation with the left
as violent as the Aba incident. Relations between Nimeiri and the
communists in the 1969–71 period were complex, confused by the
undetermined direction of the regime, the uncertain intentions of
the communists, and the nature of their uneasy alliance to crush the
right-wing opposition. Directly after the 1969 coup it seemed that

the new government would follow a political and economic course closely patterned on that of the communists. The regime adopted the general policy of the CP to extend relations with the socialist and Arab states (despite the hostility this was bound to engender in the south), to form a one-party system consolidating 'progressive' forces, and to develop national capital. Events were soon to show that this tendency of the RCC towards communist positions was based on the officers' appreciation, derived from the fate of the Transitional Government of 1965, of their broad but shallow support, which seemed to necessitate co-operation, if not identification, with the communists.

Although preoccupied between June 1969 and March 1970 with the impending showdown with the Ansar, Nimeiri nevertheless moved gradually to dilute communist influence within the government. Relations deteriorated sharply from mid-1970. In November three members of the RCC were dismissed, the officer corps was purged, and leading communist civilians were arrested. In early 1971 Nimeiri publicly accused the communists of subversion and called upon the people to 'destroy the Communist movement'. Thus by February 1971 Nimeiri felt his position strong enough to abandon his nominal allies in a calculated appeal to an underlying Sudanese antipathy to communism. In this he acted precipitately, for he had not yet conciliated either the extreme right or the important pro-Egyptian element which under the disillusioned 'Awadallah was nursing its wounds. The result of this attempt to occupy an independent middle ground exposed his position and brought Nimeiri's regime to the edge of disaster in July 1971.

On 19 July a coup was staged by Major Hashim al-'Ata', in concert with fellow officers deposed from the RCC in the previous November. Nimeiri was imprisoned, and a 'democratic' system was proclaimed, involving an 'industrial and agricultural revolution'. A new RCC was formed, and pro-communist demonstrations were staged in Khartoum. But the new revolutionary government underestimated the response of the Sudanese to an openly communist regime and the reaction of Egypt and Libya to the presence of such a regime on their borders. The Libyan leader, Colonel Gaddafi, ordered a British airliner bound for Khartoum to land in Libya, and two leading members of the new regime to be arrested. President Sadat ordered Egyptian troops stationed south of Khartoum to resist the coup. A large pro-Nimeiri force moved on the capital from

Shendi. In the meantime Nimeiri had escaped from detention and rallied forces loyal to him, and the revolt was easily crushed. Hashim al-'Ata' and his colleagues were summarily executed. Al-Shafi' Ahmad al-Shaykh, the veteran labour leader; 'Abd al-Khaliq Mahjub, the leader of the communist party; and Joseph Garang, the leading southern communist, were hanged, despite their resolute denial of involvement in the coup and in defiance of international pleas for clemency.[2] A massive purge of leftists within the army and the government was initiated, and relations with the Eastern Bloc, accused by Nimeiri of complicity, deteriorated rapidly.

The abortive coup had important long-term effects on the regime. The suppression of the Ansar and the communists undoubtedly increased Nimeiri's personal popularity, but left the regime without the strong support of any major political or sectarian grouping. Nimeiri therefore acted quickly, through changes in domestic and foreign policies, to strengthen the base of his political support and to shore up his personal position by means of a referendum on the presidency. This began on 15 September and resulted in a 98.6 per cent affirmative vote for Nimeiri, who was duly sworn into office for a six-year term as president. A new cabinet was announced, with Nimeiri as prime minister. Steps were taken to speed the establishment and organization of the Sudan Socialist Union.

An important consequence of the July 1971 coup was the recognition by Nimeiri that foreign policy should be more closely related to, and indeed contingent upon, domestic political considerations. Upon assuming power in 1969 the regime had asserted the Sudan's support for national liberation movements in Africa, closer ties with Eastern Europe and a total commitment to the Arab cause in the struggle with Israel. One of the regime's first acts was to recognize the government of East Germany, and Nimeiri embarked on tours of Eastern Europe, China, and North Korea in 1970. Trade with the Eastern Bloc increased greatly, and the Sudan looked to Moscow for the supply of arms and for economic assistance. The Sudan took a greater interest in Arab affairs, spurred by Nimeiri's attachment to views of Arab Socialism identified with those of President Nasser and Colonel Gaddafi. In December 1969 Libya, Egypt and the Sudan agreed in the Tripoli Charter to co-ordinate their foreign policies, a scheme that developed into a Federation of Arab Republics which, despite domestic opposition and his own misgivings,

Nimeiri publicly supported. Relations with the West deteriorated in the 1969–71 period, owing to continued American support for Israel, Israeli support for southern secessionists, and the government's nationalization, under unacceptable terms of compensation, of foreign, mainly British, banks and companies.

The regime's closer ties with the Arab socialist states, tending towards at least theoretical identity of foreign policies and some form of political union, were predictably deprecated in the South, and seemed yet another justification for mistrust of whatever government held power in Khartoum. The 1969 coup had raised hopes, as had previous changes in government, that a peaceful solution could be found for the 'southern problem'. A number of measures were announced to induce southern co-operation, but rhetoric outpaced action and the appearance of movement could not mask the failure of the regime to implement its announced aims, a failure blamed unconvincingly, after the 1971 coup, on the communist Joseph Garang. Nimeiri responded to continuing Anya Nya activity by recourse to a policy of suppression, which was, however, no more effective in 1969–70 than it had been under previous regimes.

Meanwhile the personal and political disputes which had long divided the southern leadership began to show signs of settlement. We have seen that in 1967 a Southern Sudan Provisional Government had been established by Aggrey Jaden. Like previous attempts to place the Anya Nya under a unified political command, this failed. In 1969 the SSPG was superseded by the Nile Provisional Government under the presidency of Gordon Mayen, a former leader of the Southern Front in Khartoum, while General Emedio Taffeng established an organization called the Anyidi State Government, which encompassed all the factions except the NPG. Under his leadership the war was stepped up, just as the Nimeiri regime was attempting to devise a peace formula. While the sophistication of the Anya Nya's campaign reached an unprecedented level under Taffeng, and attracted increasing international attention and support, the problem of maintaining a unified command arose yet again. In July 1970 Colonel Joseph Lagu, commanding the Anya Nya in Eastern Equatoria, challenged Taffeng's authority. The NPG was disbanded, and leadership of the Anya Nya was concentrated, under Lagu, in a Southern Sudan Liberation Movement. By 1971 it was clear that the renewed attempts of the government to reach a military solution were failing in the face of the Anya

Nya's growing strength, and the effective combination of the political and military wings of the movement.

The history of the conflict in the south had since its outbreak been partly contingent on the course of national politics in Khartoum. The first parliamentary regime and its military successor, while paying lip-service to the idea of some degree of southern autonomy, had never undergone the essential change of mind required to put that idea into effect. They believed not only in the maintenance of territorial integrity, but also that the future of the Sudan was as part of the Muslim Middle East, and in all that this implied. Under the Transitional Government some movement appeared likely, but momentum was lost as the old parties returned to power. Again, during the brief premiership of Sadiq al-Mahdi it had seemed that a political solution was possible, but Sadiq's weakness within his own party and the political in-fighting that characterized the second parliamentary regime had proved insurmountable. In its first two years the Nimeiri regime had followed the same haphazard course as its predecessors. It was only after the July coup that President Nimeiri, strengthened by renewed popularity but lacking the active collaboration of any major political, sectarian, or regional grouping, turned away from the policies of the past. At the same time it was appreciated that the meagre resources of the Sudan were expended pointlessly in a war which neither side seemed capable of winning in the field. The essential change when it came was therefore not merely political but moral and intellectual, a recognition that Khartoum had finally to come to terms with the fact that the Sudan was a country whose future depended upon a peaceful process of nation-building. At the same time Joseph Lagu, having finally united the political and military leadership of southern resistance, approached the regime, from a position of strength, to seek new negotiations.

In July 1971 Nimeiri appointed Abel Alier to replace Joseph Garang as minister for southern affairs. Secret meetings with southern leaders in exile led to a conference in Addis Ababa in February 1972. An agreement between representatives of the SSLM and the government was reached on the 27th. On 3 March the Addis Ababa accord became the *Regional Self-Government Act for the Southern Provinces*, and on the 12th a ceasefire was declared in the south.

The Addis Ababa agreement called for the grouping of the three southern provinces into a self-governing Southern Region with a

People's Regional Assembly and High Executive Council or cabinet. The central government would devolve upon the assembly powers over local government, education, public health, mineral and natural resources, control of the police forces, and other powers. Reserved to the sovereign national government were control of defence, foreign affairs, currency, inter-regional communications, and the broad functions of economic, social, and educational planning. The president of the republic would appoint a president (or chairman) of the High Executive Council and, in consultation with that official, the other members of the council. The regional government would derive revenues from various sources, including a Special Development Budget for the region. Juba was designated as the regional capital. The body of the Addis Ababa agreement was vague as to specifics, relying rather on the establishment and strengthening as time went on of a degree of mutual trust. Several annexes to the agreement dealt with the enshrinement of personal liberties in a future constitution, revenue, the repatriation and resettlement of refugees and, most importantly, arrangements for a ceasefire. Indeed, it was probably these last which provided the guarantee to the south that the agreement itself would be honoured. A joint commission of the government and the SSLM and representatives of other governments and international organizations would supervise implementation of the ceasefire. An important provision was that the People's Armed Forces in the south would 'consist of a national force called the Southern Command composed of 12,000 officers and men of whom 6,000 shall be citizens of the Region and the other 6,000 from outside the Region'. A gradual integration of forces was to occur under the auspices of a Joint Military Commission of three senior officers from each side. Ratification and implementation of the agreement occurred on 27 March 1972. Abel Alier was later named president of the High Executive Council, and the first Regional Assembly of sixty members was elected in November 1973.

The same degree of compromise needed to reach the Addis Ababa agreement would be necessary to establish a lasting peace between the regions. While the northern politicians were able to ensure the territorial integrity of the Sudan and to exemplify to the rest of Africa a new spirit in dealing with minorities, the south had achieved a degree of autonomy considered adequate to preserve its identity. But the conclusion of hostilities was only a first if essential step in reconciliation. The south had been ravaged, its population uprooted, its vulnerable economy all but destroyed. While the Addis Ababa agreement marked an important stage in relations between Khartoum and the south, that it could not alone ensure peace and unity was soon evident.

The new southern regional government was from the start beset by familiar problems of ethnic and personal rivalries. The integration of Anya Nya forces into the national army was inevitably fraught with danger, and was implemented remarkably well, owing in part to the continuing efforts of Joseph Lagu. Mutinous incidents at Wau and Akobo in 1976 and Juba in 1977 were exceptional. Political development was less harmonious. The government of Abel Alier gradually lost popular support as the social and economic benefits expected from the peace settlement were slow to materialize, corruption was widely perceived, and an evident Dinka dominance resented. Elections in 1978 led to Alier's resignation as president of the HEC and brought into the Regional Assembly many of his most vociferous opponents, including Joseph Oduho, Benjamin Bol and Clement Mboro. Lagu became president of the HEC, with Samuel Aru Bol as vice-president. This set the stage for a power-struggle in which Lagu, to retain his position, was forced to make important concessions to the allies of the ousted Alier. Corruption scandals further weakened the regime, and in February 1980 Nimeiri stepped in, dissolving the Regional Assembly and dismissing Lagu. Elections were held in April, and following a showdown between Alier and Aru Bol, Alier regained the presidency of the HEC.

In the early 1980s the inability or unwillingness of southern politicians to put regional interests above their own presented an opening for renewed intervention from Khartoum. President Nimeiri's proposal to 'redivide' the south into three separate 'regions' was warmly supported by Lagu and various Equatorians, but was rejected by the Regional Assembly in March 1981. Proponents of the idea pressed on, however, and in October Nimeiri dissolved the assembly, dismissed Alier, and appointed an officer, Gismalla Abdalla Rassas, to head an interim government while a referendum on the issue was prepared. Opponents of division were jailed, but in February 1982 Nimeiri cancelled the referendum, calling instead for new elections. These resulted in no clear majority, and after a series of elaborate and cynical manoeuvres the divisionists emerged triumphant and Joseph James Tombura, an Azande, was elected president of the HEC. In June 1983 Nimeiri unilaterally decreed the division of the south into three regions corresponding to the old southern provinces.

The 'redivision' issue was only one of several that divided southerners, tainted southern politics, and rekindled hostility to the central government. Some of the old Anya Nya fighters had never been reconciled to the Addis Ababa agreement which, in any case, was repeatedly ignored and openly contravened. Dissatisfaction grew in inverse proportion to the pace of economic development, which never approached the level promised. The most extensive development projects, especially the construction of the Jonglei Canal and the siting of an oil refinery in Kosti rather than in the south, where oil had been discovered, seemed to many to be of no benefit to the region. In higher education, for example, the new university at Juba did little to improve the lot of southerners: there were but four among the 158 students admitted to the scientific and technical faculties in 1984. In 1972 thirty-five of the 1641 places at the University of Khartoum went to southerners; in 1984 only nine of 1637. In the period 1972–77, only 20 per cent of the money allotted to the south under Special Development Budgets was actually spent. Economic stagnation was ironically highlighted by the rapid growth of a new bureaucracy, by corruption, inefficiency, and the local effects of an unfolding national economic crisis. Southerners (and others) watched with suspicion and dismay as President Nimeiri's early commitment to secularism gave way, especially after the 1977 'reconciliation' with the religious right, and that commitment was openly abandoned in September 1983 when the Shari'a was declared applicable to all Sudanese.

The reappearance of armed resistance to the regime in the south therefore resulted not only from the central government's disregard of the Addis Ababa agreement but also from its thinly-veiled recourse to the failed policies of previous regimes. The first such resistance, undertaken by a tribally-based separatist group calling itself Anya Nya II, was soon superseded by the far more powerful and sophisticated Sudan People's Liberation Movement, established in the summer of 1983 after the mutiny of an army battalion at Bor. Led by Colonel John Garang, the unusually highly disciplined forces of its military arm, the SPLA, won a rapid series of victories against the demoralized and poorly equipped government forces in the south, and by 1986 had taken control of most of the region. The SPLA received arms and other support from Ethiopia and, until the overthrow of Nimeiri in 1985, from Libya, but most of its war material was obtained from raids on, and defections from, government forces. The Nimeiri regime's slow initial response to the emergence of this powerful opposition was followed by an inept carrot-and-stick approach which, however, lacked credibility in the light of history. Avowedly anti-separatist, but revolutionary and leftist, the SPLM/SPLA insisted on the removal of Nimeiri himself, and to this end held secret talks with various Northern-based opposition groups.

The Addis Ababa agreement in 1972 may be seen in retrospect as an essential step in the Nimeiri regime's attempt to broaden its base of support. The maintenance of the country's political unity and the cessation of hostilities allowed the promulgation of a permanent constitution, without which successive governments had laboured since independence. This constitution formalized reforms which had already been undertaken, and aimed at legitimizing and extending a new and highly structured relationship between politics and administration.

One of the most ambitious and potentially significant programmes of the Nimeiri era was the reform of local and provincial administration. The move away from Indirect Rule by the British in the 1930s and subsequent modifications of the system of local government had nevertheless left considerable authority in the hands of tribal leaders in rural areas. These had proven a bulwark of conservatism, especially in the west where the chief Umma strength lay. The 1965 Transitional Government placed on record its intention to abolish 'native administration' and to entrust authority to responsible elected officials. Difficulties had arisen, and the system remained as before. The Nimeiri regime was determined to remove power once and for all from the shaykhs, and to integrate local administration into a new pyramidal structure closely linked with the Sudan Socialist Union. Village, rural, district and provincial councils were established. Geographical rather than tribal considerations determined local council boundaries, and while powers were devolved from the central government, Khartoum appointed provincial council chairmen and otherwise maintained control; councils had little revenue, and many had no obvious function. Mainly advisory, they further bureaucratized a system already top-heavy and inefficient. Thus while on the one hand the principle was established of divorcing traditional authority from administrative responsibility, the principle of separating politics from administration was abandoned.[3] At the pinnacle of the new administrative system was the People's Assembly in Omdurman.

Further steps towards decentralization ensued. The establishment of a semi-autonomous Southern Region involved a degree of devolution that remained controversial and was unmatched by the further 'regionalization' of the country in 1980. Then, five new regional administrations were established, and certain powers of the central government were transferred to them. This constituted a recognition of the ethnic and cultural diversity of the country, but was also an expensive innovation susceptible to abuse and hamstrung by the political machinations of the regime. 'Regionalization' added new layers of bureaucracy without providing the resources of trained staff and money these would need to function. Although promised wide powers, the new regional administrators and assemblies all served at the pleasure of the president and therefore provided the appearance but not the reality of local autonomy.

A constituent assembly elected in October 1972 drafted a constitution that was promulgated in May 1973. A lengthy document of some 225 articles, it established a presidential system concentrating great authority in the head of state. He was to be elected by 'plebiscite' to a six-year term, could rule by decree, and was invested with the right to declare a state of emergency under which he would assume vague and sweeping powers, including the right to suspend temporarily the constitution. The judiciary was made directly responsible to the president. The thorny question of whether the state should be 'Islamic' or not was sidestepped by the provision that while 'the society should be guided by Islam', the state should 'endeavour to express' the values not only of Islam but of Christianity.

The 1973 constitution proclaimed the Sudan Socialist Union as 'the sole political organization' in the Sudan. Officially inaugurated by Nimeiri in January 1972, the SSU was organized along lines both parallel to, and intersecting, those of the new administrative system, with local, district and provincial establishments. Real power, however, was vested in a Political Bureau at the centre which was appointed by Nimeiri as chairman of the SSU. Despite periodic alterations of its nominal functions and scope, the SSU remained until its liquidation in 1985 essentially a prop for Nimeiri's personal control and a vehicle for distributing patronage. It developed an enormous bureaucracy and myriad formal responsibilities, but was never a real political party. Similarly the People's Assembly, while occasionally showing flashes of independence and certainly consti- tuting a safety-valve for the expression of dissent, was, however, largely a rubber-stamp for the wishes of the president. The old parties, officially defunct, retained a shadowy existence, and prom- inent ex-members formed cores of opposition or collaboration that at least had to be taken into account by the regime. But neither the SSU nor the Assembly ever threatened Nimeiri's position of domi- nance.

The numerous coup attempts that punctuated the Nimeiri years serve to illustrate both the weakness of the opposition and the insecurity of the regime. The most serious plot occurred in 1976, when Sadiq al-Mahdi, in Britain, master-minded a coup attempt with Libyan support. This was suppressed after several days of bloody street-fighting in the capital. Over one hundred executions took place, and Sadiq and Sharif Hussayn al-Hindi, a former NUP finance minister who with other leaders of defunct political parties had established a National Front in exile, were tried *in absentia* and sentenced to death.

Although Nimeiri appeared to emerge from this violent con- frontation with renewed strength, both domestic and international politics required a reorientation of the regime and a settlement with the National Front. The opposition's surprising strength within the country, and its support in Libya and Ethiopia, promised con- tinuing instability and consequent disruption of the government's plans for foreign-financed economic development. For its part, the National Front had to recognize the durability of the regime and its likely survival as long as it retained the powerful support of the army and of Egypt, the Umma's historic enemy. Further, while basic differences continued to divide the Front and the regime, these were not of an immutable ideological character; since 1971 Nimeiri had jettisoned much of the revolutionary fervour which had so alarmed the religious right. Thus in late 1976 mediation between Nimeiri and Sadiq al-Mahdi was undertaken, and the two met secretly at Port Sudan in July 1977. Agreement was reached on certain reforms, and an amnesty was declared. Sadiq returned from exile in September. Reconciliation was incomplete, however, as Sharif al-Hindi and others continued to demand more fundamental measures of reform. The return of Sadiq al-Mahdi nevertheless greatly vitiated the strength and prestige of the opposition in exile, while the vaunted 'process' of National Reconciliation benefited the regime more than it did its erstwhile opponents.

In elections to the People's Assembly in February 1978, candidates associated with the old Umma, DUP, and Muslim Brothers won eighty of the 304 seats, while 'independents' occupied another sixty. Sadiq al-Mahdi, Hasan al-Turabi, and other former opponents were appointed to the Political Bureau of the SSU. Sadiq resigned after Nimeiri's outspoken support for the Camp David accords later in the year, but in 1979, as the regime tempered that support, relations warmed again. In 1980 the Ansar boycotted the Assembly elections and, after further defeats in the now seemingly endless reconciliation process, Sadiq al-Mahdi declared the rapprochement a failure in 1982. His arrest and imprisonment in 1983 ironically clarified his opposition and helped to restore his prestige, while at the same time the increasingly close identification of the Muslim Brothers with the regime did much to dilute their appeals to principle.

Domestic politics after 1976 thus consisted of almost constant manoeuvring, tentative and temporary alliances, cabinet reshuffles, and highly publicized new beginnings, all orchestrated by President Nimeiri who, against the background of theoretical 'reconciliation', stayed at least one step ahead of his opponents. Having failed to bring down the regime by force, they proved powerless to achieve basic reforms from within. Obviously opposed to the structure and leadership of the government, they yet found it impossible to break completely with it. The result was Nimeiri's continued personal dominance of a regime which, however, by the early 1980s, had clearly lost popular support.

Essential to the strategy of neutralizing the opposition was Nimeiri's increasing attention to the role of Islam in the Sudan's political and economic life, which deprived the old parties of that argument against him which was most likely to attract mass support. Although initially this commitment was vaguely phrased and resulted in no fundamental changes of policy, from the late 1970s a more substantive approach was adopted. The determination to bring Sudanese law into conformity with the precepts of Islam was underscored by the appointment of Hasan al-Turabi as attorney general, and more dramatically, by the comprehensive assertion of the Shari'a in 1983. While this assured the support of the powerful Muslim Brothers, it further alienated secularists, southerners, and those Muslims, notably the Republican Brothers but also many others, to whom Nimeiri's version of the Shari'a was unpalatable. Nimeiri's motives for turning towards Islam were deeply suspect, and his open association with minor *fakis* and obscure fanatics tainted the policy and the regime.

The decade of the 1970s witnessed a gradual and fairly constant shift in Sudanese foreign relations, as always closely related to domestic political developments. Following the 1971 coup attempt, relations with the Socialist Bloc declined, while those with western Europe, America, China, and most of the Arab states were strengthened. Diplomatic relations with the United States were resumed in 1972, but continued to be complicated by the Arab–Israeli dispute. In March 1973 the United States ambassador was among three diplomats killed by Palestinians in Khartoum, and Nimeiri's decision to hand over the convicted murderers to the PLO necessarily strained relations with the United States. The perceived threat of Soviet-backed regimes in Ethiopia and Libya, the increasing dependence of the Sudan on western and especially American aid, and Nimeiri's apparent belief in the domestic value of close American support, produced strong bilateral relations that lasted until the end of the regime. Relations with Egypt were similarly close, although these too were occasionally strained. A plan for 'economic and political integration' with Egypt was announced in February 1974, and in 1977 a mutual defence pact was signed. The Nimeiri regime stood out as a supporter of President Sadat's peace treaty with Israel. In October 1982 Egypt and the Sudan signed an Integration Charter establishing various unified institutions and a Higher Council with its own budget. This was thus the furthest step yet taken towards the old Egyptian ideal of the Unity of the Nile Valley, and was predictably deprecated by the Ansar, southerners, and others, who saw the Charter as proof of the Sudan's subservience to Egypt and the United States. But as relations with Libya and Ethiopia were soured by the civil war in Chad, Sudanese support for Eritrean separatists, and Ethiopian assistance to the SPLM/SPLA, this alignment became a central feature of Nimeiri's policy.

No dramatic shift in foreign relations occurred during the final years of the regime. Indeed, the economic and political crises besetting the country restricted its room for manoeuvre on the regional and international stages. Arms and aid from the United States, American influence with the international agencies, and the continuing support of Egypt were increasingly seen as props for an unpopular regime. The disclosure in 1985 that the government had collaborated in transporting Falashas (Ethiopian Jews) to Israel produced deep embarrassment in a country long publicly committed to the Palestinian cause, and seemed damning proof of deference to American wishes. Despite protestations of broad mutual concerns, relations with the United States came to be associated with Nimeiri personally, to the detriment of both American and Sudanese interests.

The Sudanese economy seemed to alternate after the 1969 revolution between periods of great optimism characterized by extravagant predictions and the launching of ambitious development projects, and periods of near bankruptcy, when foreign credit alone was able to sustain the country. This inconsistency was caused partly by factors beyond the Sudan's control: fluctuations in world market prices, slumps in demand for Sudan's exports, and the exaggerated local effects of the world recession and inflation. Problems were caused also by unbalanced investment policies, mismanagement, investors' uncertainties, and the difficulties of long-range planning when investment capital was closely tied to export performance. In the later years of the Nimeiri regime corruption was an increasing problem which, becoming rampant, had deleterious effects on the economy, while the announced implementation of the Shari'a in 1983 disrupted an already confused situation. By the mid-1980s an enormous foreign debt, inflation, shortages, devaluation and, ultimately, famine, combined to bring the Sudan to a crisis of unprecedented proportions which, in part, led to the downfall of Nimeiri.

The 1971 coup attempt was a turning point in economic policy as it was in domestic political and foreign affairs. Prior to that the regime had instituted a sweeping nationalization programme, involving both foreign-based and Sudanese companies, and the banking and insurance industries. Some of these expropriations were reversed in early 1973. Bilateral trading arrangements with socialist states, especially with Eastern Europe, expanded rapidly, and foreign assistance came predominantly from the same sources. A Five

Year Industrial Development Plan was introduced in 1970, and was later extended to seven years. After the failed coup of 1971 and the Addis Ababa agreement of 1972 the Sudan turned increasingly, for economic assistance and partnerships, to the West and to neighbouring Arab states. Emphasis shifted from state intervention to a more balanced co-operation between the government and its agencies on the one hand, and foreign companies and governments and the international agencies on the other. While efforts were made to increase the Sudan's manufacturing capacity, especially in textiles and other agriculturally-based industries, the government recognized that prosperity would depend, as in the past, on the success of agriculture. It was thus doubly unfortunate, then, that ambitious schemes for rapid development came at a time of world recession and trade dislocation. While these were beyond the government's control, its strategy for dealing with them was not. Two fundamental errors proved costly: concentration on new schemes at the expense of those already in operation, and the financing of huge, long-term projects without the financial resources to meet their short-term costs. Both of these errors were compounded by the huge increases in the price of oil in the 1970s, leaving the Sudan severely exposed.

Cotton production may serve as an example of the general problem. As always, the country continued to depend on cotton as its major cash crop. A boom in world prices in 1973 was mismanaged by the government's marketing agencies, with disastrous results for its revenues and foreign reserves. After 1974, a new emphasis on diversifying agricultural exports led to a reduction in cotton production, which had halved by the early 1980s. The Gezira Scheme itself was threatened by falling yields, rising costs and mismanagement, and in 1980 a renovation programme was undertaken with the assistance of the World Bank.

In the mid-1970s the realization that the country's vast and largely untapped reserves of cultivable land are a major asset led to a number of ambitious proposals designed to make the Sudan the 'breadbasket' of the Middle East. In 1976 only seventeen million of an estimated two hundred million acres of cultivable land were under the plough. In 1973 the government and the Arab Fund for Economic and Social Development announced a joint twenty-five-year Basic Programme for Agricultural Development in the Sudan, calling for an investment of some six billion dollars during the first ten years. A large number of projects were set in motion, but inattention to existing works, poor maintenance, shortages and other problems led to a decline in agricultural production, even as the cropped area was expanded by four million acres.

The tradition of huge development projects, begun with the Gezira Scheme and involving similar promises and risks, continued, with mixed results. Three innovative projects that have attracted special attention are the Rahad Scheme to cultivate cotton, ground-nuts and other crops on 300,000 acres of irrigated land; the Kenana sugar project, designed to satisfy the enormous Sudanese demand and to supply the Middle East market; and the Jonglei Canal scheme in the south, a plan to by-pass the Sudd, where much water is lost to evaporation, and thereby increase the Nile flow to the North and Egypt. The Jonglei project fell victim to the civil war (as did oil exploration), and construction has halted. The Rahad and Kenana schemes have been completed. At Kenana construction delays, cost overruns, and mismanagement have meant that although imports of sugar have been drastically reduced, sugar costs more to produce than to import. Sugar production generally has been hindered by poor infrastructure, shortages of spare parts and foreign currency, and the weak performance of neglected older schemes, problems common to the agricultural sector as a whole. By the end of the 1970s, the dream of the Sudan as breadbasket of the Middle East was over, and in subsequent years was replaced by the nightmare of drought and famine.

By the early 1980s the government had largely lost control of economic policy, and lacked the will to take strong recovery measures. Weak world prices for the Sudan's dwindling exports, shortages that led to inflation, black marketeering, and the crippling of production, and mismanagement and corruption on unprecedented levels, required drastic action. This was largely resisted for political reasons, but in May 1979 the government agreed to the International Monetary Fund's terms for continued support, which included cuts in public expenditure, the reduction or elimination of subsidies, and greater emphasis on exports, a programme blamed for the urban riots that erupted in August. Yet in 1980–81 an explosion in the value of imports coincided with an actual decline in exports. With the country's external debt topping $3 billion, the World Bank halted the release of aid funds, and the IMF made payment of emergency loans dependent upon the adoption of strict measures.

In November 1981 Nimeiri therefore announced a recovery programme that included yet another devaluation of the currency, increased taxes on imports, and the ending of subsidies on basic
foodstuffs, measures that temporarily satisfied foreign creditors but
fell mainly on the poor.

The expectation of export-led recovery went unfulfilled. De-
valuations increased the price of imports and thus their cost to
farmers, while shortages, transport difficulties and a lack of credit
hindered agricultural production. The value of imports continued
to rise, and rampant black-marketeering resulted. Reduced exports
led to a shortage of foreign exchange and thus reduced supplies of
oil and other requirements for agriculture. The prospects for controlling corruption were poor when high officials themselves were
its chief sponsors. When in September 1982 it had become clear that
the government could not meet its obligations, which indeed were
far higher than had been revealed, the IMF cancelled a previously
arranged 'standby credit'.

By 1984–85 the Sudan's economic problems had apparently become insoluble. Repeated rescue attempts collapsed or were unen-
forced. Foreign debts, variously estimated, but of at least $9 billion,
were in arrears. The imposition of the Shari'a in 1983 was severely
disruptive of an already disastrous situation: the replacement of
income and other taxes with *zakat* resulted in a collapse of revenue,
while the uncertain implications for business of the new laws frightened off investors and exasperated foreign governments and aid
organizations. The desperation of the regime was evident in October 1984 when Nimeiri signed away half of the country's mineral
resources and unassigned oil rights to a Saudi businessman. In
February and March 1985 another devaluation and abolition of
subsidies were decreed under pressure from the IMF. The riots that
followed form part of the drama of Nimeiri's downfall.

The collapse of the economy resulted in untold suffering. When
in 1983 hundreds of thousands of refugees entered the country from
Ethiopia, a further strain was placed on the Sudan's resources. The
drought that had forced their migration soon took its toll in the
Sudan. Unwilling to publicize the failure of the regime to feed
the people, Nimeiri continued until the end to deny or minimize the
famine that drought and government incompetence had brought.
Relief efforts were too little and too late, and were finally all but
abdicated to foreign agencies. On the outskirts of Omdurman a

huge refugee camp sprang up, matched in urban centres in the west, where the disaster was greatest. International efforts, which were dilatory and sometimes poorly conceived, were stymied by the ruined state of the railways and the inadequacy of vehicles. Estimates of the number of deaths from starvation and the effects of malnutrition vary greatly, but a figure of 500,000 may be cautiously advanced. The effects of drought were exacerbated in the south, where relief efforts became embroiled in the war between the SPLA and the government.

The neglect of established businesses in favour of new schemes; the provision of subsidized grain to the urban masses, to the detriment of the Sudan's producers; the decline of the Sudan Railways, once a proud and famous service, into virtual collapse; the bloated inefficiency of the national airline, and chaotic bottlenecks at Port Sudan; a decline in educational standards but a chronic shortage of white-collar employment; a huge elaboration of the 'black' economy; these and other developments contributed to and were symptomatic of the improvisational character of economic policy during the Nimeiri years. A disturbing and careless dependence on foreign aid, with its attendant demands on foreign policy and its predictable accompaniments of inefficiency and corruption, was bought at a high price in national confidence and purpose. The exodus of skilled workers, not only professionals but drivers, mechanics, and teachers, was mitigated only by their remittances, on which the country became dangerously reliant. Class differences developed rapidly; in the Khartoum suburbs the stunning mansions of the newly rich, financed through foreign earnings, corruption, or patronage, rose in their hundreds amid the squalor of the thousands of poor who annually migrated from the countryside. The living standards of the urban middle class, the mainstay of each regime since independence and before, declined, or were maintained only through the remittances of relatives abroad.

The deterioration of the economic and political life of the country was reflected in the decay or collapse of institutions. The education system suffered from political interference and a lack of funds. The quality and distribution of medical care declined, as resources were increasingly channelled into private clinics for the urban middle class. The press, radio and television became mere mouthpieces for the regime. Trade unions and professional associations were hamstrung, superseded by hollow official organs, or ignored, their leaders either publicly espousing the official line or subjecting themselves to periodic arrest and imprisonment without trial. Government ministries and departments proliferated, but were often façades for political patronage and were immobilized by lack of finance and direction. Political appointees to meaningless posts devalued government service. The law was disregarded and courts were reduced to mere enforcers of the president's wishes. Islam itself was mocked as Nimeiri assumed the title of Imam and described as Islamic a state and system that were in collapse. Apathy and cynicism resulted, and the conviction was widespread that nothing short of a radical change in the political structure could reverse the trend.

By the mid-1980s President Nimeiri's mastery of Sudanese politics was his last remaining claim to power; he had survived every coup attempt, every spate of strike and riot, every mutiny and rebellion, and seemed destined to rule indefinitely. His deftness in the politics of divide and rule was legend; in the course of his long rule he had collaborated with almost every political group, from the communists to the Muslim Brothers, from the ex-Anya Nya guerrillas to the traditional tribal chiefs. As often as political gossip predicted his imminent downfall, so often was he able to manipulate the hopelessly divided forces of opposition. Demoralized and without credibility, their energies spent in irrelevant ideological debate and personal intrigue, the opposition was always wide but never deep. When his personal rule collapsed in 1985 it was under the weight of an unprecedented combination of foreign pressure, economic disaster, famine, civil war, popular disgust, and the overweening self-confidence of a ruler who had come to despise his own people.

Throughout 1984, as the Nimeiri regime lurched from one crisis to another, it seemed to many that the end was at last in sight. The peculiarly Sudanese degree of tolerance, which had, despite excesses, characterized even the Nimeiri regime, seemed finally to have been exhausted. Yet still no clear focus of opposition, no party, interest group, or individual emerged to challenge him directly. Serious strikes by various professionals were followed in April by the declaration of a state of emergency. A virtual reign of terror ensued, during which specially-constituted 'courts of decisive justice', presided over by Muslim Brothers, purported to pass 'Islamic' judgements for a wide variety of novel offences. Floggings, amputations, and executions were met with incredulity and despair at home and received wide publicity abroad. When even the docile People's Assembly hesitated to rubber-stamp drastic constitutional amendments, Nimeiri dissolved it. The state of emergency ended in September, but terror tactics did not. In January 1985 Mahmud Muhammad Taha, the 76-year-old leader of the progressive Republican Brothers, who had long supported the regime but objected to its brand of the Shari'a, was arrested and, after a showtrial, was executed for 'heresy'. This outrage, perpetrated to frighten the opposition, seemed to go beyond the boundaries set even by the increasingly unpredictable Nimeiri, and deeply shocked public opinion. In March, in yet another about-face, the president turned on the Muslim Brothers, his last civilian supporters, and imprisoned their leaders on a variety of charges, including plotting to overthrow the government. Attempts, before and after this move, to acquire some new collaborative element, were unsuccessful. There remained, most significantly, the army, on which in his last resort Nimeiri had to rely. Apparently sure of its continued support he left Khartoum, amid anti-government riots, in late March for a visit to Washington.

Although in retrospect the overthrow of Nimeiri as a result of popular pressure in April 1985 appears to have been inevitable, in fact the outcome was uncertain until the army publicly abandoned him. Demonstrations in Omdurman, Khartoum North, and, massively, in Khartoum, were met by police and troops and suppressed with loss of life. A general strike was called and received an enthusiastic public response. Nimeiri cut short his visit and enplaned for Khartoum but, before he reached Cairo the commander-in-chief, General 'Abd al-Rahman Muhammad Siwar al-Dahab, announced on the national radio that the army would 'yield to the wishes of the people'. Nimeiri went into exile in Egypt, and a Transitional Military Council was constituted to rule the country. Doubts about the intentions of these officers, and about the very assumption of power of Nimeiri appointees, were drowned in the general rejoicing over the downfall of the man who had ruled the Sudan longer than any other in its modern history.

THE TRANSITIONAL GOVERNMENT AND THE RETURN TO PARLIAMENTARY RULE[1]

There are striking similarities between the overthrow of Nimeiri and the fall of the Abboud regime in 1964. Both occurred after a period of rising dissatisfaction with economic policies and in the context of civil war. In each case the end came as the result of popular fury, channelled and led by trade unions and professional associations rather than political parties. An initial attempt in each case to suppress the rising was met by determined resistance, casualties in the streets, and divided counsels within the army. In neither 1964 nor 1985 was there a concerted conspiracy, and in the transitional periods that ensued new, progressive political forces tried and failed to prevent a return to party politics as usual. Indeed, whereas in 1964 the army had fled from power, in 1985 it appropriated it, used it to protect its own position, and presided over a resumption of traditional politics.

That the overthrow of President Nimeiri was the result of a reluctant military coup and not of a revolution was clear within hours of the army's assumption of power. Reflecting the deep divisions in Sudanese society that had been so skilfully exploited by Nimeiri, the army was itself riven by factions, and the decision of the generals to topple the discredited president was the only means of avoiding coup attempts from below or revolution in the streets. United only in opposition to Nimeiri, the civilian leaders of the uprising accepted General Siwar al-Dahab's pledge of the army's transitional role, and deferred to his threat that continuation of the general strike would be treated as treason. In deciding, however suspiciously, to 'give the generals a chance', the strike leaders in effect called off the uprising, and forfeited an historic opportunity. Amid the euphoria in Khartoum, a discordant note was struck by Colonel John Garang, the SPLM leader, who in a clandestine radio address called the new leadership 'Nimeiriism without Nimeiri', and demanded that it hand over power to civilians. The political situation appeared very fluid, with no rump political party or interest group having obvious mass support, and no certainty as to what direction the generals would take. The essentially improvisational nature of the April coup was one reason for this; the continuing divisions of Sudanese politics were another.

In its first weeks in power, the officers tended to react to events rather than to guide them, but by the end of April, largely because of the ineffectiveness of civilian opposition, they were safely in command. On 9 April a fifteen-man Transitional Military Council was announced, under Siwar al-Dahab's chairmanship, to act as both head of state and source of legislation. The constitution was suspended, and the moribund SSU was dissolved. Political detainees were released after a mob stormed the notorious Kober Prison, and Nimeiri's security police were formally disbanded only after a similar mass demonstration. Although some of Nimeiri's prominent subordinates were arrested, most were not, and the trials that followed were crowd-pleasing rather than purgative. All laws remained in effect, including notably the infamous 'September Laws' of 1983, which had established Nimeiri's brand of the Shari'a, and the omnibus State Security Act. While the generals' intentions were therefore uncertain and unavoidably suspect, that they planned no radical departure from Nimeiri's policies seemed clear. An issue of much concern in the months that followed was what degree or length of collaboration with the deposed ruler should now be deemed criminal. The fact that so many prominent individuals had held office under Nimeiri favoured a forward-looking approach, and most public revulsion was reserved for the exiled ex-president.

Contributing to the upheaval of late March and early April was the Alliance of National Forces for National Salvation which, after Nimeiri's ousting, became the principal coalition of mass organizations. The Alliance's charter, signed originally by three vestigial political parties (the Umma, DUP, and communists) and trade unions, called for a three-year transitional period during which the 1956 provisional constitution, as amended in 1964, would be reinstated; basic freedoms would be restored; regional self-government would be reinstituted in the south; and the country would be freed from 'its dependence on world imperialism', while a non-aligned foreign policy would be pursued. The force of these demands, which were largely unexceptionable, was dissipated by rapid factionalization of political opinion. The powerful Islamic National

218

Front of the Muslim Brothers under Hasan al-Turabi refused to sign the charter, and some signatories soon flouted its provisions. Although the Alliance continued to represent one major strand of opinion in the ensuing political debate, the focus of attention reverted from mass meetings to back rooms, and from the 'new forces' to the old parties.

Within weeks of the coup dozens of 'parties' had announced their otherwise unnoticed existence. The Alliance's call for a relatively long transitional period, during which new political formations might occur, failed in the face of the traditional parties' opposition. The old parties, having collaborated with Nimeiri, and having had no role in his downfall, were anxious to re-establish their legitimacy through elections, much as they had been in 1965. The TMC's willingness to appoint a civilian cabinet (while retaining effective power itself) led to a lengthy and complicated series of political manoeuvres within and outside the Alliance to reach agreement on representation. The cabinet, which took office on 25 April, was headed by Dr Gazuli Dafalla, president of the doctors' union. A professional diplomat, Ibrahim Taha Ayub, was named foreign minister, and the defence portfolio went to Brigadier Uthman Abdalla Muhammad, a member of the TMC. Significantly, command of the army remained in the hands of the TMC, and was not subject to the cabinet. The refusal of newly-formed southern political groups to acquiesce in only token representation resulted in their being by-passed in favour of three politicians of the old regime, one of whom, Samuel Aru Bol, took up the meaningless post of deputy prime minister. Obviously subordinate to the TMC, this caretaker cabinet's main duties were to carry on the day-to-day affairs of administration and prepare for the election promised by the TMC within a year.

It was widely hoped that the personal inclinations of the council members, including especially Siwar al-Dahab himself, an unassuming career officer, would conform with the popular will, and that no attempt would be made from within its ranks to prolong military rule. During the transitional period, despite constant rumours and the widely recognized ambitions of certain officers, no overt coup attempt was made. A small-scale mutiny in September, which the government ineptly inflated into a 'racist coup attempt' because of the alleged involvement of southerners and Nubas, led to hundreds of arrests and the detention without charge of prominent southerners, adding fuel to the growing perception that the new government was merely a continuation of the old.

Relations between the TMC and the civilian cabinet were unguided by precedent and remained unregulated until the promulgation of an interim constitution in October. Until then, any dispute might provoke a crisis, but in the event this was largely avoided. The cabinet had no constituency and its influence inevitably declined as the elections neared which would signal its demise. Agreement on an interim constitution occurred only after a long debate. Based on the provisional constitution of 1956 as amended in 1964, the document also incorporated subsequent provisions for southern autonomy and regionalization, and included special arrangements for legislation during the transitional period. An attempt to compromise on the question of the Shari'a, and even more the retention of the 'September Laws', however leniently enforced, provoked disappointment or derision. Indeed the constitution was but one example of the transitional government's tendency to postpone difficult decisions for consideration by its successor. Although a strong case could be made for this, yet it is undoubted that the position of the new parliamentary regime would have been made considerably easier had it been presented with a few accomplished facts in such difficult areas as the Shari'a.

In promising to restore civilian rule within a year the TMC was as good as its word. Elections to a constituent assembly, which would rule until a constitution was adopted, were held in April 1986. As in 1965, a special graduates' constituency, now enlarged to encompass other 'modern forces', was devised, while the war prevented polling in thirty-seven southern constituencies. The result, as predicted, was no clear majority for any party. The Umma emerged as the largest single party and Sadiq al-Mahdi, having failed to construct a national government, formed a coalition with the DUP and several small parties. The official opposition party was the well-organized and well-financed Islamic National Front which, despite the defeat of its leader, Hasan al-Turabi, emerged from the elections with the greatest apparent increase in public support, at least as measured against the last free elections of eighteen years earlier. A five-man Supreme Council of State was named to act collectively as head of state, under the presidency of Ahmed 'Uthman al-Mirghani. Thus the government was headed by a descendant of the Mahdi, and the council of state by a scion of the Mirghani family. The TMC was dissolved and General Siwar al-Dahab went gracefully into retirement.

The restoration of parliamentary government little more than a year after Nimeiri's downfall and in the midst of multiple political and economic crises was the great achievement of the TMC and transitional government. The particularistic character of Sudanese politics, the unabated hostility of the SPLM/SPLA, the vigilance of the Alliance, and the administrative chaos left by Nimeiri were powerful brakes on the ambitions of would-be coup-makers. Yet all of the country's problems required solutions which, if practicable and fair, might restore legitimacy to parliamentary rule itself, but if merely expedient and self-serving, would surely lead to another military takeover or worse.

Although on issues such as the role of the Shari'a and the character of a permanent constitution the transitional government reserved decisions for its successor, in several fields the urgency of the Sudan's position required immediate action but allowed little room for manoeuvre. This was most obvious in connection with the economy. The need for famine relief, the crushing burden of unpayable debts, the blockage of essential foreign credit, and indeed the nature of the regime all pointed to continued co-operation with the West and the rich Arab states. Immediately after the coup Siwar al-Dahab took personal responsibility for overseeing famine relief. Foreign food aid was sufficient, but transport problems continued to plague efforts to distribute it. Abundant harvests in 1985 eased the situation in the western Sudan. In the south, however, famine was caught up with the politics of the civil war, and even the extent of the crisis was difficult to judge.

In its overall economic policy the transitional government was caught between the stark realities of virtual bankruptcy and heightened expectations. The co-operation of the Sudan's creditors was enlisted to reschedule the massive foreign debt, but the government's early acceptance of conditions set by the International Monetary Fund led to widespread dissatisfaction. Huge public-sector wage increases were demanded and promised. Some subsidies were restored, and attempts were made to control prices. The money supply was rapidly expanded. Predictably, inflation soared. The IMF's insistence on austerity, limits to the growth in money supply, an end to price controls and adoption of a market-determined exchange rate for the Sudanese pound, was resisted within the cabinet, and the finance minister therefore resigned in December 1985. Further negotiations with the IMF failed to produce agreement, and in February 1986 the Sudan was declared bankrupt. While some welcomed this open breach with the Fund, others recognized that most bilateral and multilateral donors had made their assistance conditional on the Sudan's acceptance of IMF advice. Despite assertions that the country would turn elsewhere, the Sudan had little to bargain with, except the presumed concern of other governments in preserving order and preventing a radical alteration in the country's foreign policy.

Thus despite (and partly because) of its severely restricted position, the transitional government embarked upon at least a superficial reorientation of the Sudan's foreign affairs, towards a professed policy of non-alignment. Relations with the USA and Egypt, both of which were widely and correctly seen as too-willing collaborators with Nimeiri, suffered initially, as his fall was viewed as their defeat. It is symptomatic that immediately after Nimeiri's dismissal was announced, there was fear of Egyptian or American-backed intervention. While the fate of the mutual defence pact with Egypt and especially of the much-touted Integration remained clouded, the transitional government's relations with Egypt were not seriously breached. Sudanese demands for the extradition of Nimeiri, which were refused, remained an irritant, but the ex-president's return to the Sudan was also seen as more dangerous to vested interests there than his silent absence abroad. Relations with the United States, as with Egypt, suffered after a rapidly arranged rapprochement with Libya and episodes of presumed anti-Americanism. But formal and institutional relations remained close.

The transitional government quickly set about repairing relations with the Sudan's other important neighbours, Libya and Ethiopia. The implacable hostility between Nimeiri and Colonel Gaddafi had required the disappearance of one as a condition for improved relations, and within hours of the coup Gaddafi had offered his support to the new regime. A mission to Libya in mid-April was followed first by a large Libyan delegation to Khartoum in May, and then by the unannounced arrival of Gaddafi himself. Libyan aid for the SPLA was withdrawn, and in July the Sudanese defence minister, without the consent of his colleagues, signed a military agreement with Libya, provoking strong negative reactions abroad and at home, where, however, few practical results of the pact were expected. Relations with Ethiopia were more crucially important because of the close support of the Ethiopian government for the SPLM/SPLA, and the presence in the Sudan of about one million Eritrean and Tigrean refugees. Public pronouncements of a new era were not followed by concrete evidence of closer ties. Historic and ideological differences aside, the transitional government had little to offer Ethiopia at a time when the SPLA was increasingly effective in the field and while Ethiopia's internal crises were largely unsusceptible to Sudanese intervention.

Relations with Libya and Ethiopia, the recovery of the economy and its future development, indeed the fate of the latest parliamentary regime seemed destined, in 1986, to depend on the outcome of the civil war. Early expectations in Khartoum that the SPLA's reason for existence had departed with Nimeiri were soon contradicted. The transitional government's steps towards conciliation were timid, reflecting the lack of consensus in the north and indeed within the government and the army. Thus, an offensive ceasefire was declared, amnesty extended, and a transitional Higher Executive Council appointed; yet on the critical issue of Shari'a law only 'revision' was promised, and ambivalence over the issue of redivision, the hasty efforts to improve relations with the SPLM's Ethiopian and Libyan backers, and the initial appointment to the cabinet of three discredited southern politicians, did nothing to restore confidence. In September 1985 riots followed a Muslim Brothers' demonstration in Khartoum calling for a military solution in the south, and later in the month many southerners were arrested in the wake of the alleged coup attempt. Reaffirming its determination to bring about a radical change of the Sudan's political and economic structure, the SPLM leadership meanwhile made little progress in attracting the support of non-southerners, but stepped up its military activities in the south.

The urgent priority of bringing an end to the war and establishing a new basis for national unity was fully recognized in Khartoum only by certain elements in the Alliance. Delegations and individuals went to Addis Ababa and elsewhere to consult the SPLM leadership, and a conference of Alliance members and representatives of the SPLM in May 1986 called for reinstatement of the 1956 constitution, abolition of the 'September Laws', abrogation of bilateral military pacts, and the convening of a constitutional conference. The ideological rift between the transitional government (and its parliamentary successor) and the SPLM; the lack of consensus in the north on fundamental constitutional and religious issues; and the SPLM's conviction that time is on its side; did not augur well for an early peace, or therefore for the future of the new regime in Khartoum. Having learned from experience about the value of constitutional and legal guarantees and the reliability of plans and promises of a new economic deal, southerners both within and outside the SPLM/SPLA were wary of calls for 'dialogue' by members of the traditional parties and northern elite. Those calls, meanwhile, although couched in vogue terms, continued to address the problem from a perspective which was largely outdated. Hope was therefore focused on a national conference to reach consensus on a solution, but the obvious rigidity of opinion in the north, and a revival of factionalism among southerners, were ominous.

More clearly than ever, the problems facing the Sudan are national. It is a multilingual state in which a majority speak Arabic but where demands have increased for the preservation of non-Arabic cultures. It is a multi-religious state where Islam predominates but where a large minority will not tolerate the universal application of Islamic law. It remains a multi-ethnic state wherein, however, a Sudanese identity has been recognized and can be fostered, without provocative reference to either 'Arabness' or 'Africanness'. Yet the Sudan remains subject to political paralysis, sectarian rifts, appeals to regional, ethnic, and tribal feelings. Above all there is a chasm between rich and poor which, despite the efforts of traditional political parties, is increasingly recognized as a result of traditional politics. The yawning gap between the centre and the periphery, the modern and the undeveloped, the rich and the poor, is no longer seen as accidental or natural, but as the result at least in part of the policies adopted by both parliamentary and military governments to advance the interests of the metropolitan elite. To what extent the system inherited by that elite at independence can survive in the face of continuing economic decline and the armed resistance of a substantial part of the country, is a question that cannot be avoided much longer without explosive consequences.

Despite the gloom that pervades the economic statistics and the political analyses, there is, however, a reason for hope, if not conviction, that the Sudan can survive and even prosper. The very recognition that the Sudanese can change their political and economic circumstances is proof that a traditional fatalism has limits. The emergence of a Sudanese identity, which forces every old stereotype–of Arab, African, northerner, and southerner, even Muslim and non-Muslim–to be qualified, has been sped by deep economic and social changes that are stronger than a traditional structure which, though weakened, still prevails. Demographic changes, the results of labour migration, rural poverty, civil war, and famine, have altered the old ethnic and political map. Poor northerners have begun to re-examine traditional loyalties, while younger southern intellectuals have confidently eschewed separatism and demanded equal treatment in a united Sudan. In the explosive growth of the press since the downfall of Nimeiri can be seen a deep attachment to the free expression of ideas. Restored freedom of association has led to a recrudescence of trade unionism, and to a conscious and public assertion of new affinities among, for example, women, deracinated ethnic groups, and even amputees who survived Nimeiri's 'September Laws'. All of these developments must serve to continue processes that have been under way throughout the modern era and which will put increasing pressure on the old style and content of Sudanese politics.

Old loyalties die hard. New attachments are not always easily perceived. Even the short-term effects of famine, political upheaval, and economic disaster cannot confidently be predicted. A widespread expectation of change may help to speed it, but what direction it will take is far from certain. Amid these imponderables there is one constant, the character of the Sudanese people. That it has survived the tests of the past is perhaps the best reason for hope in the future.

NOTES

INTRODUCTION: THE LAND AND THE PEOPLE

1 In 1823, the *Defterdar* Muhammad Bey Khusraw was entitled 'commander-in-chief of the Sudan and of Kordofan'. Ten years later, 'Ali Khurshid Pasha was given the title of 'governor of the provinces of the Sudan', perhaps the first official usage of the term in something like its modern sense. The Ottoman sultan's *ferman* to Muhammad 'Ali Pasha in 1841 did not mention the Sudan as such (see p. 45).

2 Barabra, the plural of *Barbari* (in English, Berberine) is the name given to the Nubians of this region.

3 See below, Ch. 2, p. 28.

4 See below, Ch. 1, p. 23.

5 See below, Ch. 2, p. 29.

6 Arbaji was an important town from the sixteenth to the eighteenth century. It was visited by Bruce, the Scottish traveller, in 1772, and was devastated by its own ruler in 1783–84.

7 *Makk* was a title given to the vassal-kings under the suzerainty of the Funj sultan.

8 John Lewis Burckhardt, a Swiss by birth, visited Shendi in 1814. See below, Ch. 2, pp. 28, 35.

9 See 'Umar al-Naqar, *The pilgrimage tradition in West Africa* (Khartoum 1972), 104–13.

CHAPTER 1: THE EASTERN *BILAD AL-SUDAN* IN THE MIDDLE AGES

1 French translations of Ibn Sulaym's account of Nubia, as transmitted by al-Maqrīzī (d. 1442), may be found in Et. Quatremère, *Mémoires géographiques et historiques sur l'Égypte et sur quelques contrées voisines* (Paris 1811), II, 1–126 (Mémoire sur la Nubie); and U. Bouriant (tr.), Maqrizi, *Description topographique et historique de l'Égypte* (Paris 1900), II, 549–53.

2 The text of the oath is given by the contemporary Arabic chronicler, Ibn al-Dawādārī, *Kanz al-durar wa-jāmi' al-ghurar,* VIII (ed. U. Haarmann, Freiburg 1971), 185–6.

3 Ibn Khaldūn, *Kitāb al-'ibar* (Beirut n.d.), v, 922–3.

4 Gaston Wiet (ed.), [al-Maqrīzī], *El-Mawā'iz wa'l-i'tibâr fî dhikr el-khitat wa'l-âthâr,* iii (Paris 1922), 263–4. By Jacobite Christianity is meant the Monophysite doctrine, held by the Coptic Church in Egypt.

5 The accepted view that 'Aydhab was destroyed by an expedition sent by the Mamluk Sultan Barsbay in 1426 is effectively challenged by Jean-Claude Garcin, 'Jean-Léon l'Africain et 'Aydhab', *Annales Islamologiques,* xi, 1972, 189–209.

Notes

CHAPTER 2: THE EASTERN *BILAD AL-SUDAN* FROM THE EARLY SIXTEENTH TO THE EARLY NINETEENTH CENTURY

1 A critical edition has been published by Yūsuf Faḍl Ḥasan, *Kitāb al-ṭabaqāt fī khuṣūṣ al-awliyā' wa'l-ṣāliḥīn wa'l-'ulamā' fi'l-Sūdān* (second edition, Khartoum 1974). A summary translation (not always accurate) with useful notes was made by Sir Harold MacMichael, *A history of the Arabs in the Sudan* (Cambridge 1922), II, 217–323. See also S. Hillelson, 'Tabaqât Wad Ḍayf Allah: studies in the lives of the scholars and saints', *Sudan Notes and Records,* VI, 1923, 191–230.

2 A late recension was published by Makkī Shibayka, *Ta'rīkh mulūk al-Sūdān* (Khartoum 1947), and a critical edition based on an early recension by al-Shāṭir Buṣaylī 'Abd al-Jalīl, *Makhṭūṭat Kātib al-Shūna fī ta'rīkh al-salṭana al-Sinnārivva wa'l-idāra al-Miṣriyya* (Cairo 1963). An annotated translation of a late recension is given by MacMichael, *History of the Arabs,* 354–430.

3 Muḥammad Ibrāhīm Abū Salīm, *al Fūnj wa'l-ard: wathā'iq tamlīk* (Khartoum 1967); P. M. Holt, 'Four Funj land-charters', *Studies in the history of the Near East* (London 1973), 104–20.

4 S. Hillelson, 'David Reubeni, an early visitor to Sennar', *Sudan Notes and Records,* XVI, 1933, 55–66.

5 Maria Teresa Petti Suma, 'Il viaggio in Sudan di Evliyā Čelebī', *Annali dell'Istituto Orientale di Napoli,* N.S. XIV, 433–52.

6 James Bruce, *Travels to discover the source of the Nile* (second edition, Edinburgh 1805), VI.

7 John Lewis Burckhardt, *Travels in Nubia* (London 1819).

8 See P. M. Holt, 'The coming of the Funj', *Studies,* 67–87.

9 J. L. Spaulding, 'The Funj: a reconsideration', *Journal of African History,* XIII/1, 1972, 39–53.

10 Wendy James, 'The Funj mystique: approaches to a problem of Sudan history', in Ravindra K. Jain (ed.), *Text and context: the social anthropology of tradition* (Philadelphia 1977), 95–133.

11 There appears to have been further fighting before the Ottoman frontier was finally established at the Third Cataract. There is an 'Abdallabi tradition of a victory on 'the Egyptian border' over Ottoman troops armed with firearms, but the chronological indications are hopelessly muddled. This may be a suitably modified version of another tradition which describes the overwhelming defeat of a 'Funj' force by a Ghuzz governor at Hannak, just above the Third Cataract. The Ghuzz leader is called Ibn Janbalan, and may be identified with Sulayman Janbulad, a Mamluk bey who, about the year 1620, became the first governor of Upper Egypt, and thereby the immediate overlord of the *kashif* of Dirr. Henceforward Hannak was the border between Ottoman and Funj territory.

12 Bruce, *Travels, VI, 372.*

13 *Ṭabaqāt,* 41. The '*idda* is the period during which, under the Sharī'a, a divorced woman may not remarry.

14 *Ṭabaqāt,* 345.

15 P. M. Holt, 'The Sons of Jābir and their kin: a clan of Sudanese religious notables', *Studies,* 88–103.

16 P. M. Holt, 'Holy families and Islam in the Sudan', *Studies,* 121–34.

17 An extract from this notice in the *Ṭabaqāt* is given and translated by S. Hillelson,

228

Sudan Arabic texts (Cambridge 1935), 194–9.

18 See Hillelson, *Sudan Arabic texts*, 174–93.

19 W. G. Browne, *Travels in Africa, Egypt, and Syria, from the year 1792 to 1798* (London 1799).

20 Muḥammad b. 'Umar al-Tūnusī, *Tashḥīdh al-adhhān bi-sīrat bilād al-'Arab wa'l-Sūdān* (ed. Khalīl Maḥmūd 'Asākir and Muṣṭafā Muḥammad Mas'ad: Cairo 1965). French translation by Dr Perron, *Voyage au Darfour* (Paris 1845).

21 Now available in translation by Allan G. B. Fisher and Humphrey J. Fisher, *Sahara and Sudan*, IV (London 1971).

22 Rudolf C. Slatin, *Fire and sword in the Sudan* (London 1896), 37–55.

23 Na'ūm Shuqayr, *Ta'rīkh al-Sūdān al-qadīm wa'l-ḥadīth wa-jughrāfiyatuh* (Cairo 1903), II, 111–47.

24 See Rex S. O'Fahey and Jay L. Spaulding, 'Hāshim and the Musabba'āt', *Bulletin of the School of Oriental and African Studies*, XXXV/2, 1972, 316–33.

25 *Makhṭūṭat Kātib al-Shūna*, 10.

26 *Makhṭūtat Kātib al-Shūna*, 26.

27 Browne, *Travels*, 307.

28 Bruce, *Travels*, VI, 345.

29 *Makhṭūṭat Kātib al-Shūna*, 79.

30 Browne, *Travels*, 212.

31 Browne, *Travels*, 215.

32 *Pièces diverses et correspondance relatives aux opérations de l'Armée d'Orient en Égypte* (Paris An IX), 187, 216, 217.

CHAPTER 3: THE INAUGURATION OF THE TURCO-EGYPTIAN REGIME: 1820–25

1 English, *Narrative*, 21.

2 Waddington and Hanbury, *Journal*, 98.

3 The name of Berber was at this time applied only to the district inhabited by the Mirafab. The complex of villages on the right bank, the predecessors of the modern town of Berber, had no common name. At the time of the conquest the village of Nasr al-Din was the effective capital of the district. Fifty years earlier, at the time of Bruce's visit, the capital had been Gooz (*al-Quz*), another village in the complex.

4 English, *Narrative*, 140.

5 This was the two-horned cap (*taqiyya umm qarnayn*) which was the particular symbol of authority in the Funj state. See above, p. 34.

6 English, *Narrative*, 159–60.

7 The date (17 Rajab 1136) is given by Jabarti (*'Ajā'ib al-āthār*, IV, 318) who also makes it clear that the objective of the expedition was Darfur, not merely Kordofan.

8 Stories of the capricious cruelty of the *Defterdar* were told to the British traveller, John Petherick, who visited Kordofan in 1847.

9 El Fasher (*al-Fashir*) means literally the courtyard before the royal palace, and was used for the successive residences of the sultans of Darfur. With the final settlement of the royal residence in the late eighteenth century, the name came to be applied to the town which grew up around the palace.

10 *Mu'allim* (Arabic: 'teacher') was the regular title of Christian and Jewish officials in this period.

229

11 Hill gives the sterling equivalent of the taxes as £2 5*s*., £1 10*s*., and 15*s*., respectively. He states that the current price at Sennar of a male slave was £3, while that of a milch cow was £1 4*s*. *Egypt in the Sudan*, 14–15.

12 MacMichael, *History of the Arabs*, II, 420.

13 MacMichael, *History of the Arabs*, II, 422, places Umm 'Uruq 'on the west bank of the White Nile close to the site of the present Commandania of Omdurman.' Shibeika, *Ta'rikh*, Notes, p. 21, thinks that it may have been a village on the Nile between Khartoum and Shendi. The Funj Chronicle distinguishes between Umm 'Uruq and Omdurman (*Umm Durman*).

14 The name of Khartoum (*al-Khurtum*) means 'the elephant's trunk'.

CHAPTER 4: SETTLEMENT AND STAGNATION: 1825–62

1 Translated from Shibayka's edition of the Funj Chronicle. The passage is omitted in MacMichael's translation.

2 Kanfu was the paternal uncle of the future King Theodore, who made himself ruler of Ethiopia in 1855 and committed suicide at the time of Sir Robert Napier's expedition to Magdala in 1868.

3 Ahmad Abu Widan was probably of Circassian Mamluk origin. He served in Muhammad 'Ali Pasha's forces in Arabia, Greece, Syria and the Sudan. Recalled from the Sudan after a difference of opinion with Khurshid, he was for a time minister of War in Egypt.

4 *Hükümdar* had long been used in Turkish in the sense of sovereign or ruler. It had not hitherto possessed any precise administrative significance, and, in the sense of governor-general, was a neologism. Muhammad 'Ali also, in 1832, conferred this title on his governor-general in Syria (information supplied by Professor M. Abu Hakima of McGill University).

5 Khurshid was appointed governor of Adana, a province at this time controlled by Muhammad 'Ali Pasha, in consequence of his successful war against the Ottoman Sultan Mahmud II. He died in 1845, in the post of governor of the Egyptian province of the Sharqiyya.

6 During the winter of 1838–9, Muhammad 'Ali Pasha paid a visit to the Sudan. His principal object was to inspect the gold-producing region of Fazughli. Disappointed with what he saw, he returned to Egypt. His visit is devoid of significance for Sudanese history.

7 Kanbal was the son of *Makk* Jawish, who had resisted the advance of Isma'il Pasha (see above, p. 50). After his death, Kanbal became a legendary figure: 'he is described, on account of his cruelty and savage deeds, constantly wandering round, without grave, rest, or peace, as the punishment of his crimes.' (F. Werne, *African wanderings* (London 1852), 177–8.) His son, Bashir, served both the Turco-Egyptian and Condominium regimes, and died in 1919.

8 Muhammad wad Dafa'allah's wife, Nasra bint 'Adlan, was a person of even greater consequence than he himself. She was the daughter of the Regent 'Adlan by a Funj princess. She held her court at Surayba, near Wad Medani, where she was visited by the German archaeologist Lepsius in 1844, and by the American Bayard Taylor in 1852.

9 These measures should undoubtedly be linked with decrees of the Ottoman Sultan 'Abd al-Majid, who in October 1854 prohibited trade in white slaves, and in February 1857 trade in negro slaves.

Notes

CHAPTER 5: THE ERA OF KHEDIVE ISMA'IL: 1863-81

1 Usually called Arabi Pasha by English writers.
2 See above, p. 67.
3 See above, p. 69.

CHAPTER 6: THE MAHDIST REVOLUTION: 1881-85

1 A supporter of 'Urabi named Ahmad al-'Awwam was banished to Khartoum after the suppression of the Egyptian revolution. He then wrote an account of recent events in Egypt, which he communicated to the Mahdi's followers. For this he was tried and put to death. His work was later lithographed in Omdurman by the Mahdist authorities. 'Awwam's book was, however, only composed at a time when the Mahdist movement was on the verge of its final successes.
2 The original Ansar were the 'Helpers' of the Prophet Muhammad in Medina. In this, as in other instances, the Mahdi patterned his movement on early Islamic history. See below, pp. 95-7.
3 The name is usually given in English works as Osman Digna. His Beja followers were the 'Fuzzy-Wuzzies' of Kipling's poem.
4 See above, p. 35.
5 Later the first Earl of Cromer.
6 Al-Siddiq, al-Faruq and al-Karrar are names traditionally given to Abu Bakr, 'Umar and 'Ali respectively.

CHAPTER 7: THE REIGN OF THE KHALIFA 'ABDALLAHI: 1885-98

1 The name has gone down in British military history as Toski.
2 Ahmad 'Ali's successor as qadi al-Islam, al-Husayn Ibrahim wad al-Zahra, who also perished in disgrace, had studied at al-Azhar in the Turco-Egyptian period, and was a literary poet of repute.
3 For information on the diplomatic background of the Dongola Campaign see G. N. Sanderson, England, Europe and the Upper Nile 1882-1899 (Edinburgh 1965).
4 Later Earl Kitchener of Khartoum.
5 The name is often distorted to Surgham.

CHAPTER 8: PACIFICATION AND CONSOLIDATION: 1899-1913

1 The capitulations were originally treaties by which the Ottoman sultans had conceded virtually autonomous status and trading rights to European mercantile communities within the empire. With the decline of Ottoman power they had become in effect charters of extra-territoriality for any person who could claim citizenship or protection of European states or of the United States.
2 Cromer, Modern Egypt, II (London 1908), 549.
3 The Mixed Tribunals had been set up in the reign of Khedive Isma'il to try civil suits in which Europeans were concerned. They were independent of the Egyptian government.
4 The incident in which the three Ashraf were killed has been the subject of a controversy as to whether they were shot while trying to escape custody, or were executed after the failure of an escape attempt.

Notes

5 See Gabriel Warburg, *The Sudan under Wingate, administration in the Anglo-Egyptian Sudan, 1899–1916* (London 1971), 129–33.

CHAPTER 9: WAR AND REVOLT, 1914–24

1 See A. B. Theobald, *'Alī Dīnār, last sultan of Darfur, 1898–1916* (London, 1965), 174–6.

2 The title of high commissioner superseded that of agent and consul-general when Egypt was declared a protectorate in 1914.

3 At Wingate's suggestion, Stack was named acting sirdar and acting governor-general until the conclusion of the war. The dual appointment was confirmed in May 1919.

4 See below, p. 136.

5 The title of khedive was superseded by that of sultan at the beginning of the war. Sultan Ahmad Fu'ad became king after independence in 1922.

6 The Sudanese feddan = 1.038 acres.

CHAPTER 10: A PERIOD OF REACTION, 1925–36

1 Sir J. Maffey, 'Minute by His Excellency the Governor-General', 1 January 1927, Sudan Government Archives, CIVSEC 1/9/33.

2 Sir J. Currie, 'The educational experiment in the Anglo-Egyptian Sudan, 1900–1933', *Journal of the Royal African Society,* XXXIV, 1935, 49.

3 R. Bence-Pembroke, 'Proposals for the introduction of the policy on native administration', 23 January 1927, Sudan Government Archives, CIVSEC 1/20/60.

4 *Khalwa* (literally, 'a place of seclusion') means primarily a retreat for Sufi initiates. The Sudanese usage, to signify a place for religious instruction, is a surviving trace of the Sufi character of the islamization of the Sudan. During the early Condominium period, the government subsidised *kuttabs* (elementary schools), employing government-trained teachers, in an attempt to improve standards.

5 'Graduate' in this context meant one who had completed a course of study at the Gordon College or an intermediate school.

CHAPTER 11: THE DEVELOPMENT OF SUDANESE NATIONALISM, 1937–1952

1 Meaning in modern Arabic 'nation', *Umma* still carries overtones of its original significance, i.e. the community of Islam in the time of the Prophet and subsequently. Hence *Umma* has sometimes been rendered misleadingly as 'communist'.

2 See Conrad C. Reining, *The Zande Scheme* (Evanston, Illinois 1966).

3 See Gabriel Warburg, *Islam, Nationalism and Communism in a traditional society, the case of Sudan* (London 1978), 96–8.

4 See Saad ed din Fawzi, *The labour movement in the Sudan, 1946–1955,* (London 1957).

CHAPTER 12: SELF-GOVERNMENT AND SELF-DETERMINATION, 1953–56

1 An interesting account is in the memoirs of Anthony Eden, *Full Circle,* (London 1960), 272–4.

2 See below, pp. 175–6.

3 An official enquiry determined that the disturbances had been caused by, among other things, the results of sudanization, the interference in politics of northern administrators, and the circulation of provocative rumours concerning the disposition of southern army units. See Sudan Government, *Southern Sudan Disturbances*, August 1955 (Report of the Commission of Enquiry) (Khartoum 1956).

CHAPTER 13: THE FIRST PARLIAMENTARY AND MILITARY REGIMES, 1956–64

1 See G. N. Sanderson, 'Sudanese nationalism and the independence of the Sudan', in Michael Brett (ed.), *Northern Africa: Islam and modernization* (1973) 97–109.
2 The Sudanese pound (£S), divided into one hundred piastres and one thousand milliemes, was in early 1978 worth about £1.50 sterling.
3 See Peter Bechtold, *Politics in the Sudan* (New York 1976), 195.
4 The agreement of the major parties to consider federal status had led to the southern MPs' support for the declaration of independence in 1955.
5 Government of the Sudan, Ministry of Irrigation and Hydro-Electric Power, *The Nile Waters Question* (Khartoum 1955).
6 For details of the resettlement, see Hassan Dafalla, *The Nubian Exodus* (London 1975).
7 See Warburg, *Islam, nationalism and communism*, 93–140.

CHAPTER 14: THE TRANSITIONAL GOVERNMENT AND THE SECOND PARLIAMENTARY REGIME, 1964–69

1 For the events leading up to the Round Table Conference of March 1965, and relevant documents, see M. O. Beshir, *The Southern Sudan, background to conflict* (London, 1968).
2 For information relating to the Sudan's economy during this period, see Ali Mohamed El Hassan (ed.), *An introduction to the Sudan Economy,* (Khartoum 1976).

CHAPTER 15: THE REGIME OF JAAFAR AL-NIMEIRI

1 The account of political and economic developments in this chapter is based on private information and on Peter Bechtold, *Politics in the Sudan*; Ruth First, *The barrel of a gun* (London 1970); Gabriel Warburg, *Islam, nationalism and communism*; and on reports in the periodical press.
2 For a discussion of communist involvement in the coup, see Warburg, *Islam, nationalism and communism*, 132–4.
3 For a discussion of local government reforms, see John Howell (ed.), *Local government and politics in the Sudan* (Khartoum 1974).

CHAPTER 16: THE TRANSITIONAL GOVERNMENT AND THE RETURN TO PARLIAMENTARY RULE

1 This chapter is based on press reports and private information.

APPENDIX

Governors-General of the Anglo-Egyptian Sudan, 1899–1955

1 Horatio Herbert (Lord) Kitchener: January-December 1899
2 Sir Francis Reginald Wingate: 1899–1916
3 Sir Lee Stack: 1917–24 ('acting', 1917–19)
4 Sir Geoffrey Archer: 1924–6
5 Sir John Maffey (later Lord Rugby): 1926–33
6 Sir George Stewart Symes: 1934–40
7 Sir Hubert Huddleston: 1940–47
8 Sir Robert Howe: 1947–55
9 Sir Alexander Knox Helm: 1955

Heads of Government of the Independent Sudan, 1956 onwards

1 Isma'il al-Azhari: 1954–July 1956
2 'Abdallah Khalil: July 1956–November 1958
3 Ibrahim Abboud: November 1958–October 1964
4 Sirr al-Khatim al-Khalifa: October 1964–May 1965
5 Mohammed Ahmed Mahgoub: May 1965–July 1966
6 Sadiq al-Mahdi: July 1966–May 1967
7 Mohammed Ahmed Mahgoub: May 1967–May 1969
8 Babikr 'Awadallah: May–October 1969
9 Jaafar al-Nimeiri: October 1969–April 1985
10 'Abd al-Rahman Siwar al-Dahab: April 1985–May 1986
11 Sadiq al-Mahdi: May 1986–

MAPS

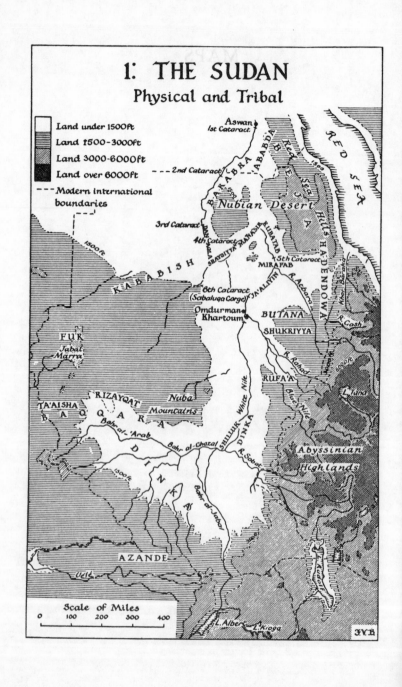

1: THE SUDAN
Physical and Tribal

Land under 1500ft
Land 1500-3000ft
Land 3000-6000ft
Land over 6000ft
- - - Modern international
boundaries

Aswan
1st Cataract

RED SEA

- - - 2nd Cataract

BARABRA   ABABDA

Red Sea Hills   HADENDOWA

Nubian Desert

3rd Cataract

4th Cataract

SHAIQIYYA RABASIA

5th Cataract

RUBATAB

MIRAFAB

R. Atbara

R. Gash

6th Cataract
(Sabaluqa Gorge)

JA'ALIYIN

Omdurman
Khartoum

BUTANA

SHUKRIYYA

KABABISH

FUR

Jabal
Marra

RIZAYQAT

Nuba
Mountains

RUFA'A

R. Rahad

Blue Nile

L. Tana

TA'AISHA

BAQQARA

Bahr al-'Arab

SHILLUK White Nile

DINKA

R. Sobat

Abyssinian

Highlands

DINKA

Bahr al-Ghazal

Bahr al-Jabal

AZANDE

Uelle

R. Kibali

Scale of Miles
0   100   200   300   400

L. Albert   L. Kioga

J.V.B.

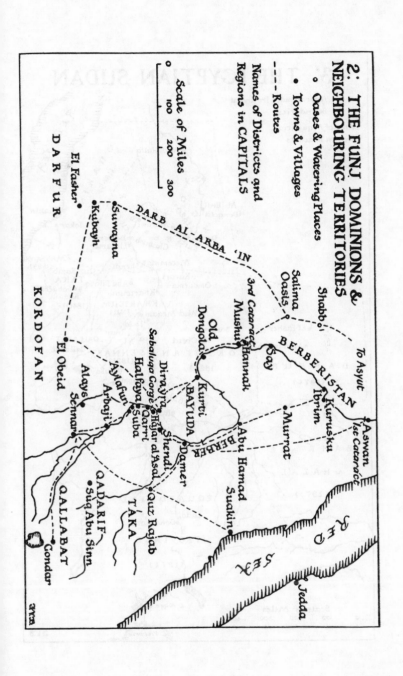

2: THE FUNJ DOMINIONS & NEIGHBOURING TERRITORIES

- ○ Oases & Watering Places
- ● Towns & Villages
- --- Routes

Names of Districts and Regions in CAPITALS

Scale of Miles
0 100 200 300

DARB AL-ARBA'IN

DARFUR

El Fasher
Kubayh
Suwayna

KORDOFAN

El Obeid
Alays
Sennar
Arbaji
'Aylafun
Suba
Qarri
Halfaya
Hajar al'Asal
Sabaluqa Gorge
Dirayra
Shendi
Damer
QALLABAT
QADARIF
Suq Abu Sinn
TÁKA
Quz Rajab
Gondar

3rd Cataract
Mushu
Hannak
Old Dongola
Kurti
BAYUDA
Abu Hamad

Salima Oasis
Shabb

Say
Kuruska
Ibrim
BERBERISTAN
Murrat
BERBER

Aswan
1st Cataract
To Asyut

Suakin

RED SEA

Jedda

2a

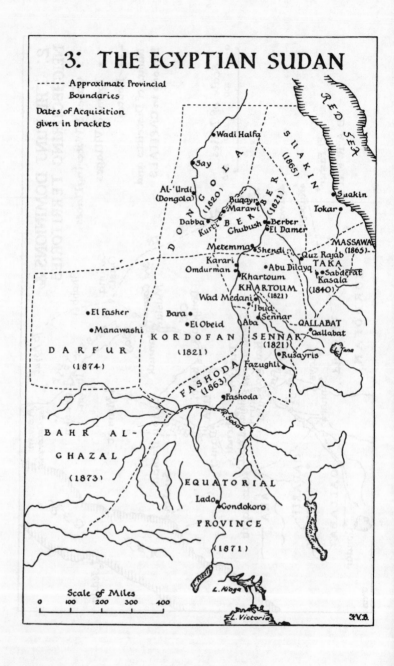

3: THE EGYPTIAN SUDAN

- - - - Approximate Provincial
         Boundaries

Dates of Acquisition
given in brackets

RED SEA

• Wadi Halfa

• Say

SUAKIN
(1865)

Al-'Urdi
(Dongola)

D O N G O L A
(1820)

• Suakin

Buqayr•
Marawi•
Dabba•
Kurti•
Chubush•

B E R B E R
(1821)

• Tokar

• Berber
• El Damer

MASSAWA
(1865)

Metemma• • Shendi

• Quz Rajab

Karari
Omdurman•
• Khartoum
Wad Medani•

• Abu Dilayq

TAKA

• Sabderat
Kasala
(1840)

KHARTOUM
(1821)

• El Fasher

Bara •

• Ibud
• Sennar
Aba•

QALLABAT
• Qallabat
L. Tana

• Manawashi

• El Obeid

KORDOFAN
(1821)

SENNAR
(1821)

• Rusayris

D A R F U R
(1874)

FASHODA
(1863)

Fazughli•

• Fashoda

B A H R   A L -
G H A Z A L
(1873)

Sobat

E Q U A T O R I A L

Lado•
• Gondokoro

P R O V I N C E

(1871)

L. Albert

L. Kioga

Scale of Miles

0   100   200   300   400

L. Victoria

H.V.B.

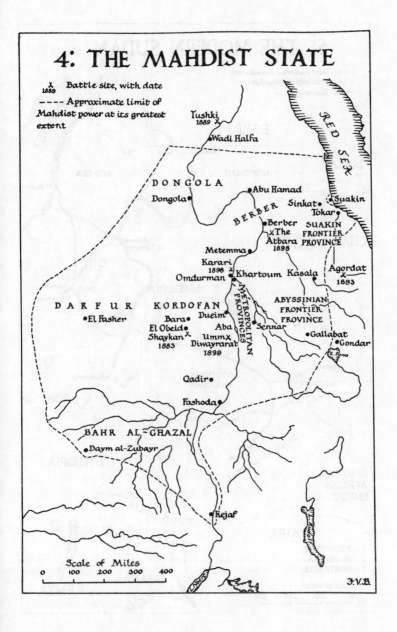

4: THE MAHDIST STATE

X
1889 Battle site, with date

- - - - Approximate limit of
Mahdist power at its greatest
extent

RED SEA

Tushki X
1889

●Wadi Halfa

DONGOLA

●Abu Hamad

Dongola ●

Sinkat ●Suakin

BERBER Tokar

●Berber SUAKIN
x The FRONTIER
Atbara PROVINCE
1898

Metemma ●

Karari
1898
X
Omdurman ● ● Khartoum Kasala ● Agordat
X
1893

METROPOLITAN PROVINCES

DARFUR KORDOFAN ABYSSINIAN
FRONTIER
●El Fasher Bara ● Dueim PROVINCE

El Obeid ● Aba ● Sennar
Shaykan X Umm X ●Gallabat
1883 Diwayrarat ●Gondar
1899 L. Tana

Qadir ●

Fashoda ●

BAHR AL-GHAZAL

●Daym al-Zubayr

●Rejaf

Scale of Miles
0   100   200   300   400

J.V.B.

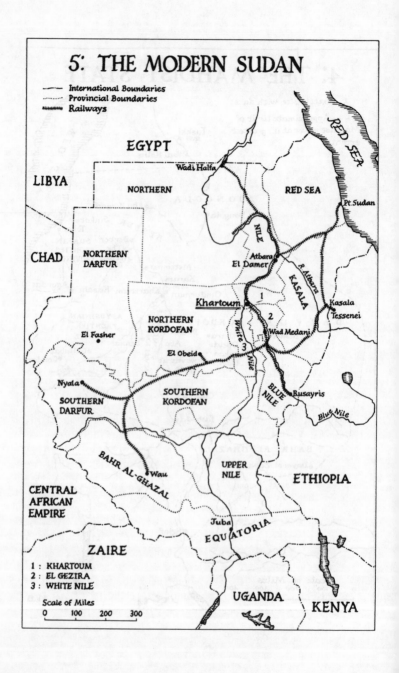

5: THE MODERN SUDAN

- - - International Boundaries
.... Provincial Boundaries
++++++++ Railways

EGYPT

LIBYA

NORTHERN

RED SEA

Wadi Halfa

Pt. Sudan

CHAD

NORTHERN
DARFUR

NILE

Atbara
El Damer

KASALA

Khartoum

1

Kasala
Tessenei

El Fasher

NORTHERN
KORDOFAN

White Nile

2

Wad Medani

El Obeid

3

BLUE
NILE

Busayris

Nyala

SOUTHERN
DARFUR

SOUTHERN
KORDOFAN

Blue Nile

BAHR AL-GHAZAL

Wau

UPPER
NILE

ETHIOPIA

CENTRAL
AFRICAN
EMPIRE

Juba

EQUATORIA

ZAIRE

1 : KHARTOUM
2 : EL GEZIRA
3 : WHITE NILE

Scale of Miles
0   100   200   300

UGANDA   KENYA

SELECT BIBLIOGRAPHY

INTRODUCTION

Two essential and comprehensive bibliographical works are R. L. Hill, *A bibliography of the Anglo-Egyptian Sudan from the earliest times to 1937* (London 1939) and Abdel Rahman el Nasri, *A bibliography of the Sudan 1938–1958* (London 1962). A recent general bibliography is M. W. Daly, *Sudan* (Oxford and Santa Barbara 1983). Reference should also be made to the relevant sections of J. D. Pearson, *Index Islamicus 1906–1955* (Cambridge 1958) and its *Supplements* (Cambridge 1962–   ), which list materials in periodicals, *Festschriften* and similar works. *Sudan Notes and Records* (Khartoum 1918–   ) is a specialist periodical and a mine of information on all aspects of Sudanese studies, but its articles vary in quality. *Sudan Texts Bulletin*, edited by Ali Osman and Robin Thelwall at the New University of Ulster (annually from 1980) presents the text and translation of documents from the pre-Islamic period onwards. There are relevant articles in the *Encyclopaedia of Islam* (second edition, Leiden and London 1960–   ) and Yūsuf Fadl Ḥasan (ed.), *Sudan in Africa* (Khartoum 1971). The geography of the Sudan is fully treated in K. M. Barbour, *The republic of the Sudan: a regional geography* (London 1961).

There is no general history of the Sudan available in English, but a short survey forms part of J. Spencer Trimingham, *Islam in the Sudan* (London 1949). The account given of Sudanese Islam, which forms the main portion of the book is extremely valuable. H. A. MacMichael, *A history of the Arabs in the Sudan* (Cambridge 1922), is a collection of materials from classical, Arabic and Sudanese sources, not a systematic history, and incorporates much genealogical and tribal tradition. Of more limited scope is the same writer's *The tribes of central and northern Kordofan* (Cambridge 1912). Another tribal history is A. Paul, *A history of the Beja tribes of the Sudan* (Cambridge 1954). Among recent Arabic monographs on tribal subjects are Aḥmad ʿAbd al-Rahīm Naṣr, *Taʾrīkh al-ʿAbdallāb min khilāl riwāyātihim al-samāʿiyya* (Khartoum 1969); Ādam al-Zayn, *al-Turāth al-shaʿbī li-qabīlat al-Musabbaʿāt* (Khartoum 1970); and Muhammad Aḥmad Ibrāhīm, *Malāmiḥ min turāth Ḥamar al-Shaʿbī* (Khartoum 1971). The history of a small western sultanate is investigated in detail by Lidwien Kapteijns, *Mahdist faith and Sudanic tradition: the history of the Masālīt sultanate, 1870–1930* (London 1985). Richard Hill, *A biographical dictionary of the Sudan* (second edition, London 1967) is indispensable.

243

Select Bibliography
PART I: BEFORE THE TURCO-EGYPTIAN CONQUEST

The pre-Islamic past is surveyed in A. J. Arkell, *A history of the Sudan to 1821* (second edition, London 1961). The standard work on Christian Nubia is Ugo Monneret de Villard, *Storia della Nubia cristiana* (Rome 1938). A recent study incorporating archaeological data is Giovanni Vantini, *Christianity in the Sudan* (Bologna 1981). The arabization of the northern Sudan is studied in Yūsuf Faḍl Ḥasan, *The Arabs and the Sudan from the seventh to the early sixteenth century* (Edinburgh 1967). An outline of subsequent developments is included in P. M. Holt, 'Egypt, the Funj and Darfur', *Cambridge History of Africa*, 4 (Cambridge 1975), 14–57, 623–6, 653–5. O. G. S. Crawford, *The Fung kingdom of Sennar* (Gloucester 1951) assembles valuable data, and is still important. The Funj and Kayra sultanates are the subject of R. S. O'Fahey and J. L. Spaulding, *Kingdoms of the Sudan* (London 1974). A more specialized account of the Funj is given in Jay Spaulding, *The heroic age in Sinnār* (Michigan 1985). Detailed studies of aspects of the Kayra sultanate are provided by R. S. O'Fahey, *State and society in Dār Fūr* (London 1980), and R. S. O'Fahey and M. I. Abu Salim, *Land in Dār Fūr* (Cambridge 1983). For a critique by a social anthropologist of the vexed question of Funj origins, see Wendy James, 'The Funj mystique: approaches to a problem of Sudan history', in Ravindra K. Jain (ed.), *Text and context. The social anthropology of tradition* (Philadelphia 1977). Several articles are collected in P. M. Holt, *Studies in the history of the Near East* (London 1973). The 'Abdallabi shaykhdom is the subject of an Arabic monograph by Muḥammad Ṣāliḥ Muḥyī al-Dīn, *Mashyakhat al-'Abdallāb* (Beirut and Khartoum 1972). Editions and translations of the Arabic primary sources are given in the notes to Chapters 1 and 2 above. An important pioneer study of trade in the late Funj period is Terence Walz, *Trade between Egypt and Bitad as-Sūdān 1700–1820* (Cairo 1978).

There were few European travellers in the Sudan before the Turco-Egyptian conquest. The journey of Charles Jacques Poncet, who visited Sennar at the end of the seventeenth century, has been reprinted by Sir William Foster (ed.), *The Red Sea and adjacent countries at the close of the seventeenth century* (Hakluyt Society, Second Series, No. C, London 1949). The classical description of the Funj sultanate in its decline was given by James Bruce, *Travels to discover the source of the Nile* (vol. VI, second edition, Edinburgh 1805). The earliest English traveller in Darfur was W. G. Browne, *Travels in Africa, Egypt, and Syria, from the year 1792 to 1798* (London 1799). Conditions on the main Nile before the Turco-Egyptian conquest are described in John Lewis Burckhardt, *Travels in Nubia* (London 1819).

PART II: THE TURCO-EGYPTIAN PERIOD

A short survey is included in P. M. Holt, 'Egypt and the Nile valley', *Cambridge history of Africa*, 5 (Cambridge 1976), 13–50, 497–500, 540–2.

Select Bibliography

The only general account in English is Richard Hill, *Egypt in the Sudan, 1820–1881* (London 1959), largely based on unpublished materials including the Egyptian archives. The same author's bibliographical article, 'Historical writing on the Sudan since 1820', in Bernard Lewis and P. M. Holt (eds.), *Historians of the Middle East* (London 1962), is of interest. Parts of the period are treated in full by G. Douin in *Histoire du Soudan égyptien*, I (Cairo 1944–all published), and in *Histoire du règne du Khédive Ismaïl*, III (Cairo 1936–41). An Arabic work covering the period is Muḥammad Fu'ād Shukrī, *Miṣr wa'l-Sūdān* (Cairo 1963), and the same author examined a more limited topic in an earlier work, [M. F. Shukry], *The Khedive Ismaïl and slavery in the Sudan (1863–1879)* (Cairo 1938). The opening-up of the south in this period is described by Richard Gray, *A history of the southern Sudan 1839–1889* (London 1961). Anders Bjørkelo, *From king to kāshif. Shendi in the nineteenth century* (Bergen 1983) examines the impact of the Turco-Egyptian regime on the principal town of the Ja'aliyyin.

Accounts by travellers become increasingly numerous in this period. *A narrative of the expedition to Dongola and Sennaar* (London 1822), by 'an American in the service of the viceroy', was written by G. B. English, an officer in the Egyptian artillery at the time of the conquest. The Turco-Egyptian invasion coincided with 'an antiquarian visit to Egypt and Nubia, and an attempt to penetrate as far as Dóngola' by George Waddington and Barnard Hanbury, described in *Journal of a visit to some parts of Ethiopia* (London 1822). Two other early travel accounts are those of L. M. A. Linant de Bellefonds, *Journal d'un voyage à Méroé dans les années 1821 et 1822*, ed. Margaret Shinnie (Khartoum 1958), and G. A. Hoskins, *Travels in Ethiopia* (London 1835). Manuscript source materials on the Turco-Egyptian Sudan by contemporary European visitors and residents have been translated and edited by Richard Hill, *On the frontiers of Islam* (Oxford 1970), and Paul Santi and Richard Hill, *The Europeans in the Sudan 1834–1878* (Oxford 1980). John Petherick, *Egypt, the Soudan and Central Africa* (Edinburgh and London 1861), describes early travels in the Bahr al-Ghazal. Two books by Sir Samuel W. Baker, *The Nile tributaries of Abyssinia* (London 1874), and *The Albert N'yanza* (London 1877) are records of exploration, which throw some light on conditions in the Sudan, while his *Ismailïa* (London 1874) is his account of his mission to the southern Sudan on behalf of Khedive Isma'il. There is some interesting material in T. Douglas Murray and A. Silva White, *Sir Samuel Baker, a memoir* (London 1895), while a modern biography has been written by Dorothy Middleton, *Baker of the Nile* (London, 1949).

The immense and still growing literature about Charles George Gordon began in this period. It is surveyed in Richard Hill, 'The Gordon literature', *Durham University Journal*, New Series, XVI/3 (1955), 97–103. The essential study of Gordon's work in the Sudan is Bernard M. Allen, *Gordon and the Sudan* (London 1931). Material on Gordon's activities in the country before the Mahdia is found in G. Birkbeck Hill (ed.), *Colonel Gordon in Central Africa, 1874–1879* (London 1881) and M. F. Shukry (ed.), *Equatoria under Egyptian rule* (Cairo 1953). The career of Gordon's lieutenant in the Bahr al-Ghazal is described in the autobiographical work of Romolo Gessi (ed. Felix Gessi), *Seven years in the Soudan* (London 1892). Another Italian servant of the khedive described his adventures in Gaetano Casati, *Ten years in Equatoria* (London 1891). A collection of the letters and journals of Emin Pasha (Eduard Schnitzer), the last khedivial governor of Equatoria, is offered in G. Schweinfurth, F. Ratzel, R. W. Felkin and G. Hartlaub (eds.), *Emin Pasha in Central Africa* (London 1888). For his biography, see Georg Schweitzer, *Emin Pasha, his life and work* (Westminster 1898). An important account of the Kayra sultanate in Darfur, shortly before its overthrow, was given by Gustav Nachtigal (tr. Allan G. B. Fisher and Humphrey J. Fisher), *Sahara and Sudan*, IV (London 1971). Materials left by two leading Europeans from the last phase of the Turco-Egyptian regime have been edited by M. W. Daly, *The road to Shaykan: Letters of ... Hicks Pasha written ... 1883* (Durham 1983), and by Richard Hill, *The Sudan memoirs of Carl Christian Giegler Pasha 1873–1883* (London 1984).

PART III: THE MAHDIA

A general history, which makes extensive use of the Mahdist archives, is P. M. Holt, *The Mahdist state in the Sudan, 1881-1898* (second edition, Oxford 1970). A detailed study of events in the south is provided by Robert O. Collins, *The southern Sudan 1883-1898* (New Haven and London 1962). The diplomatic background to the Reconquest is examined in detail in G. N. Sanderson, *England, Europe and the Upper Nile 1882-1899* (Edinburgh 1965). Research in the Mahdist archives has resulted in a number of important Arabic monographs. Muḥammad Ibrāhīm Abū Salīm, *al-Ḥaraka al-fikriyya fi'l-Mahdiyya* (Khartoum 1970), is basically a study of the Mahdist chancery and documents, while the same author's *al-Arḍ fi'l-Mahdiyya* (Khartoum 1970) is an exposition of the land-law. The propaganda debate between the Mahdi and the orthodox *'ulamā'* who served the Turco-Egyptian administration is the subject of 'Abdallāh 'Alī Ibrāhīm, *al-Ṣirā'bayn al-mahdī wa'l-'ulamā'* (Khartoum 1968). Three regional studies are Mūsā al-Mubārak al-Ḥasan, *Ta'rīkh Dār Fūr al-siyāsī* (Khartoum [1971]); Muḥammad Sa'īd al-Qaddāl, *al-Mahdiyya wa'l-Ḥabasha* (Khartoum 1973); and 'Awaḍ 'Abd al-Hādī al-'Aṭā, *Ta'rīkh Kurdufān al-siyāsī fi'l-Mahdiyya 1881-1899* (Khartoum 1973).

Published Arabic primary sources include a selection of Mahdist documents by Muḥammad Ibrāhīm Abū Salīm (ed.), *Manshūrāt al-Mahdiyya* ([?Beirut] 1969). The same scholar has also edited three despatches of 'Uthmān Diqna to the Mahdi in *Mudhakkirāt 'Uthmān Diqna* (Khartoum 1974) and the contemporary hagiography by Ismā'īl 'Abd al-Qādir al-Kurdufānī, *Sa'ādat al-mustahdī bi-sīrat al-imām al-mahdī* (Khartoum and

Select Bibliography

Beirut 1972). Of this last, a condensed paraphrase is available in Haim Shaked, *The life of the Sudanese Mahdi* (New Brunswick 1978). Abu Salim and Muḥammad Sa 'īd al-Qaddāl have jointly edited Ismā'īl 'Abd al Qādir al-Kurdufānī's sequel (*al-Ṭirāz al-manqūsh bi-bushrā qatl Yuḥannā malik al-Ḥubūsh*) dealing with the reign of the Khalifa, as *al-Ḥarb al-Ḥabashiyya al-Sūdāniyya* (Khartoum 1972). The first of three volumes of autobiography by a Sudanese participant in the Mahdia, Bābikr Badrī, *Ta'rīkh ḥayātī* ([?Khartoum] 1959–61), has been translated by Yousef Bedri and George Scott, *The memoirs of Babikr Bedri* (London 1969).

Among contemporary works in English, three form a group on their own: F. R. Wingate, *Mahdiism and the Egyptian Sudan* (London 1891) and *Ten years' captivity in the Mahdi's camp, 1882-1892, from the original manuscripts of Father Joseph Ohrwalder* (London 1892); also Rudolf C. Slatin, *Fire and sword in the Sudan* (London 1896). For a critique of these as war-propaganda, see P. M. Holt, 'The source-materials of the Sudanese Mahdia', *St. Antony's Papers, Number 4; Middle Eastern Affairs, Number One* (London 1958). An independent account by a European prisoner of the Mahdia is Charles Neufeld, *A prisoner of the Khaleefa* (London 1899). For an account of events in the south in addition to those mentioned in the previous section, see A. J. Mounteney-Jephson, *Emin Pasha and the rebellion at the Equator* (London 1890). A modern study is Iain R. Smith, *The Emin Pasha Relief Expedition 1886-1890* (Oxford 1972). Published primary sources on the siege of Khartoum and the relief expedition are A. Egmont Hake (ed.), *The journals of Major-Gen. C. G. Gordon, C. B., at Kartoum*, covering only part of the siege, and Lord Wolseley's journal in Adrian Preston (ed.), *In relief of Gordon* (London 1967). The Reconquest produced a great amount of journalistic narrative, of which G. W. Steevens, *With Kitchener to Khartoum* (Edinburgh and London 1898) is the best-known example.

Biographies of persons important during and after the Mahdia include H. C. Jackson, *Osman Digna* (London 1926), which does not use the Arabic material cited above. The account of Kitchener in Sir George Arthur, *Life of Lord Kitchener* (London 1920) may be compared with the presentation in Sir Philip Magnus, *Kitchener, portrait of an imperialist* (London 1959). Cromer's attitude to the Mahdia and the Reconquest is revealed in his *Modern Egypt* (London 1908).

Special mention should be made of the history written by a Lebanese officer in Egyptian Military Intelligence under Wingate, Na'ūm Shuqayr, *Ta'rīkh al-Sūdān al-qadīm wa'l-ḥadīth wa-jughrāfīyatuh* (Cairo [1903]), which is particularly valuable for the period of the Mahdia.

PART IV: THE CONDOMINIUM

Accounts of the Condominium period have chiefly been written by former members of the Sudan political service and tend to lack detachment. The

Select Bibliography

most useful are K. D. D. Henderson, *Sudan Republic* (London 1965), which also covers the period up to and including the October 1964 revolution, Sir Harold MacMichael, *The Sudan* (London 1954), and J. S. R. Duncan, *The Sudan's path to independence* (Edinburgh 1957).

Political developments of the period have in recent years attracted attention. M. W. Daly, *Empire on the Nile* (Cambridge 1986) is a general history of the period up to 1934. Gabriel Warburg, *The Sudan under Wingate* (London 1971) describes the establishment and structure of the Condominium government. M. W. Daly, *British administration and the Northern Sudan* (Leiden 1979) and G. M. A. Bakheit, *British administration and Sudanese nationalism, 1919–1939* (Cambridge Ph.D. 1965) deal with the political history of the inter-war years and the rise of Sudanese nationalism. The White Flag League is studied in 'Abd al-Karīm al-Sa'īd, *al-Liwā' al-abyaḍ* (Khartoum 1970). Especially useful for political development during and after the second world war are Muddathir Abd al-Rahim, *Imperialism and nationalism in the Sudan* (Oxford 1969), K. D. D. Henderson, *The making of the modern Sudan, the life and letters of Sir Douglas Newbold* (London 1953), Sir James Robertson, *Transition in Africa, from direct rule to independence* (London 1974), and Peter Woodward, *Condominium and Sudanese nationalism* (London 1979). The Sudan's role in Anglo-Egyptian relations is covered in John Marlowe, *A history of Egypt and Anglo-Egyptian relations, 1800–1956* (London 1965). A case study is Hassan Ahmed Ibrahim, *The 1936 Anglo-Egyptian Treaty* (Khartoum 1976).

Memoirs and biographies contain much useful information. In addition to those cited above, Ronald Wingate, *Wingate of the Sudan* (second edition, Westport, Conn, 1975), Richard Hill, *Slatin Pasha* (London 1965), Ṣādiq al-Mahdī (ed.), *Jihād fī sabīl al-istiqlāl* (Khartoum n.d.), and Edward Atiyah, *An arab tells his story* (London 1946) are informative.

In recent years increasing attention has been paid to the Southern Sudan, by Sudanese and others. In *Land beyond the rivers, the Southern Sudan, 1898–1919* (New Haven 1971), R. O. Collins discusses the conquest and pacification of the south and the foundations of administration, while in *Shadows in the grass* (New Haven 1983) he brings the story down to 1956. L. S. P. Sanderson and G. N. Sanderson have described in detail *Education, religion, and politics in Southern Sudan 1899–1964* (London 1981). Much anthropological work can be found in *Sudan Notes and Records* and in more specialized periodical publications.

Important works on social, economic and educational developments during the Condominium period include J. D. Tothill (ed.), *Agriculture in the Sudan* (London 1948), Arthur Gaitskell, *Gezira, a story of development in the Sudan* (London 1959), and H. C. Squires, *The Sudan Medical Service, an experiment in social medicine* (London 1958). Conrad Reining discusses *The Zande Scheme, an anthropological case study of economic development in*

248

Select Bibliography

Africa (Evanston, Illinois 1966). Developments in Muslim law are outlined in J. N. D. Anderson, *Islamic Law in Africa* (London 1954). Educational development is covered by V. L. Griffiths, *An experiment in education* (London 1953) and Mohamed Omer Beshir, *Educational development in the Sudan, 1898-1956* (Oxford 1969). The history of trade unionism is studied in Saad ed Din Fawzi, *The labour movement in the Sudan, 1946-1955* (London 1957).

PART V: THE INDEPENDENT SUDAN

The political history of the post-independence period is studied, by detailed reference to the development of parties and to their electoral performance in Peter Bechtold, *Politics in the Sudan* (New York 1976). The role of the army is discussed in Ruth First, *The barrel of a gun: political power in Africa and the coup d'état* (London 1970). Sectarian politics and the history of communism in the Sudan are dealt with in Gabriel Warburg, *Islam, nationalism and communism in a traditional society: the case of Sudan* (London 1978). Specialized studies of Sudanese tribes include Talal Asad, *The Kababish Arabs* (London 1970), Ian Cunnison, *Baggara Arabs* (Oxford 1966), Abd al-Ghaffar Muhammad Ahmed, *Shaykhs and followers* (Khartoum 1974), Abbas Ahmed Mohamed, *White Nile Arabs* (London 1980), Francis Mading Deng, *The Dinka of the Sudan*, and, among his many works, E. E. Evans-Pritchard, *The Azande* (Oxford 1971) and *The Nuer* (Oxford 1974). The Sudan Research Unit has undertaken further work, and has actively collected oral data. It has issued an important study of developments in the independence period and before, Yusuf Fadl Hasan (ed.) *Sudan in Africa* (Khartoum 1971). Several provincial histories have appeared. Among them Muḥammad Ibrāhīm Abū Salīm has written *Ta'rīkh al-Khurṭūm* (Khartoum 1971). Local government since the inception of the Condominium is studied in John Howell (ed.), *Local government and politics in the Sudan* (Khartoum 1974).

The southern problem has been the subject of many recent studies, some of which show a northern or southern bias. Among the most useful works are R. O. Collins, *The Southern Sudan in historical perspective* (Tel Aviv 1975), which also surveys the history of the south from pre-Turco-Egyptian days. The subject of Oliver Albino, *The Sudan, a Southern viewpoint* (London 1970) is evident in its title. Mohamed Omer Beshir, *The Southern Sudan, from Conflict to Peace* (London 1975) describes the negotiations leading to the Addis Ababa accord. An interesting study is Francis Mading Deng, *Dynamics of identification: a basis for national integration in the Sudan* (Khartoum 1974).

A comprehensive and reliable economic history of the Sudan has yet to appear, but a useful series of articles is in Ali Mohamed El Hassan (ed.), *Growth, employment and equity* (Khartoum n.d.), and Adel Amin Beshai,

249

Select Bibliography

Export performance and economic development in Sudan 1900–1967 (London 1976) is valuable.

Current events are best viewed by reference to publications of the government of the Sudan and to the periodical press. Annual surveys appear in *Africa contemporary record* (Exeter). *Sudanow* is a monthly news magazine published by the Sudan's ministry of information. *The Middle East Journal* (Washington) is also useful.

INDEX

Index

257

Index